The Food Lover's Handbook To
The Southwest

BOOKS BY DAVE DEWITT

The Fiery Cuisines (with Nancy Gerlach)
Fiery Appetizers (with Nancy Gerlach)
Texas Monthly Guide to New Mexico
Just North of the Border (with Nancy Gerlach)
The Whole Chile Pepper Book (with Nancy Gerlach)
Hot Spots

The Food Lover's Handbook To

The Southwest

Dave DeWitt and Mary Jane Wilan

With help from Colette and John Bancroft in Tucson, Elaine Corn in El Paso, Elin Jeffords in Phoenix, Jim Peyton in San Antonio, and Robb Walsh in Austin.

Prima Publishing
P. O. Box 1260DEW
Rocklin, CA 95677
(916) 786-0426

Production by Carol Dondrea, Bookman Productions
Typography by Recorder Typesetting Network
Interior design by Michael Yazzolino
Jacket design by The Dunlavey Studio
Photography by Dave DeWitt, Chel Beeson, and Jim Peyton

Prima Publishing
Rocklin, CA

Library of Congress Cataloging-in-Publication Data

DeWitt, Dave.
    The food lover's handbook to the Southwest / Dave DeWitt, Mary
    Jane Wilan
       p. cm.
    Includes index.
    ISBN 1-55958-171-9 :
    1. Restaurants, lunch rooms, etc.—Southwest, New—
Guide-books. 2. Grocery trade—Southwest, New—Guide-books.
3. Cookery. American—Southwestern style. 4. Southwest, New—
Description and travel—1981—Guide-books. I. Title.
TX907.3.S69D49 1992
647.9579—dc20   91-46473
                                            CIP

92 93 94 95 RRD 10 9 8 7 6 5 4 3 2 1

Printed in the United States of America

Dedication For Ann Wilan, a Santa Fe tourist in
1940 and a great cook

Acknowledgments Thanks to all the people who helped with this project:

Colette and John Bancroft, Jennifer Basye, Chel Beeson, Pete Benavidez, Lia Bijnsdorp, Jeffree Brooks, Jane Jordan Browne, Jane Butel, Gregory Jay Byfield, Red Caldwell, Cindy Castillo, Elaine Corn, David Garcia, Nancy Gerlach, Antonio Heras-Duran, Elin Jeffords, José Marmolejo, Mark Miller, John Roger Morton, Nancy Parsons, Sam Pendergrast, Jim Peyton, Miguel Ravago, Robert Spiegel, Mick Vann, Robb Walsh, and all the other food lovers in the Southwest who shared information with us.

Contents

FOREWORD *ix*

INTRODUCTION *xi*

PART ONE THE NATIVE SOUTHWEST *1*

    CHAPTER 1 NATURE PROVIDES *3*

PART TWO SOUTHWESTERN TEXAS *23*

    CHAPTER 2 LONE STAR CUISINE *25*

    CHAPTER 3 AUSTIN AND THE HILL COUNTRY *49*

    CHAPTER 4 SAN ANTONIO *88*

    CHAPTER 5 EL PASO AND CIUDAD JUÁREZ *114*

PART THREE NEW MEXICO *135*

    CHAPTER 6 AN ENCHANTED FEAST *137*

    CHAPTER 7 LAS CRUCES *159*

    CHAPTER 8 ALBUQUERQUE *179*

    CHAPTER 9 SANTA FE AND NORTHERN NEW
MEXICO *207*

PART FOUR ARIZONA *241*

    CHAPTER 10 DESERT DINING *243*

    CHAPTER 11 PHOENIX AND SCOTTSDALE *259*

    CHAPTER 12 TUCSON *284*

PART FIVE APPENDICES *309*

    APPENDIX 1 MAIL-ORDER SOURCES FOR
SOUTHWESTERN FOOD ITEMS *311*

    APPENDIX 2 GLOSSARY OF SOUTHWESTERN COOKING
TERMS AND INGREDIENTS *314*

    APPENDIX 3 ADDITIONAL READING *320*

    INDEX *323*

FOREWORD

The Southwest is a region with many culinary treasures, the most important of which is the chile. It is revered here as nowhere else and is ever-present in the food. Chiles are an ingredient with bravado that also display qualities of elegance and subtlety. They provide a true sense of connection with the land and help shape the people of this region. Most Southwesterners eat chiles every day—sometimes three times a day.

In the Southwest, chiles are inescapable. They appear in virtually every New Mexican dish except desserts. Chiles abound in salsas, jerky, popcorn, nuts, honey and even beer! Chileheads commonly carry bags of chile pods and bottles of hot sauce with them when they leave the area. Those few outcasts who don't eat chile peppers are regarded as heretics, so tourists should consider themselves forewarned.

Two types of tourists visit the Southwest. Some sightsee in new jeans, boots, hats, and turquoise jewelry; drive around and take pictures of Indian pueblos; do lots of shopping; visit the museums; and eat a couple of Southwestern meals. But others come to experience more deeply a culture vastly different from home and to seek adventure, challenge, and change.

I call the latter group the "tasteseekers," those who know there's more to life than white bread and pasta, those searching for the answer to life's Big Question: Shouldn't food have more flavor? They're on a taste pilgrimage; for this group, especially, this book is a veritable treasure map. With it, the reader will be able to find the distinctive regional cooking that still reigns in the Southwest—from famous restaurants to authentic holes-in-the-wall where the food is more important than the setting.

Dave DeWitt and Mary Jane Wilan have accumulated a vast amount of information from years of living and traveling in the Southwest, and this book is an invaluable guide to those of us who live here and to the legions of tasteseekers who travel here to enjoy the wonderful food.

MARK MILLER
Santa Fe, New Mexico
March 1992

Introduction

Where Is the Southwest?

The Southwest can include as few as two states—or as many as eleven. There is no debate about the location of Arizona and New Mexico, but demographers have long pondered California's location (Southwest or Far West?) and that of Texas as part of the Midwest, South, or Southwest. Guidebooks often graft Utah, Nevada, Colorado, and Oklahoma onto the Southwest; and amazingly enough, a popular national travel guide once included Kansas, Missouri, and Arkansas in the region!

Such geographical quandaries fade when confronted with culinary facts because, face it, no one really associates states like Nevada with Southwestern cuisine—although local restaurants may serve their own versions of "Mexican" food. Heavily populated Southern California deserves its own guide, and the cities in northern and eastern Texas have such diverse culinary influences that they are beyond our Southwestern focus.

So, for the purposes of this handbook, the Southwest is defined as Southwestern Texas, New Mexico, and Arizona—those areas most influenced by Native American and northern Mexican cookery, as well as American imports and techniques. These are the traditional locations for a unique cuisine—dating to prehistory—that continues to evolve.

What Is Southwestern Cuisine?

Mexican and *Southwestern,* the two terms used most often to describe the cuisine of the region, are misnomers in a way, yet they remain as the only food descriptors that make any sense. The term *Mexican cooking* is inadequate to describe the cuisine of the Southwest and too general to characterize the incredibly diverse dishes prepared in Mexico. We avoid that term because it conjures up visions of very poor food served by national restaurant chains.

Our Austin correspondent, Robb Walsh, makes a good case against the term *Southwestern cuisine,* which he says is a "fad and fading fast." Walsh points out that such nomenclature was invented by California chefs who opened "Southwestern restaurants . . . that carefully ignored the Mexican traditional uses of the ingredients, lest they be confused with Mexican restaurants."

When the Southwestern trend spread across the country, innovative chefs incorporated all sorts of non-traditional ingredients and styles, which is why Dean Fearing, executive chef at the Mansion on Turtle Creek in Dallas, claims *his* Southwest cuisine includes elements of Plains Indian, Asian, and Cajun cooking. Walsh agrees with Stephan Pyles of the Routh Street Cafe in Dallas that because there are at least twenty-five national and ethnic influences on Texas cookery, the correct term for the food served there should be *Texas cuisine.*

The only problem with that thinking is that soon we will have fifty (or more) independent cuisines in the United States and the newest rage will be restaurants in Manhattan serving "South Dakota pronghorn cuisine." There is no doubt that the Texas, New Mexico, Arizona, and California versions of Mexican cooking differ, yet the fact remains that the ingredients used are mostly the same; it is the *techniques* that differ.

It gets even more confusing when we realize there are sub-cuisines within some states. For example, since the styles of cooking vary radically from south to north in New Mexico, to be perfectly accurate, we'd have to adopt descriptors such as the Mexican- and Native American-influenced cuisine of New Mexico, Taos-style. And since no one's going to choke on that one, there simply is no better general term to describe the food of the entire area than *Southwestern cuisine.* We agree with Walsh, however, that the term is misused outside the region—especially in California.

We often think of Southwestern cuisine as imported from Mexico, but we must remember that parts of the Southwest belonged to Mexico for more than 200 years. In fact, as recently as 1824, New Mexico was united with the states of Durango and Chihuahua. As Jim Peyton, our San Antonio correspondent and an expert on northern Mexican cuisine, points out: "The cooking of New Mexico was not brought across the border by immigrants; the border was moved south, leaving the cuisine intact." The same is true of Texas, which evolved its own version of northern Mexican cooking that was heavily influenced by Native American and early Anglo cultures. The situation was different in Arizona, as we shall see.

How This Book Was Compiled

When Jennifer Basye, our editor at Prima Publishing, suggested this project, we were immediately confronted with a challenge. The only way to become intimately familiar with the food of a specific region or city is to live there for years and years and experience all aspects of it. We have decades of this sort of seasoning in New Mexico, but our training in Texas and Arizona was limited to frequent travel—which, though educational, barely tasted the delights of a particular city.

So we decided to find like-minded correspondents with similar food experiences in other regions and depend on their judgment to select the best food of the Southwest. They are

- Robb Walsh, food editor of the *Austin Chronicle,* who covered the Austin area
- Jim Peyton, author of *El Norte: The Cuisine of Northern Mexico,* who investigated San Antonio
- Elaine Corn, native of El Paso and former food editor of the *Sacramento Bee,* who returned home to assist us
- Elin Jeffords, former restaurant critic of the *Arizona Republic,* who explored Phoenix and Scottsdale
- Colette Bancroft, Starlight editor of the *Arizona Daily Star,* who with her husband, John, a food writer, researched Tucson

We covered New Mexico and traveled to other cities several times to do research, but for the most part our correspondents determined which establishments to include in this guide. As it was impossible to visit or dine at every single establishment in each city, we could not, of course, include everyone—that would be a duplicate of the Yellow Pages rather than a guide. So, we limited ourselves to the establishments we felt were unique or the overall best in their fields of interest. In some cases, restaurants were selected for their historical significance, decor, or funkiness in addition to the quality—or authenticity—of their food. We also occasionally suggest particularly interesting restaurants where the reader can escape from the Southwest during travels there.

Readers and travelers should remember that life goes on during the lengthy process of book writing, production, and publication. Although it is unlikely the mountains will move or the border with Mexico will change position, new shops and restaurants will open, old ones will go out of business, telephone numbers and addresses will change, and travel conditions often fluctuate. We apologize in advance for any discrepancies and suggest that it's always a good idea to phone ahead before risking a long journey to visit a particular establishment.

With those caveats in mind, it's time to explore the great—and tasty—Southwest.

PART

ONE

THE NATIVE SOUTHWEST

Ussen (God) told Child-of-the-Water and White-Painted Woman: "You must live on yucca fruit, piñon nuts, and all other wild plants."

—CHIRICAHUA APACHE LEGEND

CHAPTER

—✦—

I

NATURE PROVIDES

When the first Spanish explorers ventured north from Mexico City in the sixteenth century and wandered into what is now the Southwest, they discovered that the indigenous Native Americans made excellent use of nearly every edible animal and plant substance imaginable. For protein, the Native Americans hunted and trapped deer, rabbits, quail, pronghorn, bison, and many other mammals and birds. However, some tribes such as the Apaches had taboos against eating certain animals they regarded as repulsive: snakes, fish, and owls, for example. Later, after the appearance of European food animals, game was viewed as poor man's meat. Today, of course, game has made a comeback because of its exotic nature and appeal to an adventurous audience.

The food plants eaten by the Native Americans were divided into two categories: those harvested in the wild and those cultivated plants that had managed to adapt to the dry desert climate or were irrigated. Harvested wild plants included acorns; berries such as chokecherry and Juniper; yucca fruits; various herbs such as wild mint; mushrooms; mesquite seeds (sometimes called beans); and agave hearts (*mescal*), which were roasted in pits by the Mescalero Apaches and other tribes. Three other very important uncultivated crops in Native-American cooking (and most commonly used today) are cacti, piñon nuts, and chiltepins (wild, berry-like chile peppers).

Various species of cactus were collected and eaten, including the fruits from the huge Saguaros, but the most commonly used cacti were the varieties of the genus *Opuntia*, the prickly pears. The pads of the prickly pear were stripped of spines and then boiled or fried. The fruits of these cacti (*tunas*) were picked when they were ripe and eaten raw as a snack or dessert. Today, prickly pear pads (*nopales)* can be found canned or fresh in some local markets, and many brands of cactus jellies and jams are made from the tasty fruits.

Another wild plant, the piñon tree, was fully used. The tough piñon tree (*Pinus edulis*), New Mexico's state tree, was nearly as important to Native Americans of the Southwest as the bison was to the tribes of the Great Plains. The Ramah Navajo, for example, utilized all parts of the tree in their daily lives and gave credit in legend to the squirrel for planting the first piñon tree. The nuts, a food staple, were collected, traded, and sold at market, but that was just the beginning. The Ramahs used the wood for fuel and the logs for building hogans, fences, and corrals. Saddle horns were fashioned from the roots, and piñon resin was chewed as gum and used as a binder and dye in pottery making and basket making. The branches and needles of the tree were important in tribal rituals, and the dried buds were used as medicines to ease suffering from burns, earaches, coughs, and fever.

The only problem with the nuts of the piñon is their scarcity. The crop is dependent on the moisture received each year, and insufficient rainfall in the years preceding flowering means a scant supply of nuts. The cones containing the nuts mature during the second year after flowering; and this fact, combined with weather variations, results in a good crop of nuts in the same region only every four or five years.

Piñon trees are evergreen survivalists because of their drought resistance and slow growth. But this toughness causes a skimpy and undependable supply of nuts. And once ripe, the tasty nuts are devoured in great quantities by deer, turkeys, javelinas, bears, birds, squirrels, and other rodents. In fact, an old trick used by Native Americans is to wait for a snowfall and follow the tracks of ground squirrels to their burrows, where sometimes as much as a twenty-pound cache of piñons can be found, stored by the hoarding little squirrel. But probably the most voracious consumer of piñons is mankind, cracking some 3 to 5 million pounds of the nuts a year collected in the Southwest and Mexico.

1-1 A Metate for Grinding Corn

The ripe piñon is contained in a pitchy cone and is usually collected by spreading blankets beneath the trees and shaking the branches until the nuts separate from the cones. The shells can be cracked with the teeth or stronger implements, and the nuts are roasted by spreading them in a single layer on a shallow tray and baking them in a 350-degree oven for eight to ten minutes. An alternate method is to bake them in the shells, which makes the shells brittle and easier to crack (and prevents frequent trips to the dentist).

Gastronomically speaking, piñon nuts are usually eaten raw or roasted and are also used in butters, candies, soups, and stuffings. There are about 200 calories per ounce of nuts, and the roasted nuts are high in unsaturated fats. It is a simple matter to mash them into a butter. They also contain significant amounts of vitamins A and B, protein, calcium, and phosphorus. They are available in shops and from street vendors in Albuquerque and Santa Fe and by mail order.

The third important wild crop is wild chile peppers, called chiltepins (*Capsicum annuum* var. *aviculare*), which are the closest surviving species to the earliest forms of chiles that developed in Bolivia and southern Brazil long before mankind arrived in the

New World. The small size of the fruits was perfect for dissemination by birds, and the wild chiles spread across South and Central America and to what is now the U.S. border millennia before the domesticated varieties arrived.

The pod shapes vary wildly, from tiny ones the size and shape of BBs to elongated half-inch pods. By contrast, domesticated piquins have much longer pods, up to three inches. The chiltepins, the most prized in Mexico, are spherical and measure five to eight millimeters in diameter. They are among the hottest chiles on Earth, rating up to 100,000 Scoville units.

In Sonora and southern Arizona, chiltepins grow in microhabitats in the transition zone between mountain and desert, which receive as little as ten inches of rain per year. They grow beneath "nurse" trees such as mesquite, oak, and palmetto, which provide shelter from direct sunlight, heat, and frost. During the summer, there is higher humidity beneath the nurse trees, and legumes such as mesquite fix nitrogen in the soil—a perfect fertilizer for the chiltepins. The trees also protect the plant from grazing by cattle, sheep, goats, and deer. Chiltepins planted in the open, without nurse trees, usually die from the effects of direct solar radiation.

Although the chiltepin's average height is about four feet, there are reports of individual bushes growing ten feet tall, living twenty-five to thirty years, and having stems as big around as a man's wrist. Chiltepins are resistant to frost but lose their leaves in cold winter weather. New growth will sprout from the base of the plant if it is frozen back.

Quite a bit of legend and lore is associated with the fiery little pods. In earlier times, the Papago Indians of Arizona traditionally made annual pilgrimages into the Sierra Madre range of Mexico to gather chiltepins. Dr. Gary Nabhan of Native Seeds/SEARCH, a seed-preservation organization, discovered that the Tarahumara Indians of Chihuahua value the chiltepins so much that they build stone walls around the bushes to protect them from goats. Besides their use as a spice for food, Indians use chiltepins for antilactation, whereby nursing mothers put chiltepin powder on their nipples to wean babies. Chiltepins are also an aid in childbirth because when they are powdered and inhaled they cause sneezing. And, of course, the hot chiles induce gustatory sweating, which cools the body during hot weather.

In 1794, Padre Ignaz Pfeffercorn, a German Jesuit living in Sonora, described the wild chile pepper: "A kind of wild pepper which the inhabitants call *chiltipin* is found on many hills. It is placed unpulverized on the table in a salt cellar and each fancier takes as much of it as he believes he can eat. He pulverizes it with his fingers and mixes it with his food. The *chiltipin* is the best spice for soup, boiled peas, lentils, beans, and the like. The Americans swear that it is exceedingly healthful and very good as an aid to the digestion." In fact, even today, chiltepins are used— amazingly enough—as a treatment for acid indigestion.

Padre Pfeffercorn realized that chiltepins are one of the few crops left in the world that are harvested in the wild rather than cultivated. (Others are piñon nuts, Brazil nuts, and wild rice.) This fact has led to concern for the preservation of the chiltepin bushes because the harvesters often uproot entire plants or break off branches. Nabhan believes the chiltepin population is diminishing because of overharvesting and overgrazing. In Arizona, plans are under way to establish a chiltepin reserve near Tumacacori at Rock Corral Canyon in the Coronado National Forest. Native Seeds/SEARCH has been

AMERICANS DISCOVER PIÑONES

Before the Santa Fe Trail was officially opened for commerce between the United States and New Mexico, Americans were already exploring the region. In the 1820s, Josiah Gregg recorded that a wagon train headed to Missouri carried two gallons of piñon nut oil and noted that the "delicate, sweet flavor generated when these nuts are roasted would make it a serious rival to sesame oil."

Lt. John Abert reported in 1846 that piñones were "sometimes used for the manufacture of oil which may be used as a substitute for lamp oil. . . . They form the chief article of food of the Pueblos and New Mexicans."

granted a special use permit from the National Forest Service to initiate the permanent marking and mapping of plants, ecological studies, and a management plan proposal.

Even though wild crops were important, the ancient Anasazi culture of the Southwest—and later the Pueblo Indians—depended on some important domesticated crops: corn, beans, squash, and, some experts say, chile peppers other than chiltepins. It is not a coincidence that these foods are the foundation of Southwestern cuisine. Although domesticated in Mexico and Central America, these crops had moved north to what is now New Mexico long before the Spanish arrived.

Maize, what we now call corn, is of Mexican origin and was first domesticated about 5,000 years ago. Early man must have had to grow tons of it, for the cobs were about the size of pencil erasers. Maize moved north as the size of the cobs increased. In 1948, primitive ears of corn one to two inches long were discovered in the Bat Cave archaeological site in New Mexico and were dated to 3,500 years ago. By selectively breeding for larger ears, prehistoric farmers had developed over 200 varieties before Columbus arrived in the New World.

As the size of the cobs increased, maize became an increasingly important food plant in Native-American culture and acquired religious as well as culinary usage. Its pollen was used in numerous ceremonies, and various colors of corn were aligned with the four compass directions: blue with the west; red, the south; white, the east; and yellow, the north. It was grown in both dry field and irrigated plots and was much hardier than the hybrids of today.

Recently, there has been a resurgence of interest in non-hybridized varieties of corn, especially blue corn. Blue corn tortillas and chips are everywhere these days, and home gardeners are experimenting with an astounding variety of strains that have been rescued from hybridization. These include Isleta Blue, Santo Domingo Blue, Hispanic Pueblo Red, and Rainbow.

Most of the corn grown in the Southwest, however, is hybridized. It still forms the basis for what is called the corn cuisine of the Southwest, for the kernels are ground into corn meal and corn flour, which are used in breads and tortillas. And, tortillas, of course, are the foundation of a number of Southwestern entrees, such as enchiladas.

1-2 The Giant Saguaro Has Tasty
Fruits

Domesticated beans predate corn and were tamed about 10,000 years ago in Peru and apparently moved north into Mexico and eventually to the Southwest and to the rest of the country. When the Europeans arrived, the common bean, *Phaseolus vulgaris*, was being grown everywhere in what is now the United States. In the Southwest, another species, *P. acutifolius* or the tepary bean, was more popular because it was a rapid grower and resistant to drought and alkalinity. Black varieties of tepary beans, such as the Mitla Black Bean, are used in the famous black bean soups.

Pinto beans are commonly used in Southwestern cuisine, and farmers grow three or four different varieties, mostly in the Estancia Valley and the Four Corners area of New Mexico. (An interesting fact about pinto beans is that they must be cooked at the same altitude where they were grown. Beans grown at a lower altitude will not cook at higher altitudes and will simply rattle around in the pot no matter how long they are boiled.) Pinto beans are generally boiled, mashed, and then refried in oil or lard and spiced with red chiles. Traditionally, they are not used as an ingredient in chili con carne but rather are served as a side dish.

In addition to beans, another early vegetable was squash, which was first domesticated in Central America about 9,000 years ago and eventually spread over all the Americas. It was a staple of the Anasazi and Hohokam cultures and was passed down to the Navajos and Pueblo Indians, who loved them so much they incorporated the shape of the squash flowers into artwork and silver necklaces called squash blossoms. Several ancient squash varieties are still grown today, including the blue-fruited Acoma Pumpkin, the green-striped Santo Domingo Squash and the Calabaza Mexicana, or the long-neck pumpkin. Southwestern farmers and home gardeners grow squash in profusion—mostly zucchini, a late arrival to this cuisine.

Early Native-American recipes show that squash was a common ingredient of soups and stews. In addition to the squash fruits, the blossoms were also eaten. They were added to soups and stews or were boiled and mashed with corn kernels. Today, squash is sauteed with green chile and corn, baked whole, or added to casseroles. Pumpkins are a common ingredient of stews, and early New Mexican recipes also show how to make pumpkin candies. Incidentally, an early preservation method is baking winter varieties, slicing them thin, and drying them in the sun. The slices can be put in soups and stew or rehydrated with hot water.

The various uses of squash are probably secondary compared with those of chile peppers, which were domesticated in Mexico and South America at least 10,000 years ago, and, like many other food plants, migrated northward. Although a debate rages over whether domesticated chile peppers were introduced into New Mexico by Native Americans or the Spanish (see Chapter 6), there is no doubt that the wild chiltepins were growing in Arizona and Texas long before the European invaders arrived. Most chile pepper seeds sold today are hybridized varieties that were developed through selective breeding, long before the advent of genetic engineering. However, some seed companies collect and sell the wild chiltepin seeds from Sonora and Arizona (see Appendix 1).

During the past decade, a conservation movement has been growing in the Southwest; its goal is preserving and promoting the use of the traditional native crops that are thousands of years old. Home gardeners are being urged to forgo the hybridized and genetically altered commercial varieties of corn, beans, squash, and chiles and to plant, instead, the ancient American types. As

TRADITIONAL FOODS COMBAT DIABETES

After World War II, the Pima Indians of Arizona developed the highest incidence of Type II diabetes in the world. At first, doctors were baffled, but they soon realized that the cause was quite obvious. The Pimas had stopped eating native plants and had switched to a non-traditional diet loaded with sugary and fatty fast-food; the result was that their metabolism could not handle the change.

Studies by Native Seeds/SEARCH indicate that native desert food plants control blood sugar levels because they are slow-release carbohydrates that are converted to glucose at a much slower rate than other foods. In fact, mesquite pods and acorns rank among the top 10 percent of all foods ever analyzed for their effectiveness in controlling blood sugar.

Now, all that's needed to reduce diabetes among the Pimas is to switch them back to native foods—and that's not an easy task. Native Seeds/SEARCH representatives speak at conferences, health fairs, and schools and have even produced a video entitled "Desert Food Is Healthy Food." They have also designed recipes for such "new" delicacies as prickly pear juice, mesquite tea, and a cool bean salad with cholla buds.

Margaret Visser points out in *Much Depends on Dinner*: "Worst of all, varieties of corn are disappearing by the dozen even as these words are being written [1985]. A corn not being planted is a corn which ceases to exist."

Leading the movement to preserve ancient food plants is Native Seeds/SEARCH of Tucson. It provides seeds for an astounding number of varieties of traditional crops and publishes a quarterly newsletter, "The Seedhead News." The organization is listed under Mail-Order Sources in Appendix 1. "The food crops of this region," notes its catalog, "are not only delicious and nutritious but better adapted to the harsh environments of the low hot deserts and dry rocky uplands than most modern vegetables."

Exhibits and Demonstration Gardens

DESERT BOTANICAL GARDEN

1201 N. Galvin Parkway, Phoenix, AZ 85008 (602-941-1225). *Open daily, 9 a.m.–sunset (8 a.m.–sunset in June, July, and August).* ADMISSION CHARGE.

Over 10,000 desert plants representing 2,500 different species are planted in this fascinating garden. Of note to food lovers is the People and Plants of the Sonoran Desert Trail and its hands-on demonstrations of the ways early desert people collected and grew their food. On display are native food plants, demonstration gardens, mescal-roasting pits, *metates*, mescal pod pounders, and more. The gift shop offers books on food, cooking, and native plants.

TUCSON BOTANICAL GARDENS

2150 North Alvernon Way, Tucson, AZ 85712 (602-326-9255). *Open daily, 8 a.m.–4:30 p.m.* ADMISSION CHARGE.

The highlight here is the Native Seeds/SEARCH Garden, which is planted with traditional crop seeds gathered from the Southwest. Native-American gardening techniques are re-created in miniature. The gift shop is a celebration of chiles, featuring books, T-shirts, and food products. The gardens sponsor the annual Fiesta de los Chiles, held the third weekend in October.

PIMA COUNTY COOPERATIVE EXTENSION GARDEN CENTER

4040 North Campbell Avenue, Tucson, AZ 85719 (602-628-5628). *Open Monday–Friday, 9 a.m.–5 p.m. except holidays.* FREE ADMISSION.

1-3 Native Plantings at Tucson Botanical Gardens

This garden center is affiliated with the University of Arizona and has a demonstration garden of Arizona crop plants, particularly chiles (fourteen varieties). The center also carries a useful collection of gardening pamphlets.

Cultural Centers and Restaurants

INDIAN PUEBLO CULTURAL CENTER

2401 12th Street NW, Albuquerque, NM 87104. (505-843-7270). *Open Monday–Saturday, 9 a.m.–5:30 p.m.*

The Cultural Center features a permanent exhibit explaining the history of New Mexico from the point of view of the state's nineteen Indian pueblos. The restaurant specializes in Native-American dishes such as green chile stew and Indian fry bread.

OTHER NATIVE FOOD PLANTS OF THE DESERT

Yucca.   About thirty species of this relative of the lily grow in the Southwest, and virtually every part of the plant was utilized by Native Americans. The fruits, seeds, and petals were used as food, medicine, and dye; baskets, rope, cloth, and mats were made from the fibers and leaves; and the roots were pounded into pulp for a soap.

Jojoba.   Early desert dwellers were roasting and eating jojoba nuts for centuries before the Spanish arrived. After the frontier was settled, the plant was called the coffee bush because its seeds look like coffee beans—and indeed, it was often used as a coffee substitute by Anglo pioneers in Arizona. It has recently been produced commercially, but not for food. The fruit is about 50 percent oil, which is a substitute for sperm whale oil, and it is also used in the manufacture of shampoos and body oils.

Mesquite.   The beans of this plant were more important than even corn to the Native Americans of the Sonoran desert. The ripe beans were dried on rooftops, then stored. Later, the beans were ground into a flour for making drinks, breads, gruel, and cakes. Mesquite wood and charcoal are favorites for grilling meats and poultry in the Southwest.

TIGUA RESTAURANT

Ysleta del Sur Pueblo Tigua Indian Reservation, 122 S. Old Pueblo Rd., El Paso, TX 79915 (915-859-3916). *Open daily (except Mondays) 11 a.m.–4 p.m. (lunch only).* MAJOR CREDIT CARDS; BEER AND WINE LICENSE.

This restaurant first started serving food to Pueblo people in 1860 and opened to the general public 108 years later. The Indian bread served is made in adjacent *hornos*, and the aroma of fresh bread wafts through the restaurant. The restaurant boasts a red tile floor, corner fireplaces, and colorful murals. The food ranges from traditional (their red chile stew was named best in the world by *People* magazine) to shark fajitas (the shark comes from Corpus Christi).

GILA RIVER ARTS AND CRAFTS CENTER

Gila River Reservation, I-10, Exit 175, on Casablanca Road between Tucson and Phoenix (602-963-3981). *Open daily, 6 a.m.–5 p.m.* MAJOR CREDIT CARDS; NO LIQUOR.

The Gila River Reservation cultural center offers exhibits on the history and artifacts of the Pima and Maricopa tribes. The gift shop sells baskets, pottery, and rugs. The restaurant specialties are (of course) Indian fry bread, plus red and green chile, and Navajo tacos. Daily specials highlight white Indian beans and *posole*.

Recipes

MESQUITE BEAN CAKE

This recipe is one of the simplest Native Southwestern dishes imaginable, one that undoubtedly is tens of thousands of years old.

6 cups ripe, dried mesquite beans
Water

Grind the mesquite beans between two rocks, or with a mortar and pestle, until they reach a flour-like consistency. Add water and mix until a stiff dough is achieved. Pat the dough flat, cut it into squares, and dry the squares in the sun. Serve with coffee or milk.

SERVES: **2 TO 4**

1-4 The Fiery Chiltepin

Prickly Pear Jam

A Navajo legend holds that in order not to offend the spirit of the plant when the *tunas* are being picked, the gatherer must pluck a hair from his or her head—a sacrifice indeed for balding men! The prickly pear fruits are often available in border markets such as the Centro Mercado in Ciudad Juárez. The *Opuntia* cacti are easily grown in well-drained xeriscape gardens in most temperate parts of the country and usually produce plenty of fruits.

14 to 20 ripe prickly pear fruits
1 cup water
3 tablespoons lime juice
2 cups mesquite honey (more or less to taste)

If the fruits have spines, remove them by holding the fruit with tongs over an open flame until the spines burn off. Peel the fruits, remove as many seeds as possible, chop fine, and place in a pan with water. Simmer the fruit until it is soft and pulpy.

Add the lime juice, honey, and more water, if needed. Simmer until the jam is thick, about 30 minutes, taking care not to burn the mixture.

Remove from heat, cool, and place in sterilized jars.

YIELD: **2 CUPS OR MORE, DEPENDING ON THE SIZE OF THE FRUIT**

SALSA CASERA (CHILTEPIN HOUSE SAUCE)

This diabolically hot sauce is also called chiltepin *pasta* (paste). It is used in soups and stews and to fire up *machaca*, eggs, tacos, tostadas, and beans. Because it is so hot, the amount of sauce in this recipe can last for years when stored in the refrigerator.

2 cups chiltepins (yes, 2 cups)
8 to 10 cloves garlic
1 teaspoon salt
1 teaspoon Mexican oregano
1 teaspoon coriander seed
1 cup water
1 cup cider vinegar

Combine all ingredients in a blender and puree on high speed for 3 to 4 minutes. Refrigerate for 24 hours to blend the flavors before using. From then on, it keeps indefinitely in the refrigerator.

YIELD: **2 CUPS**
HEAT SCALE: **EXTREMELY HOT**

PUEBLO BLUE CORN-CHILE BREAD

The addition of green chiles to corn bread is an ancient Pueblo tradition. Blue corn is making a comeback in products such as chips and cornmeal.

1½ **cups blue cornmeal**
2 **tablespoons sugar**
2 **teaspoons baking powder**
½ **cup green chiles, chopped**
¾ **cup milk**
1 **egg**
2 **tablespoons bacon fat, or substitute cooking oil**

Combine the first three ingredients and mix well. In a separate bowl, combine the next four ingredients and mix well. Add the liquid ingredients to the dry ingredients and mix well.

Pour the mixture into a greased 8-inch-square baking dish. Bake at 350° for 30 minutes.

SERVES: **4 TO 6**
HEAT SCALE: MILD

PIÑON-GRILLED VENISON CHOPS

This tasty grilled dish features native New World game, chiles, tomatoes, and wild piñon nuts.

5 **tablespoons roasted piñon nuts**
3 **cloves garlic**
1 **tablespoon red chile powder**
½ **cup tomato paste**
¼ **cup olive oil**
3 **tablespoons lemon juice or vinegar**
4 **thick-cut venison chops, or substitute thick lamb chops**

Puree all the ingredients, except the venison, in a blender.

Paint the chops with this mixture and marinate at room temperature for 1 hour.

Grill the chops over a charcoal and piñon wood fire until done, basting with the remaining marinade.

SERVES: **4**

HEAT SCALE: **MILD**

BORDER BEANS

Beans are so ubiquitous in Southwest cuisines that there are literally hundreds—if not thousands—of recipes for them. This version originated in El Paso.

> **3 cups cooked pinto beans (canned or dried, simmered for hours until tender)**
>
> **1 onion, minced**
>
> **2 tablespoons lard (or substitute vegetable oil)**
>
> **5 slices bacon, minced**
>
> **¾ cup chorizo sausage**
>
> **1 pound tomatoes, peeled, seeded, and chopped**
>
> **6 serrano chiles with stems removed, minced**
>
> **1 teaspoon cumin**

Sauté the beans and onion in the lard (or oil) for about 5 minutes, stirring constantly. In another skillet, sauté the bacon and chorizo. Drain.

Combine the beans and onion with the drained bacon and chorizo in a pot; add the other ingredients and simmer for 30 minutes.

SERVES: **4**

HEAT SCALE: **MEDIUM**

1-5 A Stone and Wood Mesquite Pod Crusher

SPICY CALABACITAS

This recipe, by *Chile Pepper* magazine food editor Nancy Gerlach, combines three Native-American crops: squash, corn, and chile. It is one of the most popular dishes in New Mexico and is so colorful and tasty that it goes well with a variety of foods.

   3 zucchini squash, cubed
  ½ cup chopped onion
   4 tablespoons butter or margarine
  ½ cup green New Mexican chiles with stems removed, roasted, peeled, and chopped

2 cups whole kernel corn
1 cup milk
½ cup grated Monterey jack cheese

Sauté the squash and onion in the butter until the squash is tender. Add the chiles, corn, and milk. Simmer the mixture for 15 to 20 minutes to blend the flavors. Add the cheese and heat until the cheese is melted.

SERVES: **4 TO 6**
HEAT SCALE: **MEDIUM**

Indian Fry Bread

Fry bread is very similar to *sopaipillas*, which are smaller and puffier. These large round pieces of bread are used as a basis for Navajo tacos and can also be folded over a stuffing and eaten as a sandwich. At fairs, festivals, and rodeos throughout New Mexico, they are cooked in large round frying pans over open fires by Native Americans and are easily found due to the wonderful aromas.

3 cups flour
1½ teaspoons baking powder
½ teaspoon salt
1⅓ cups warm water
Vegetable oil for frying

Mix the flour, baking powder, and salt together. Add water and knead the dough until soft.

Roll out the dough until it is ¼ inch thick. Cut out 8-inch-diameter rounds.

Fry the bread in 2 to 3 inches of hot oil until puffed and browned on both sides.

YIELD: **4 PIECES OF FRY BREAD**

—NANCY GERLACH

PART

TWO

SOUTHWESTERN TEXAS

So many requests came in for the recipe [her Pedernales River chili] that it was easier to give the recipe a name, have it printed on a card and make it available. It has been almost as popular as the government pamphlet on the care and feeding of children.

—LADY BIRD JOHNSON

Chili concocted outside of Texas is usually a weak, apologetic imitation of the real thing. One of the first things I do when I get home to Texas is have a bowl of red. There is simply nothing better.

—PRESIDENT LYNDON B. JOHNSON

CHAPTER

―◆―

2

―

LONE STAR CUISINE

President Johnson didn't have to return to Texas for his favorite bowl o' red—he always carried a supply of Lady Bird's Pedernales River Chili aboard Air Force One. Such is the devotion to just one of the famous foods that originated in the Lone Star State.

Since Texas is larger than many countries, it is not surprising that its food should be varied and influenced by many different ethnic sources. But even as diverse as the state's cooking is, few people would suspect the culinary history of Texas began with wine.

From Grapes to Heifers

In the rugged land the Spanish called El Norte, the only route to the territories of Nuevo México and Tejas was the Camino Real—the rough trail romantically called the Royal Road—which ran from Mexico City to Chihuahua to El Paso del Norte to Santa Fe. In 1622 Franciscan monks planted vineyards at Ysleta Mission in El Paso, and this event was the beginning of the post-Columbian culinary history of Texas.

Winemaking moved north into New Mexico (see Part III), and it also spread across Texas as the Spanish attempted a spiritual conquest of Texas through the founding of missions. Trade routes were established from El Paso to the center of Texas, resulting in

25

the founding of San Antonio in 1718. The first wines were sacramental; it wasn't until the mid-1800s that commercial vineyards were planted.

Meanwhile, the major symbol of Texas, the longhorn steer, was becoming entrenched on the land and in the stomachs of Texans. The first known cattle to enter Texas were 500 head brought by Coronado in 1541 as he searched for the mythical city of Quivira. Many cows escaped from that herd and formed the nucleus of the wild herds that later roamed the state. Both the explorers and the settlers brought cattle to Texas, and, by 1757, the town of Reynosa had a human population of 269 and a cattle population of 18,000. Cows were worth a mere four pesos in those days, yet the cattle ranches flourished.

Modern cattle growing evolved mostly in east Texas, and, by 1860, the cattle population of the state exceeded 3 million head. The introduction of Brahma cattle from India proved to be momentous because these cows were immune to tick fever. In 1874, the first Brahmas were crossed with the native stock, resulting in a much hardier breed. But by that time, because the Civil War had prevented cattle from being shipped out, Texas was overrun with longhorns, and their value had dropped considerably.

But the establishment of huge ranches and cattle drives to other states soon changed that situation; suddenly, it seemed everyone was flocking to Texas to buy ranches, and even English earls became cattle barons. About this time, the buffalo were being slaughtered for their hides, and, in addition, their tongues were in demand by restaurants, which paid $9 a dozen for them.

It wasn't only the new types of cattle that thrived in Texas— the wine industry thrived as well. Beginning in 1876, the wine industry was assisted by Thomas Munson, who settled near Dennison and developed more than 300 new grape varieties. When the French vineyards were decimated by the plant louse in the 1880s, Munson sent carloads of Texas grape rootstock to France. The French grafted their vines onto the Texan rootstock, and the resulting plants were louse-resistant. Munson thus saved the French wine industry, and, with his colleague, Hermann Jaeger, became the only Americans to receive membership in the French Legion of Honor.

Munson was also instrumental in the development of the Texas wine industry. Because of his work, twenty-six wineries were operating at the turn of the century, and nearly thirty Texas win-

2-1 The Influence of Mexico Appears Everywhere
in the Southwest

eries were operating when Prohibition began in 1919. When Prohibition was repealed seventeen years later, only one winery—Val
Verde of Del Rio—had survived. As if recalling the origins of Texas
wines, it owed its existence to the sale of sacramental wine and
the sale of grapes to home winemakers.

The wine industry was re-established in Texas in 1975 when
the Schlaraffenland Winery (now Guadalupe Valley Winery) began
production. The industry's growth has been phenomenal since
then, with the number of wineries in the state growing to twenty-
six and having a total production of a million gallons in 1990. It
is interesting to note that Texas Cabernet Sauvignons are now
commonly served with fine, aged Texas beef.

Barbecues and Fajitas

Given the preponderance of beef in Texas, it's no wonder Texans
have perfected many different ways of cooking it. Perhaps their

TEXAS FOOD CELEBRATIONS

Carnival del Rio, a carnival of music, food, and fun along the Riverwalk in San Antonio in early February (512-227-4262).

Taste of the Sun Country, a restaurant fiesta in El Paso in March (915-541-4920).

The Texas Hill Country Food and Wine Festival, held in Austin in early April at the Four Seasons Hotel, is the premier food and wine event in the state and includes the induction ceremony for the Who's Who in Food and Wine in Texas awards (512-474-1889).

Fiesta San Antonio, held the third week in April, is a mega-event that lasts at least a week and features food, fun, and parades (512-227-5191).

Cinco de Mayo celebrates the expulsion of the French from Mexico with food and fun, May 5, in San Antonio Market Square (512-299-8600).

Return of the Chili Queens, a chili celebration in San Antonio on Memorial Day weekend (512-299-8600).

St. Anthony's Day at Tigua Indian Reservation offers traditional Native-American fare in El Paso on June 13 (915-859-3916 or 7913).

Texas Folklife Festival, held the first week in August at the Institute of Texas Cultures at HemisFair Plaza in San Antonio, showcases the ethnic diversity of the state with crafts, food, music, and dancing (512-226-7651).

Diez y Seis de Septiembre, Mexican Independence Day celebration in San Antonio Market Square and La Villita, September 16 (512-299-8610).

continued

Republic of Texas Chilympiad, in San Marcos, third weekend in September (512-396-2495).

Oktoberfest, in Fredericksburg, first weekend in October (512-997-4810).

Fredericksburg Food and Wine Festival, last weekend in October (512-997-7521).

Wurstfest, actually the "bestfest" for sausage, in New Braunfels, first week in November (512-625-9167).

crowning achievement is the Texas barbecue, which has been influenced by the Southern states in the United States, by German immigrants, and by Mexican-style barbecue. In Zavala County, between San Antonio and the border, there is a *norteño*-style (northern) barbecue known as *barbacoa*. In the early evening, a whole cow's head is wrapped in soaked burlap bags, set on top of the coals of a mesquite fire in a pit, and the pit is filled with dirt.

Twelve to eighteen hours later, the head is dug up and eaten for breakfast. The tongue, brains, and cheeks are served with jalapeños, refried beans, and guacamole. Some sources say Spanish soldiers created this dish and imported the technique when Texas was part of Mexico. This method is still commonly used in northern Mexico and in any *norteño* restaurant in the United States, such as Seis Salsas in Austin or El Norteño in Albuquerque. If you ask for *barbacoa*, don't expect a pork sandwich. You will probably get parts of *cabeza de vaca* (cow's head), which is delicious.

Beef is not the only meat barbecued in Texas. German immigrants have perfected the slow cooking of pork (see restaurant listings for Austin and the Hill Country, Chapter 3). *Cabrito*, or barbecued kid, is popular during the spring in Mexican-American communities, and lamb is also barbecued. Texas ranch barbecues are legendary for their huge size, with whole goats, pigs, and sides of beef being cooked for days over low heat.

The difference between grilling and barbecuing is important to remember: Grilling uses high heat and quick cooking, while barbecuing is "cooking meat with hot smoke," in the words of Red

Caldwell, author of *Pit, Pot & Skillet*. He says, "Closed pit barbecue involves building a fire at one end of an enclosed pit and forc-
ing the smoke to travel the length of the pit to an exit. Somewhere
in between, barbecue happens."

More precise is the USDA's catchy little definition: "Meat that
shall be cooked by the direct action of heat resulting from the
burning of hard wood or the hot coals therefrom for a sufficient
period to assume the usual characteristics . . . which include the
formation of a brown crust."

The earliest barbecues (the Virginia Burgesses mentioned
them in 1610, and George Washington went to one in 1769) were
undoubtedly whole hogs that were slow-cooked in pits in the
ground. Similar pits can still be used, but they tend to mess up
the lawn. The pits most commonly used today are specially constructed smokers that separate the meat from the direct heat of
the fire.

As Caldwell observes: "There are countless designs running
from huge brick units to various large-diameter pipe fabrications
to the ubiquitous fifty-five-gallon drum, various commercial config-
urations designed for urban dwellers, even the odd converted refrigerator (not a bad cooker, actually)."

Another important distinction between barbecue and grilling
is that barbecue sauces are used to baste barbecued or smoked
meats but generally are not placed on grilled meats because their
sugar content causes them to burn easily. In Texas, the sauces
tend to be tomato- and chile-based, rather than the vinegar-based
sauces of the Deep South.

A fairly recent innovation in Texas cooking is fajitas, which
are prepared with skirt steak—a pretty fancy term for beef dia-
phragm muscle. Fajitas have their roots in the dish *carne asada*,
thin steaks that are roasted or grilled until well done. But fajita
skirt steak is marinated first in jalapeño juice and port wine, or
various other concoctions prepared by innovative cooks. The name
means little belts, an allusion to the fact that after grilling the
steak is cut across the grain into thin strips. These strips are
placed on flour tortillas and are topped with fresh salsa, cheese,
tomatoes, and sometimes guacamole.

Fajitas probably originated on the vast *ranchos* surrounding
Monterrey, Mexico, and gradually worked their way north. In the
late 1960s, Sonny Falcon learned the butcher's trade in the Lower
Rio Grande Valley before he moved to Austin. Although most Texas

2-2 A Little Texas Food Humor

butchers threw the beef skirt steak section in with the ground meat, Mexican butchers from the valley put them aside for clients who liked to grill them for "fajita tacos."

While working in Austin, Falcon experimented with many methods of tenderizing the fajita meat and finally arrived at his butterfly slicing technique. In 1969, he began selling his grilled fajita tacos on weekends at an outdoor festival in Kyle, Texas. His fajitas became a favorite at fairs and outdoor events all over Texas, and he became known as Sonny "Fajita King" Falcon.

Soon, restaurants were making their own versions of fajitas. Pharr's Roundup Restaurant in Matamoros began serving them in 1977; five years later, the Austin Hyatt Regency was serving 13,000 orders of fajitas a month. But the chef at the Hyatt had no luck with skirt steak, so he substituted sirloin. Falcon would argue that a "steak taco" was not a "fajita taco," but no one paid much attention to the fine points of Spanish translation. As a result, anything served with fillings and tortillas came to be called fajitas, including chicken fajitas, shrimp fajitas, fish fajitas, and fajita pitas. Whether such phrases are translated as "fish skirt steaks" or "little chicken belts," all are completely meaningless to Spanish speakers and to Mexican butchers who use the word *fajita* only to describe beef skirt steak. In other words, *chicken fajitas* is a contradiction in terms.

The "National Dish" of Texas

Perhaps the most famous Tex-Mex creation is that bowl o' red, chili con carne, a dish most writers on the subject say did *not* originate in Mexico. Even Mexico disclaims chili; the *Diccionario de Mejicanismos*, a Mexican dictionary published in 1959, defines it as "a detestable food passing itself off as Mexican and sold from Texas to New York City."

Despite such protestations, the combination of meat and chile peppers in stew-like concoctions is not uncommon in Mexican cooking. Mexican *caldillos* and *adobos* often resemble chili con carne in appearance and taste because they use similar ingredients: various chiles combined with meat (usually beef), onions, garlic, cumin, and occasionally tomatoes.

E. De Grolyer, a scholar and chili aficionado, believed Texas chili con carne had its origins as the "pemmican of the Southwest" in the late 1840s. According to De Grolyer, Texans pounded together dried beef, beef fat, chile peppers, and salt to make trail food for the long ride to San Francisco and the gold fields. The concentrated, dried mixture was then boiled in pots along the trail as an "instant chili."

A variation of this theory holds that cowboys invented chili while driving cattle along the lengthy and lonely trails. Supposedly, range cooks planted oregano, chiles, and onions among patches of mesquite to protect them from foraging cattle. The next time they passed along the same trail, they would collect the spices, combine them with beef (what else?), and make a dish called trail drive chili. Undoubtedly, the chiles used with the earliest incarnations of chili con carne were the chiltepins, called chilipiquíns in Texas, where they grow wild on bushes—particularly in the southern part of the state.

Probably the most likely explanation for the origin of chili con carne in Texas comes from the heritage of Mexican food combined

IS IT SOUTHWESTERN, REGIONAL, OR THE NEW TEXAS CUISINE?

Most food writers still call the best regional cooking in Texas Southwestern cuisine, but the best chef in Texas, Stephan Pyles of Dallas' legendary Routh Street Cafe, makes a convincing case that modern Texas cuisine is something unique. Part of the difference is the diversity of cultures within the state. Although west Texas "cowboy culture" resembles the rest of the Southwest, east Texas is part of the culture of the Old South. It is said that the bayou region from Port Arthur and Orange west to Houston now contains more Cajuns than Louisiana. The south Texas Gulf ports of Galveston and Corpus Christi have also given the state continuous contact with the Caribbean. German food is popular in the Hill Country, where German settlers founded New Braunfels and Fredericksburg in the mid-1800s.

Visitors may think of Texas food as barbecue, chili, and Tex-Mex; however, Pyles writes in the August 1991 issue of *Food & Wine:* "In fact there are at least twenty-five national and ethnic influences on Texas cookery, including Belgian and Filipino. . . . After centuries, the result is a cuisine built, layer by layer, from various cultures, which maintain their individual characteristics." Pyles told me on the phone, "I told *Bon Appetit* in 1986 that I didn't like the umbrella term [*Southwestern*], and I said I like my food to be called Texas cuisine." And so it is: Pyle's new cookbook is titled *The New Texas Cuisine*.

—ROBB WALSH

with the rigors of life on the Texas frontier. Most historians agree that J. C. Clopper, who lived near Houston, wrote the earliest description of chili during a visit to San Antonio in 1828: "When they [poor families of San Antonio] have to pay for their meat in the market, a very little is made to suffice for the family; it is generally cut into a kind of hash with nearly as many peppers as there are pieces of meat—this is all stewed together."

Except for this quote, which does not mention the dish by name, historians of heat can find no documented evidence of chili in Texas before 1880. Around that time in San Antonio, a municipal market—El Mercado—was operating in Military Plaza. Historian Charles Ramsdell noted that "the first rickety chili stands were set up in this marketplace, with the bowls of red sold by women who were called 'chili queens.'"

The fame of chili con carne began to spread, and the dish soon became a major tourist attraction, appearing in Mexican restaurants all over Texas—and elsewhere. The first known recipe appeared in 1880 in *Mrs. Owen's Cook Book*. She got it all wrong, of course, referring to the bowl o' red as "the national dish of Mexico" and adding ham, carrots, celery, and cloves to it.

At the Chicago World's Fair in 1893, a bowl o' red was available at the San Antonio Chili Stand, and, in 1896, the first U.S. Army recipe appeared in the *Manual for Army Cooks*. Incidentally, Army chili contained both rice and onions. Given the popularity of the dish, some commercialization was inevitable. In 1898, William Gebhardt of New Braunfels, Texas, produced the first chili powder and began canning his chili con carne, Gebhardt Eagle. By 1918, Walker Austex was producing 45,000 cans a day of Walker's Red Hot Chili Con Carne and 15,000 cans a day of Mexene Chili Powder.

The chili queens were banned from San Antonio in 1937 for health reasons—public officials objected to the flies and poorly washed dishes. They were restored by Mayor Maury Maverick (his real name, folks) in 1939, but their stands were closed again shortly after the start of World War II. But Texans have never forgotten their culinary heritage, and, in 1977, the Texas Legislature proclaimed chili con carne the "Official Texas State Dish."

Today there is a movement afoot by the International Chili Society (in California, of all places!) to have Congress name chili the official national dish, but the idea isn't new. In the mid-1970s,

Craig Claiborne wrote, "We thought for years that if there's such a thing as a national American dish, it isn't apple pie, it's chili con carne. . . . In one form or another, chili in America knows no regional boundaries. North, South, East, and West, almost every man, woman, and child has a favorite recipe."

Chili con carne is still enormously popular in Texas and other states, and huge chili cookoffs are held. Teams of cooks use highly guarded secret recipes to compete for thousands of dollars in prizes while having a good ol' time partying. Some traditionalists, however, scorn the cookoff-style chili con carne as too elaborate and are promoting a return to the classic, "keep it simple, stupid" cafe-style chili.

Sam Pendergrast of Abilene is such a purist. In his landmark article, "Requiem for Texas Chili," which appeared in *Chile Pepper* magazine in 1989, he noted: "I have a theory that real chili is such a basic, functional dish that anyone can make it from the basic ingredients—rough meat, chile peppers, and a few common spices available to hungry individuals—and they'll come up with pretty much the same kind of recipe that was for most of a century a staple of Texas tables. So all we have to do to get back to real chili is to get rid of the elitist nonsense."

Incidentally, chili lovers will rejoice to learn that San Antonio has been staging what they call historic re-enactments of the chili queens, complete with some of the original queens like songstress Lydia Mendoza, who serenades the chili eaters. Called the Return of the Chili Queens Festival, the event is held each Memorial Day weekend in old San Antonio. The fiesta re-creates the era of the chili queens and celebrates the dish that, no matter what its origin, will live forever in the hearts, minds, and stomachs of Texans everywhere.

The Advent of Tex-Mex

Throughout the Southwest, each state has its own version of Mexican cooking. With a few exceptions, the same basic dishes—enchiladas, tacos, and the like—have become very popular but do not truly represent the cooking of Mexico. Rather, they have become Mexican-American versions of cooking from the northern states of Mexico, which developed when the states were a part of

2-3 Smoking Meats the Old Way at Kreuz Market
in Lockhart

Mexico and evolved in their own directions, based on regional ingredients and cooking styles.

The first Mexican restaurant to open in Texas was the Old
Borunda Cafe in Marfa in 1887, closely followed by the Original
Mexican Restaurant in San Antonio in 1900. Restaurants had a
great influence on the development of Tex-Mex cooking. As Texas
food writer Richard West explains: "The standard Tex-Mex foods
(tacos, enchiladas, rice, refried beans, and tamales)—and newer
editions, like chiles rellenos, burritos, *flautas*, and *chalupas*—
existed in Mexico before they came here. What Texas restaurant
cooks did was to throw them together and label them Combination
Dinner, Señorita Dinner, and the hallowed No. 1. In so doing, they
took a few ethnic liberties and time-saving shortcuts. For example:
Tex-Mex tacos as we know them contain ground, instead of shredded, meat. And chile gravy is most often out of the can, instead of
being made fresh with *chiles anchos* and special spices."

The chile peppers most commonly used in homemade Tex-
Mex cuisine are *poblanos* from Mexico (and their dried version,
anchos), which are tasty and mild. The fresh ones are usually
served relleno-style; the serranos for fresh salsas; the chilipiquín

(chiltepin) for soups and stews; and, of course, the ubiquitous ja-lapeño. This fat and fiery pepper is popular everywhere and is served raw, pickled, stuffed, chopped in salsas, and even in cooked sauces for topping enchiladas and huevos rancheros, which are served with fried eggs and salsa ranchera over corn or wheat tor-tillas. New Mexican chiles are gradually making an appearance in Tex-Mex cooking, especially the dried red form. For example, Chuy's Restaurant (see listing, p. 61) in Austin now brings in 10,000 pounds of fresh green New Mexican chiles from Hatch, New Mexico, and has a roasting and peeling fiesta.

In addition to the standard Tex-Mex food items, a few others deserve mention. *Menudo*, a bowl of tripe and hominy soup fla-vored with *anchos* or chilipiquíns and a calf's or pig's foot, is es-pecially popular with Mexican Americans, who regard it as a hangover cure. They call it "the breakfast of champions" and tease Anglos about their aversion to eating "variety meats." Contrary to popular belief, *menudo* is not cows' intestines, but rather the lin-ing of the second stomach chamber, called honeycomb tripe. How-ever, it is definitely an acquired taste.

Posole, a hominy and chile stew, is also a popular dish, as are tamale pie, guacamole, fried jalapeños, *quesadillas*, *cabrito asado* (braised kid), and desserts such as *flan*, *capirotada* (bread pud-ding), and *buñelos*.

Some recent inventions such as nachos (cheese-and-jalapeño-coated tostada chips) seem to have originated sometime during World War II at the Victory Club in Piedras Negras, although anoth-er source credits the invention to a restaurant in Villa Acuna, Mex-ico. The snack was served at the 1966 Texas State Fair in Dallas, and Arlington Stadium, home of the Texas Rangers, introduced the dish to baseball fans in 1975. From there, nachos spread to stadiums all over the country, but some customers complained that the jala-peños were too hot. No problem, said Dr. Ben Villalon at the Texas Agricultural Experiment Station at Weslaco, and he proceeded to develop a non-pungent jalapeño specifically for the nacho market.

No discussion of Texas food would be complete without men-tioning beans. They are cooked in many different ways and are served with all the major Texas food groups: barbecue, chili, and Tex-Mex. One of the greatest celebrators of Texas beans was the famous author, professor, and naturalist, J. Frank Dobie. "A lot of people want chili with their beans," he wrote in the 1949 Nie-mann-Marcus book, *A Taste of Texas*. "Chili disguises the bean

THAT LEGUMINOUS TREE WITH THE GREAT SMOKE

You either love mesquite or hate it, depending on whether you're a farmer, hunter, cook, rancher, or woodworker. Farmers and ranchers hate the tree, of course, because it chokes out needed grazing grass; and, as a result of its extensive root system, it is nearly impossible to remove from pastures. The ranchers, however, were at least partially responsible for the spread of mesquite over 55 million acres in Texas because their cattle passed the mesquite seeds through their digestive systems unharmed and deposited them in a perfect, natural fertilizer!

Yes, mesquite is tenacious, and its thorns can puncture tires—that's the bad side. The good side is that the tree prevents erosion and forms a microhabitat for birds and animals in an otherwise harsh environment. A clump of mesquite trees provides shade, humidity, and food for such animals as doves, deer, javelina, and rabbits, which is why hunters like the tree. The tree, a legume like the peanut, is nitrogen-fixing, so it serves as a host tree for other wild plants such as chiltepins.

The mesquite beans, which are sugar-rich, provide food for animals and man and once provided up to 40 percent of the food in the diet of Native Americans in Texas. The wood of the tree is variously shaded, which is why woodworkers love it for making sculptures, gunstocks, parquet floors, and other hardwood products.

continued

Cooks love mesquite because its wood produces a sweet smoke that imparts a great flavor to grilled meats. Most mesquite trees these days are being cut down for wood chips and to make charcoal, but there's such an abundance of trees that there is no threat to mesquite.

Throughout Texas and the Southwest, travelers will have little trouble finding mesquite-grilled foods. But a hint to the home cook—the wood is used for grilling but is considered too acrid for the lengthy smoking or barbecuing of meats. For that, pecan or hickory wood is suggested. And if you're grilling with mesquite, be sure to use aged wood because the green wood is too oily.

just as too much barbecue sauce destroys the delectability of good meat. For me, chili simply ruins good beans, although I do like a few chilipiquíns cooked with them. I believe, however, that the chilipiquíns make a better addition after the beans are cooked. I add about three to a plate of beans and mash them up in the plate along with a suitable amount of fresh onion. A meat eater could live on beans and never miss meat. When a Mexican laborer is unable to lift a heavy weight, his companions say he 'lacks frijoles.' As you may deduce, I am a kind of frijole man. On the oldtime ranches of the border country, where I grew up, frijoles were about as regular as bread, and in some households they still are."

Today, Texas cuisine is somewhat of a melting pot, a tossed salad kind of cooking, with many different influences vying for top honors. In addition to the cooking styles mentioned above, Texas is influenced greatly by Gulf Coast and Louisiana cooking, Southern cooking (particularly in eastern Texas), Midwestern styles, and even New Mexican cuisine in West Texas. One of the great things about traveling through Texas is the opportunity to sample a wide variety of Southwestern cooking.

Recipes

LADY BIRD JOHNSON'S PEDERNALES RIVER CHILI

This recipe originally contained beef suet, but that ingredient was omitted after LBJ's severe heart attack when he was Senate majority leader. Remember to skim the fat off the chili.

4 pounds coarsely ground beef
1 large onion, chopped
2 cloves garlic, chopped
1 teaspoon oregano
1 teaspoon ground cumin
6 teaspoons red chile powder (or more for heat)
2 16-ounce cans tomatoes
2 cups hot water
Salt to taste

Combine the beef, onion, and garlic in a skillet and sear until the meat is lightly browned. Transfer this mixture to a large pot, add the remaining ingredients, and bring to a boil. Reduce the heat and simmer for 1 hour.

When done, transfer the chili to a bowl and place it in the refrigerator. When the fat has congealed on top, remove it with a spoon.

Reheat the chili and serve it as LBJ liked it—without beans and accompanied with a glass of milk and saltine crackers.

SERVES: **12**
HEAT SCALE: **MILD TO MEDIUM**

BARBECUED BRISKET

Most barbecue in Texas revolves around beef, and more specifically, brisket. When selecting your brisket, choose only 10- to 12-pound packer-trimmed briskets. The smaller briskets don't have enough fat to tenderize them, and the larger ones could have come off of a tough old range bull that no amount of cooking will *ever* tenderize. Avoid closely trimmed or value-packed brisket pieces. The fat that was cut off to make them pretty is the very stuff that would have made them tender! All briskets have a fat cover on one side. Ignore this! Squeeze the thick end with both thumbs until you find the brisket with the smallest fat kernel; that's the one for you. Take it home and build the fire. While the fire is getting going—I build mine out of a mixture of mesquite and oak—rub the brisket with a dry rub. Make sure the meat is thoroughly coated. This helps seal the meat and adds a flavorful crust. Never use salt, as it dries and toughens the meat. Use tongs instead of a fork to turn the meat because piercing allows the juices to flow out, leaving a tougher brisket.

2-4 Scholz Garten Circa 1900 (*Credit:* Austin History Center)

DRY RUB

Lemon juice (about ¼ to ½ cup per brisket)
1 11-ounce can of finely ground, light chili powder
1 tablespoon ground cayenne powder
2 tablespoons (rounded) black pepper
4 tablespoons (rounded) garlic powder

Thoroughly coat all surfaces of the brisket with lemon juice and rub in well. Combine the dry ingredients in a bowl and sprinkle generously over the brisket, rubbing in well. Make sure the brisket is entirely covered. Store leftover rub in a tightly sealed container in the refrigerator.

When the wood has burned down, move the coals to one side of the pit, place the meat *away* from the direct heat, *fat side up* (let gravity and nature do the basting), and close the pit. Some cooks add a pan of water near the coals to provide added moisture, but I don't. Now, *don't touch* the meat for about 12 hours. Just drink a few beers, cook a pot of beans, and tend your fire. Hold the cooking temperature around 210° in the brisket cooking area. Since helpers usually show up at the first whiff of smoke, you probably ought to put some of the leftover rub on a couple of racks of pork ribs, toss them on the pit—in the hotter end—and baste and turn them for 4 or 5 hours, just to keep the animals at bay.

After 12 hours, generously slather the brisket with a *basting* sauce (not a barbecue sauce), wrap it tightly in aluminum foil, and return it to the pit. Close all the air supplies to the fire and allow the meat to "set" in the pit for 3 or 4 hours. This step really tenderizes the meat. Here's a good basting sauce recipe to get going.

RED'S BASTING SAUCE

1 pound butter or margarine
2 onions, peeled and thick-sliced
5 cloves garlic, peeled and crushed
1 12-ounce bottle of beer (Shiner preferred)
4 lemons, quartered
1 bunch parsley tops, chopped
1 pint cooking oil
2 tablespoons commercial chili powder
½ teaspoon cayenne powder
¼ cup Worcestershire sauce
2 bay leaves

Melt the butter, add the onions and garlic, and sauté for 4 to 5 minutes to soften. Add the beer, squeeze in the lemon juice, and add the lemon rinds to the pot. When the foam subsides, add all the remaining ingredients and bring to a boil. Reduce the heat to medium-low and simmer for 20 minutes.

By the way, notice there are no tomatoes, ketchup, or sugar in this recipe, which caramelize and burn quickly, giving the meat a *nasty* taste.

Serve the brisket with beans, cole slaw, jalapeños, onions, pickles, and plenty of bread. Cold beer or iced tea are the traditional beverages of choice.

YIELD: A 10-POUND BRISKET WILL YIELD 8 TO 16 SERVINGS, DEPENDING ON THE INDIVIDUAL BRISKET AND THE SIZE OF THE GUESTS' APPETITES.
HEAT SCALE: MILD

—RED CALDWELL

2-5 100th Anniversary Party at Scholz Garten, 1966 (*Credit:* Austin History Center)

SAM PENDERGRAST'S ORIGINAL ZEN CHILI

I have a theory that real chili is such a basic, functional dish that anyone can make it from the basic ingredients—rough meat, chile peppers, and a few common spices available to hungry individuals.

> **1 pound fatty bacon**
> **2 pounds coarse beef, extra large grind**
> **½ cup whole cominos (cumin seed—yes, ½ cup!)**
> **½ cup pure ground red New Mexico chiles**
>   **Water**
> **1 teaspoon cayenne powder**
>   **Salt, pepper, and garlic powder to taste**
>   **Paprika**

Render the grease from the bacon; eat a bacon sandwich while the chili cooks. (Good chili takes time.)

Sauté the ground beef in bacon grease over medium heat. Add the cominos and begin adding the red chiles until what you are cooking smells like chili. (This is the critical point. If you add all the spices at once, there is no leeway for personal tastes.) Let the mixture cook a bit between additions and don't feel compelled to use all of the red chiles.

Add water in small batches to avoid sticking; add more later for a soupier chili. Slowly add the cayenne powder until smoke curls your eyelashes. Palefaces may find the red chiles alone have enough heat.

Simmer the mixture until the cook can't resist ladling a bowlful for sampling. Skim excess fat for dietetic chili, or mix the grease with a small amount of cornmeal for a thicker chili.

Finish with salt, pepper, and garlic powder to individual taste; add paprika to darken. Continue simmering until served; continue reheating until gone. (As with wine, time enobles good chili and exposes bad.)

The result should be something like old-time Texas cafe chili: a rich, red, heavily cominesque concoction with enough liquid to welcome crackers, some chewy chunks of meat thoroughly permeated by the distinctive spices, and an aroma calculated to lure strangers to the kitchen door.

SERVES: **6**
HEAT SCALE: **HOT**

Variation:

For cookoff contest chili, drink bad tequila two days before starting the chili; burn the mixture frequently; sprinkle it occasionally with sand and blood; serve it cold to a dozen other drunks and call them judges; and keep telling yourself you're having a great time.

—SAM PENDERGRAST

TEXAS GREEN SAUCE

When you order green sauce in Texas, this is what you will be served. It differs from New Mexico's green sauce because the color is derived from tomatillos rather than from green chiles. This sauce can be used as a dipping sauce, with enchiladas, or as a topping for grilled poultry or fish.

3 **pounds tomatillos**

1 **bunch green onions**

1 **small bunch cilantro**

1 **tablespoon garlic in oil**

2 **teaspoons sugar**

2 **teaspoons lime juice**

1 **tablespoon chicken base dissolved in 2 tablespoons water**

6 **serrano chiles, stems removed**

Roast the tomatillos in a roasting pan under the broiler until they are brown and squishy. Turn them over with a pair of tongs and repeat the process. Combine the roasted tomatillos, including all the liquid from the roasting process, with the remaining ingredients in a food processor and puree.

Simmer for 10 minutes before serving or incorporating into another recipe.

YIELD: 4 CUPS
HEAT SCALE: MEDIUM

—MICK VANN

TEX-MEX ENCHILADAS

Throughout this guide, we'll try to distinguish among the various styles of Southwestern Mexican cooking. Therefore, we have included four totally different recipes for "red" enchiladas—one from Texas, one from New Mexico, and two from Arizona. Cooks can decide for themselves which one is best, but we already know the answer. Here is the first recipe, as prepared in Southwestern Texas.

- **2 tablespoons shortening**
- **3 tablespoons flour**
- **2 tablespoons red chili powder (or more for heat)**
- **3 cups warm water**
- **2 tablespoons vegetable oil**
- **12 corn tortillas**
- **2 onions, chopped**
- **4 cups grated longhorn cheese**

Melt the shortening in a skillet, stir in the flour, and make a roux. Add the chili powder and water; stir and cook until this chili gravy is thick. Keep warm on the stove.

Lightly grease a glass, ovenproof casserole dish and preheat the oven to 450°.

Heat the oil in a skillet and, using tongs, lightly fry each tortilla for about 5 seconds on each side. Do not overcook or they will get rubbery. Drain on paper towels.

Dip each tortilla in the gravy, put some of the onion and cheese on the tortilla, roll it up, and place it with the seam side down in a casserole dish. Repeat until all 12 tortillas have been rolled.

Pour the chili gravy over the tortillas, top with more cheese, and bake for 10 minutes.

SERVES: 4
HEAT SCALE: **MILD**

FRIJOLES À LA DOBIE

This recipe for J. Frank Dobie's beans originally appeared in 1949.

  1 **pound dried pinto beans, picked clean and washed thoroughly**
1½ **inch cube salt pork**
 12 **chilipiquíns (chiltepins)**
  4 **teaspoons grated raw onion**
     Vinegar

> Soak the beans overnight; then drain and rinse. Place beans in a pot with the salt pork and enough water to cover; cook over medium heat until tender. Drain the beans and keep them warm.
>
> Divide the beans into four servings; for each serving, mash three chilipiquíns into the beans with 1 teaspoon of raw onion, and sprinkle with vinegar.
>
> SERVES: **4**
> HEAT SCALE: **HOT**

MACHO NACHOS

Although non-pungent jalapeños have been developed for wimpy palates, please remember only pungent peppers are permitted in this recently invented snack.

 12 **corn tortillas**
     Vegetable oil
 ½ **pound grated cheese (cheddar, longhorn, jack)**
 10 **pickled jalapeños or 15 pickled serranos, cut into rings**

> Stack the tortillas and cut the stack into quarters. Fry the quartered tortillas in hot oil until they are crisp, turning as necessary. Drain on paper towels.
>
> Lay the chips on a baking sheet and cover with the cheese and one or two rings of chiles per chip. Bake at 350° just until the cheese melts.
>
> SERVES: **4 TO 6**
> HEAT SCALE: **MEDIUM TO HOT**

CHAPTER

✦

3

___

AUSTIN AND THE HILL COUNTRY

Austin is not a typical tourist town, but it most certainly is a food lover's town. Austin has no Sea Worlds or Disneylands, but there are more than enough sights and interesting places to entertain most adventurous people.

Besides being the state capital and home of the University of Texas, Austin is probably best known for its music scene, which is concentrated mostly around 6th Street (also called Little Bourbon Street), where there are about seventy shops, restaurants, and nightclubs.

The city has produced such music legends as Willie Nelson, Stevie Ray Vaughan, Jerry Jeff Walker, and the Fabulous Thunderbirds, plus the best Texas (and probably U.S.) reggae group, the Killer Bees. While visiting Austin, be sure not to miss a trip to one of the clubs to enjoy some country, blues, rock, conjunto, or other eclectic music.

Some places to visit include the Texas State Capitol (off Congress Avenue downtown), with its dome that is 7 feet higher than that of the U.S. Capitol; the Lyndon Baines Johnson Library and Museum (2313 Red River Street); the Texas Confederate Museum (112 E. 11th Street); the O. Henry House and Museum (409 E. 5th Street), the Laguna Gloria Art Museum (3809 W. 35th Street); the Huntington Art Gallery (21st Street and Guadalupe) with its Michener Collection of twentieth-century American painting; and the oldest building in the capital complex, the Governor's Mansion (11th and Colorado Streets).

Lovers of outdoor sports will truly enjoy Austin, where they will find great facilities for running, bicycling, tennis, and golf. But the main attractions are the nearby lakes, including Town Lake that runs through the city, and Lake Travis, with its spectacular scenery. Boating, sailing, water skiing, scuba diving, and fishing are all available around Austin.

For additional information on Austin and vicinity, contact the Austin Convention and Visitors Bureau, P.O. Box 2990, Austin, TX 78769 (512-478-0098).

A Capsule History of Austin Eating

In 1841, the king of France's chargé d'affaires, "Count" Jean Peter Isidore Alphonse de Saligny, arrived in Austin to discuss business with politicians in the newly founded Texas Republic. He brought with him a servant, a driver, and Austin's first French chef de cuisine. The house Saligny built, the French Legation, is today a fascinating museum. It is located just east of I-35 at 802 San Marcos Street, just off 8th Street (open Tuesday–Sunday, 1 p.m.–5 p.m.).

In 1966, the French Legation's kitchen was equipped with a collection of antique, French-made kitchen equipment brought to the New World by French-American families and their chefs. This museum reproduction of Count Saligny's original fully equipped kitchen is the finest example anywhere of a French creole kitchen. Saligny remained in Texas until 1845, wining and dining the new republic's politicians and talking them into signing a friendship treaty with France. During the process, Saligny and his chef began the tradition of fine dining in Austin and in the Republic of Texas.

In 1866, Austin's oldest existing restaurant, Scholz Garten, opened not far from the State Capitol. It's a German beer garden that is still popular with state legislators and is listed on the National Register of Historic Places.

Wining and dining Texas politicians has been the Austin restaurant scene's main spectator sport throughout the city's history. But the lobbyists have always complained that it's hard to spend enough money to impress anybody in Austin. Although a sprinkling of fine dining experiences is available, most Austin restau-

3-1 The Shelves Are Jammed with Spicy Foods at Sambet's Cajun Store

rants are in the lower price ranges. Mexican food, barbecue, and Southern cooking are particularly well represented. Of special interest in Austin and the surrounding rural towns are the funky old joints, places that seem like time capsules from another era.

Kreuz Market in Lockhart, a meat market that became a barbecue joint, is a good example of a funky, historic eatery. Opened in 1900 just off the Lockhart Town Square, Kreuz became famous for its smoked meats and sausage. Ask for a tour; the owners will gladly take you to the basement to see the old ammonia-powered refrigeration units, or out to the woodpile to explain the aging system for the post oak used in the open fire pits.

Louis Mueller's Barbecue in downtown Taylor is another historic spot with great food. Built in the 1930s, Mueller's is still owned by the family of the original owner. Try the pork ribs if you can get there early enough—Mueller sells barbecue until it runs out, and he often runs out early!

Kreuz and Mueller were descendants of the many German immigrants who arrived in south and central Texas in the early 1800s, a wave of immigration encouraged by Mexico in an attempt to settle the sparsely populated state of Texas by giving away land. During the time Stephen F. Austin brought large groups of Southerners to Texas with their traditions of farming and Southern cookery, many Germans and Czechs also arrived, bringing with them their traditions of brewing beer and smoking meats. Thus, beer and barbecue have as long a history in central Texas as Southern-fried chicken, chicken-fried steak, and black-eyed peas.

By the early 1900s, the success of the ranching business in Texas had provided a cheap, plentiful supply of beef. But unlike the tender corn-fed beef that made New York strip steak famous, Texas beef was as tough as it was flavorful. It was best when cooked for a long time, as in barbecue brisket, or cut up into tiny chunks for chili. Dr. J. H. Salisbury of England, who discovered his famous Salisbury steak was an aid to digestion, helped increase the popularity of ground meat around the turn of the century. In Texas, where tough beef was so plentiful, the hamburger soon became ubiquitous. During the Great Depression, hamburgers sold for a nickel.

The 1920s and 1930s were the golden age of hamburger joints in Austin. Dirty's, also known as Martin's Kum-Back Burgers, opened on Guadalupe near the University of Texas in 1926. It's still a favorite of many Austin old-timers, and it was one of the most popular drive-ins in town during the drive-in craze. But the best example of the hamburger joints of that era is Hut's Hamburgers on West 6th Street—described by *Texas Monthly* magazine as "a living museum." Hut's walls feature newspaper advertisements from the building's grand opening as Sammy's Drive-in in 1939.

Homer Hudson, who would eventually move Hut's into the Sammy's building in 1964, opened his original Hut's Hamburgers on Congress Avenue in 1939. Hamburger joints are still Austin's most popular eating institutions—as one might expect in a city dominated by college students. Mad Dog & Beans, just off the campus on 24th Street, and the Waterloo Ice House on Lamar at 6th are two good examples of the modern joints where Austinites eat burgers.

Austin's oldest existing Tex-Mex eateries were built in the 1950s. The Tex-Mex style has undergone major changes since the eateries opened. Although we used to order the No. 2 dinner, today we opt for fajitas or green enchiladas—choices that didn't exist in the Tex-Mex restaurants of the 1950s. Lady Bird Johnson's favorite Mexican restaurant, El Patio on Guadalupe at 30th Street, hasn't changed much since it opened in 1954. If you are interested in tasting old-fashioned Tex-Mex food that defines this much maligned style, you can still get it there. The Señorita Platter is the most asked for item, and pralines are still 10 cents. Located close to campus, the building was originally famous for its co-ed carhops when it opened as the Toonerville Drive-in in 1935.

La Tapitia at 1501 East 6th Street has a similarly ancient history—it is the oldest of the east side Tex-Mex joints. Matt's El Rancho, the king of Austin Tex-Mex restaurants, which once dominated the downtown restaurant scene, has moved to a quieter spot at 2613 South Lamar, where the funky environs and funky food have given way to a clean and modern decor and a somewhat more modern-style Mexican food.

HOW DO YOU SPELL *BBQ*?

A fierce debate rages not only in Texas, but all over the United States, about the spelling of the word symbolized by the acronym BBQ.

Hundreds of establishments proclaim themselves "barbeque" restaurants. But are they really? According to all major dictionaries, the word is properly spelled b-a-r-b-e-c-u-e, with the *c* correct and the *q* a weird aberration.

So, what gives? Are the "ques" taking over from the "cues"? And, if so, should this trend be reversed? Should we start a campaign to rename all these restaurants?

Forget it. Etymologists (as opposed to entomologists, who only work on *b*'s), tell us the evolution of the English language is a natural occurrence, and we should not worry about such trivial changes.

But what we do worry about is Rudy's BBQ in Leon Springs, Texas, that sells its own Bar-B-Q *Sause*.

Austin's oldest existing fine dining establishment is Green Pastures, opened in 1946. Ken Koock, one of the current owners, is the son of the restaurant's founder, Mary Faulk Koock. Koock grew up in the Southern mansion that houses the restaurant, and, for many years, the family lived on the upper floor. In 1978, Green Pastures was named one of the 100 Best Restaurants in America by the late James Beard. Beard had a long association with the restaurant through his cookbook projects. Green Pastures remains one of Austin's best restaurants, and its Sunday brunch has been called the best in Texas. Its history and fine food—as well as the landscaped grounds, complete with strutting peacocks—make it a unique place to dine.

In recent history, Austin claims to be the place that made fajitas famous. Sonny Falcon, the Fajita King, has a restaurant here. Austin has also added its own twist to the New Southwestern cuisine, mainly by making it affordable and available in more casual surroundings. In fact, eating out anywhere in Austin is extremely casual—there isn't a restaurant in the entire city that requires men to wear ties. Austin is also well known for hot sauces and tortilla chips. Several tortilla factories are located here, including Guiltless Gourmet, the company that manufactures fat-free corn chips.

Austin hot sauces are among the best in the Southwest. Rose's Salsa is a local favorite, but it is sold only in the refrigerator case of grocery stores, as it is made without preservatives. Austin is also the home of the food industry giant, Adam's Extracts.

—ROBB WALSH

The Hill Country

No one seems to know exactly what its boundaries are, but one of the great attractions of the Austin area is the vast Hill Country. Some sources include the plains east of Austin in the Hill Country, which seems odd because the land is as flat as the proverbial pancake. The true Hill Country is west and south of Austin and is truly a fascinating region for food lovers.

But before we get to food, a brief description of the region is in order. Geologically, the hills exist because of the Balcones Escarpment, a fault zone that separates the flat coastal plains to the east from the Edwards Plateau to the west. The Hill Country is a land of artesian wells, caverns, rock formations, forests, rivers, lakes, ranches, and small towns.

Historically, the region was settled by German immigrants in the 1830s and 1840s, which is why there is such a German flavor to towns like New Braunfels and Fredericksburg. In some areas, German is spoken as commonly as English, and there are the inevitable combination words such as *der jalapeño*.

For travel lovers, the Hill Country has much to offer: wildflower festivals, rodeos, bed and breakfast inns, exotic animals on game farms, hunting and fishing, golf, horse racing, guest ranches, scenic caverns, cowboy art galleries, resorts, shopping in towns like Fredericksburg, and food—lots of food.

First and foremost are the meats. The German tradition of smoked meats and sausages is very strong in the Hill Country, and it fits well with Texans' love of barbecue. Although the two cooking techniques are technically different because the Germans don't use tomato-based sauces, in reality smoked meat is just that, and sauces can always be added by the diner. There are quite a few meat markets in the region (some nearly a century old), and one or two sell *tons* of smoked meat every week. Also in the German tradition is a love of baking, and bakeries abound, especially in Fredericksburg.

The Hill Country is also a land of fruit, with grapes and peaches taking top billing. There are numerous vineyards and wineries in the region, and some of the wine produced is award-winning. Ten wineries are within an hour's drive of Austin or San Antonio. Most offer tours and tastings, and vintners predict that tours of Hill Country wineries could eventually become as popular as those of California's Napa Valley, which draws more tourists than Disneyland. Peaches are commonly grown in the Hill Country, especially around Stonewall, so it follows that peach preserves and jellies are found everywhere in retail shops. In fact, several shops in Fredericksburg specialize in fruit jams or in Texas products.

It is interesting to experience the collision of culinary cultures in the Hill Country, with influences from Germany, Mexico, and the Deep South. At some times during the year, the Hill Country resembles a Germanland theme park because of the huge influx of tourists for such events as Oktoberfest. So, if you're visiting Austin or San Antonio, don't miss a drive through one of the most fascinating regions in the country.

Hill Country listings appear after the Austin listings. For more information on the Hill Country, contact the Fredericksburg Convention and Visitor's Bureau, P.O. Box 56, Fredericksburg, TX 78624 (512-997-6523).

Austin Area Markets, Retail Shops, and Bakeries

AUSTIN COUNTRY FLEA MARKET (*LA PULGA*)

9500 Highway 290 E (512-929-2795). *Open Saturday and Sunday, 8 a.m.–dusk.* NO CREDIT CARDS; BEER AVAILABLE.

La Pulga (the flea) resembles a Mexican *mercado*. In the beginning it was just another American flea market where households sold garage sale items on the weekends. But the huge Hispanic population in the area preferred shopping in this style of market more than in the American supermarket environment, so the flea market acquired more and more Mexican grocery items. Tiny booths selling Mexican brand name hot sauces, canned chiles, candied papaya, caramel and brown sugar, and other hard-to-find Mexican items started to take over. Today, La Pulga has several merchants who import Mexican produce items directly to their stands. They include ingredients that can be found nowhere else, such as loose chipotle peppers, bulk spices and medicinal herbs, three varieties of prickly pear fruit, and five or six kinds of bananas. Texas Spice Company in La Pulga sells the largest selection of dried and processed chile peppers in Austin, including African bird peppers, ground *ancho*, and New Mexican chiles. They also have such tough-to-find ethnic spices as fenugreek. La Pulga is also a fun place to shop for weird souvenirs.

SIMON DAVID

9742 Great Hills Trail (across the street from the Stouffer Hotel) (512-338-4250). *Open daily, 7 a.m.–midnight.* CREDIT CARDS; BEER AND WINE.

Simon David boasts an enormous bakery with good bagels and excellent pastry, the city's best selection of smoked fish, a huge selection of top wines, prepared salads, pâtés, deli meats, and a full-service butcher complete with a barbecue take-out section. It has a great selection of locally produced

3-2 Dave DeWitt and Robb Walsh Judge the Pepper Competition at the Travis County Farmer's Market

items such as honeys, jams, and hot sauces. The produce section includes hard-to-find fruits and vegetables, plus herbs, mushrooms, and gourmet greens like raddichio and Belgian endive. It is, in short, a good place to stock a picnic basket— and yes, they sell picnic baskets too.

TRAVIS COUNTY FARMER'S MARKET

6701 Burnet Road (512-454-1002). *Open daily, 8 a.m.–5 p.m.* NO CREDIT CARDS.

Recognized as one of the ten best farmers' markets in the country by Judith Olney's *Farmer's Market Cookbook*, the Travis County Farmer's Market is the best place to buy fresh Texas produce in Austin. On Saturday mornings during peak growing seasons, the market is full of unusual herbs and unique vegetables; local honey; jams and jellies; gift baskets of jalapeños, salsas, relishes, and mustards; and other great things to eat like heads-on Gulf shrimp. Visitors to Texas will find this is a good place to buy Hill Country peaches, citrus from the Rio Grande Valley, onions, and several varieties of native pecans to ship home. Throughout the year, the market hosts eleven festivals, including a chile pepper fiesta. Call for festival dates.

SAMBET'S CAJUN STORE

8644 E. Spicewood Springs Road, in the Spicewood Springs Shopping Center (512-258-6410). *Open Monday–Friday, 10 a.m.–7 p.m.; Saturday, 10 a.m.–5 p.m.* MAJOR CREDIT CARDS, NO LIQUOR.

In addition to Cajun products of every description, Sambet's has a fine selection of Southwestern foods, particularly items made in Texas. They are justifiably proud that they carry more than 150 different varieties of hot sauces and salsas and are always looking for more. Sambet's is Austin's hot and spicy headquarters.

AMANDINE BAKERY AND CAFE

8015 Shoal Creek Blvd. (512-467-7400) and 917-A W. 12th Street (512-476-1956). *Open Monday–Friday, 7 a.m.–6 p.m.; Saturday, 7 a.m.–5 p.m.* NO CREDIT CARDS.

Alain Braux is a native of France, where he learned the fine art of baking pastry and became a certified master baker and a certified executive pastry chef. You will find him at the Shoal Creek location baking French-style pastries and ornate cakes for weddings and special events like Valentine's Day. Amandine is a great place for lunch; it also makes some of Austin's best ice creams.

UPPER CRUST BAKERY

4508 Burnet Road (512-467-0102). *Open Monday–Saturday, 7 a.m.–6:30 p.m.; Sunday, 7 a.m.–3 p.m.*

Elephant ears, sticky rolls, jalapeño croissants, and huge breakfast sandwiches are just a few of Upper Crust's early morning attractions. This is a favorite breakfast hangout for artists, bicyclists, and students.

Austin Area Breweries and Wineries

CELIS BREWERY

Tours and tasting room, 2431 Forbes Drive, off Highway 290 near the Main Post Office (512-835-0884). *Open: Hours vary; call for more information.*

In 1966, Pierre Celis opened his De Kluis Brewery in the Belgian village of Hoegaarden with a first-year production of 350 barrels. When Celis sold the brewery in 1990, he was making 300,000 barrels a year. In 1992, the Celis Brewery in Austin began production with 12,000 barrels of three new premium American beers: Celis White, Celis Pale Bock, and Celis Golden. Some beer experts predict Celis will soon become one of the most popular European-style brews made in the United States. Someday Celis hopes to introduce such brewing exotica as fruit lambics (beers flavored with fruit instead of hops) to the U.S. market.

SPOETZL BREWERY

603 E. Brewery, Shiner (southwest of Austin on U.S. 90A) (512-594-3852). *Open Monday–Friday, 10 a.m.–12 noon and 1 p.m.–4:30 p.m. Free tours at 11 a.m. and 1:30 p.m.*

This brewery, founded in 1909, brews the best beer made in Texas, Shiner Bock. There is a hospitality room with tastings and two tours daily (call ahead for group reservations). No retail sales.

HILL COUNTRY CELLARS

Winery, tasting room, deli, and picnic grounds, 1700 N. Bell in Cedar Park (512-259-2000). *Open Tuesday–Saturday, 11 a.m.–5 p.m.; Sunday, noon–5 p.m. Deli open Tuesday– Saturday, 11 a.m.–3 p.m.; tours Tuesday–Thursday, 1 p.m.; Friday–Sunday, 1 p.m.–4 p.m. (on the hour).*

The vineyard and winery of Hill Country Cellars is just north of Austin on U.S. 183. Tours and tastings are free. This is a pleasant lunchtime diversion: you can take a tour and eat lunch on the picnic tables outside with a bottle of their fine Riesling or a wine spritzer.

SLAUGHTER-LEFTWICH

Winery, tasting room, and picnic grounds, 4301 James Lane (just off U.S. 620 in the Lake Travis area) (512-266-3331). *Open Monday–Thursday, 1 p.m.–5 p.m., for tastings and sales; Friday–Sunday, 1 p.m.–5 p.m., for tours, tastings, and sales.*

Slaughter-Leftwich relocated its headquarters to Austin from Lubbock, where the vineyards are planted. Winemaker Russell Smith makes small quantities of very interesting varietals such as his Ruby Cabernet. The winery is best known for its Austin blush and the state's award-winning Chardonnay.

Austin Area Restaurants

EL AZTECA

2600 E. 7th Street (512-477-4701). *Open Monday–Saturday, 11 a.m.–10:30 p.m.* MAJOR CREDIT CARDS; LIQUOR LICENSE.

El Azteca features original velvet paintings, Aztec maiden calendars for sale, the city's best stand of banana trees, and some of Austin's most outstanding Mexican food. A relative newcomer, El Azteca opened in 1963, in the heart of the Mexican barrio. All food is cooked to order, and it's worth the wait. Inexpensive, funky, and fun, El Azteca is everybody's favorite—and the only restaurant in town where *cabrito* is always served.

CAFE SERRANOS

300 W. Ben White (512-447-3999); 3010 W. Anderson Lane (512-454-7333); 12636 Research Boulevard (512-250-9555); and 1111 Red River (Symphony Square) (512-322-9080). *Open Sunday–Thursday, 11 a.m.–10 p.m.; Friday and Saturday, 10 a.m.–11 p.m.* VISA, MC; LIQUOR LICENSE.

Four of the most popular Tex-Mex restaurants in Austin are the brainchildren of Adam Gonzales, who offers—in addition to Tex-Mex specialties like enchiladas—mesquite-grilled meats and fajitas. In fact, his restaurant won the Tenth Annual State Fajita Cookoff! The restaurants have their own line of Cafe Serranos salsas, including an excellent chipotle salsa and chile con queso. The products are sold at the restaurant.

CAPTAIN QUACKENBUSH'S ESPRESSO CAFE

2120 Guadalupe (512-472-4477). *Open Monday–Friday, 7 a.m.–1 a.m.; Saturday, 8 a.m.–1 a.m.; Sunday, 9 a.m.– midnight.* NO CREDIT CARDS; NO LIQUOR.

Quackenbush's gets its coffee from Shapiro Brothers, New York's premier custom espresso roaster. They bake their own pastries, cakes, and cookies on the premises. Soups, sandwiches, and rice and pasta dishes are served at lunch. Shakes, smoothies, and twenty different herb teas are also available. It is Austin's leading late-night hangout for slackers and neo-beatniks. Be prepared to discuss deconstructivist symbolism in the Polish cinema or postexistential philosophy in the twenty-first century.

CASTLE HILL CAFE

1101 W. 5th Street (512-476-0728). *Open Monday–Friday, 11 a.m.–2:30 p.m. (lunch); Monday–Saturday, 6 p.m.– 10 p.m. (dinner).* MAJOR CREDIT CARDS; BEER AND WINE.

Owner/chef David Dailey describes his menu as "regionally inspired cuisine," a combination of new American cooking, central Mexican ideas, Southwestern-style creations, and the best of ingredients and preparations from around the globe. The blackboard menu changes weekly, but no entrees cost more than $10. Such truly inspired cooking at such a reasonable price is almost unbelievable.

CHUY'S

1728 Barton Springs Road (512-474-4452) and 10520 N. Lamar (512-836-3218). *Open Sunday–Thursday, 11 a.m.– 10:30 p.m. (bar open until midnight); Saturday and*

Sunday, 11 a.m.–midnight (bar is open until 1 a.m.). MAJOR
CREDIT CARDS; LIQUOR LICENSE.

Chuy's eccentric Mexican food is consistent, and the place is
always thick with UT students and other fun-lovers. The original Barton Springs location near Zilker Park features an Elvis shrine and postserious art. The north location is home to
the world's largest collection of lava lamps. Favorite dishes
include "burritos as big as your face," Chuy's special blue corn
enchiladas, and excellent crunchy-style chicken-stuffed *chile
rellenos*. Green chiles are roasted by the road, New Mexico–
style, during the annual Green Chile Festival in September.

DOT'S PLACE

13805 Orchid Lane (512-255-7288). *Open Monday–Friday,
11 a.m.–2 p.m. (lunch only).* NO CREDIT CARDS; NO LIQUOR.

To get to this Southern lunchroom, go north on MoPac until
the highway ends, 15 or 20 minutes from downtown. Take a
right at Howard and turn right again just past the General
Cinema. Watch for the sign and turn right onto Orchid Lane.
Leave yourself enough time to get lost. While you're driving
around, think of Dot's chicken and fluffy, light dumplings
with incredible gravy, or chicken and dressing. Imagine Dot
hand-carving smoked roast beef. Fantasize about the classic
chicken-fried steak. And remember the vegetables are excellent, especially the stewed okra (yes, okra). In the dessert
department, Dot's sweet potato pie is unbeatable. It's a long
drive, but always worth it.

L'ESTRO ARMONICO (BELGIAN RESTAURANT)

3520 Bee Caves Road (512-328-0580). *Open Monday–Friday,
11:30 a.m.–2 p.m. (lunch); Monday–Thursday, 6 p.m.–
10 p.m. (dinner); Friday and Saturday, 6 p.m.–11 p.m.
(dinner); closed Sunday.* MAJOR CREDIT CARDS; BEER AND
WINE.

Need to escape from Southwestern food for a change? This is
it. Don't let the shopping center exterior fool you; L'Estro Armonico is probably Austin's most romantic dinner house. The

featured Belgian specialties resemble French cooking with rich sauces and delicate flavors. The European-style service is extremely gracious, and each woman guest is presented with a rose after dinner. A great selection of wine is offered, and wine buffs will appreciate the added attraction of having The Cellar, one of Austin's premier wine shops, next door.

FAJITA KING

6519 N. Lamar (512-452-5020). *Open Monday–Thursday, 11 a.m.–9 p.m.; Friday and Saturday, 11 a.m.–11 p.m.* MAJOR CREDIT CARDS; LIQUOR LICENSE.

Sonny Falcon, the man the *Laredo Times* called the "Fajita King," started selling fajitas at fairs and festivals in 1969. He claims to be the first person in Texas or the United States to sell fajitas; so far, his claim is uncontested. Falcon has made a major concession to popular usage in his new restaurant on Lamar. After years of fighting against the misnomer *chicken fajitas*, he surrendered to this bastardization of the Spanish language and started serving them. Falcon's beef fajitas are outstanding and are the real thing. Never marinated, they are simply trimmed, butterflied, and seasoned on the grill.

FONDA SAN MIGUEL

2330 North Loop Blvd. (512-459-4121). *Open Tuesday– Friday, 11:30 a.m.–2 p.m. (lunch); Sunday–Tuesday, 5:30 p.m.–9:30 p.m. (dinner); Friday and Saturday, 5:30 p.m.–10:30 p.m. (dinner); Sunday, 11:30 a.m.–2 p.m. (brunch).* MAJOR CREDIT CARDS; LIQUOR LICENSE.

This lovely restaurant graciously serves fine central Mexican cuisine in a magnificent setting. Sample the ceviche, calamari, and other *antojitos* among the tropical plants in the solarium. Admire the Mexican art collection in the main dining room while you savor Chef Miguel Ravago's Pork in Achiote Cooked in Banana Leaves. Homemade tortillas are made before your eyes. Don't miss the *cajete*, a rich goat's milk caramel sauce with ice cream. Finish the evening with an espresso at the copper-covered bar. The highly recommended Sunday brunch features nearly every item on the menu in a huge buffet.

GREEN PASTURES

811 W. Live Oak (512-444-4747). *Open Monday–Saturday, 6 p.m.–10 p.m.; Sunday, 11 a.m.–2 p.m.* MAJOR CREDIT CARDS; LIQUOR LICENSE.

In 1978 James Beard ranked Green Pastures on his list of 100 Best Restaurants in America. Today, Green Pastures is known for having one of the best Sunday brunches in the state (although the staff prefers to call it a luncheon buffet since no egg dishes or other typical breakfast items are served). Peacocks roam the grounds of this beautiful old mansion in south Austin, a monument to Southern charm. New regional-style dishes include Smoked Duck Texana with Poblano Peppers and Apple-Cured Bacon.

HUDSON'S ON-THE-BEND

3509 FM 620N (512-266-1369). *Open Sunday, 6 p.m.– 9 p.m.; Tuesday–Thursday, 6 p.m.–10 p.m.; Friday and Saturday, 5:30 p.m.–10 p.m.* MAJOR CREDIT CARDS; LIQUOR LICENSE.

Hudson's is a charming stone house in the Lake Travis area. It serves outstanding Hill Country game dishes including venison, quail, wild boar, pheasant, and rabbit. Chef Jeff Blank is well known for imaginative creations like Smoked Steak and Poblano Roulade and his beautiful Swordfish Vegetable Terrine. Excellent sauces and relishes complement the exotic meats and fish. An extensive wine list offers a variety of Zinfandels, Pinot Noirs, and other lesser known selections. Sauces, condiments, and vinegars are also available for sale.

THE INN AT BUSHY CREEK

I-35, Taylor Exit, Round Rock (512-255-2555). *Open Thursday–Sunday, dinner by reservation only.* MAJOR CREDIT CARDS; NO LIQUOR, BUT FREE CORKAGE.

Here is the perfect romantic getaway—if you bring your own wine. This restored 1850s-vintage stone-house-turned-restaurant offers thirteen Continental-style entrees and some of the best desserts in the area.

JAMBALAYA

6801 Burnet Road (512-453-8574). *Open Monday–Friday, 11:30 a.m.–2 p.m. (lunch); Monday–Thursday, 6 p.m.– 10 p.m.; Friday and Saturday, 6 p.m.–11 p.m. (dinner); Sunday, 5:30 p.m.–9:30 p.m. (dinner).* MAJOR CREDIT CARDS; LIQUOR LICENSE.

This is the place to go for Austin's best cajun and creole food featuring oysters; fresh, unfrozen shrimp in season; great étouffée and fish dishes; and a knockout fillet of beef with peppercorn and brandy cream sauce. Don't miss the hot bread pudding with Scotch whiskey sauce. Some of Austin's best jazz artists play the baby grand piano on Wednesday and Sunday nights.

3-3 Chef Miguel Ravago Prepares Sunday Brunch at the Fonda San Miguel

JEFFREY'S

1204 West Lynn (512-477-5584). *Open Monday–Thursday,
6 p.m.–10 p.m.; Friday and Saturday, 6 p.m.–10:30 p.m.*
MAJOR CREDIT CARDS; LIQUOR LICENSE.

Chef Raymond Tatum is a Texas original. His food is sophisticated and full of flavor, yet straightforward and unpretentious—and the menu is excitingly unpredictable. On any given night, you might find Thai Lamb Curry, Texas Redfish in Tangerine Chipotle Sauce, Ancho Pepper Stuffed with Goat Cheese, or a duck gumbo that will knock your socks off. Jeffrey's has been recognized by the *Wine Spectator* for its outstanding wine list.

JOE'S BAKERY AND COFFEE SHOP

2305 E. 7th Street (512-472-0017). *Open daily, 7 a.m.; closing times vary.* VISA, MC; NO LIQUOR LICENSE.

This is a classic Mexican breakfast hangout in a Mexican neighborhood. It features great huevos rancheros, breakfast tacos, plus *menudo, lengua,* and other exotic Mexican breakfast foods. The bakery is best known for *empanadas de camote* (sweet potato–filled pastries). Joe's dad started the family baking business in 1938; breads and cookies are available to go.

KREUZ MARKET

Courthouse Square, Lockhart (south of Austin on U.S. 183) (512-398-2361). *Open Monday–Friday, 7 a.m.–6 p.m.; Saturday, 7 a.m.–6:30 p.m., closed Sunday.* NO CREDIT CARDS; BEER AVAILABLE.

Kreuz Market ("The Meat Market" to locals), was originally a German meat market that opened in 1900. Smoking sausage and other meat was a typical sideline for German butchers. At Kreuz, the smoked meats became so famous the barbecue soon eclipsed the meat market. Kreuz Market features an ancient dining hall with knives chained to the counter where patrons have worn wells into the wood from nearly a century of enthusiastic brisket carving. The two oak fires at either end of an L-shaped brick oven are exposed to view. Bring your camera and a big appetite. The meats, particularly the smoked pork loin, are among the best smoked meats anywhere, but the Germans don't really think of them as barbecue. German-style smoked meat differs from standard barbecue, both in cooking procedure and the lack of barbecue sauce; however, hot sauce is provided. Don't let the fine distinctions get in the way of lunch, however.

LOUIS MUELLER BARBECUE

206 W. 2nd Street in Taylor (north of Austin on U.S. 79) (512-352-6206). *Open Monday–Saturday, 9 a.m. until all the barbecue's gone.* NO CREDIT CARDS; BEER AVAILABLE.

Going to Louis Mueller's barbecue restaurant in downtown Taylor is a trip to a bygone era. The walls can't possibly have been painted since the place opened in 1939. Don't come if you're in a rush. The pace of life in Taylor is positively glacial, although the people are warm and friendly. Relax, sit back, enjoy the smoky atmosphere and the overheard conversations, and pretend you're doing yoga—pork rib yoga.

PINCH-A-POLLO

7917 Burnet Road (near the corner at Andersen Lane) (512-452-3088). *Open Monday–Thursday, 11 a.m.–9 p.m.; Friday and Saturday, 11 a.m.–9:30 p.m.* NO CREDIT CARDS; BEER AND WINE.

Pinch-a-Pollo features *achiote*-marinated, grilled chicken with beans, rice, tortillas, and your choice of sixteen freshly made hot sauces! Healthy and thirst-quenching *aguas frescas* are a very popular drink here. They come in exotic flavors including *tuna* (prickly pear), *jamaica* (flower tea), and *tamarindo* (tamarind bean).

PINCH-A-POLLO'S SIXTEEN HOT SAUCES

The following sixteen sauces are served at the best salsa restaurant in Texas, Pinch-a-Pollo in Austin.

Mild

Table Sauce.   A fresh vegetable salsa, mild and tart, and the kind Austinites eat with spoons when the chips run low.

Roja Sauce.   Tomato and serranos—very pleasant.

Verde Sauce.   A tart tomatillo flavor—very mild; a kid's hot sauce.

Pasilla Sauce.   Made with the dried form of the Mexican *chilaca* chile.

Guajillo Sauce.   A tobacco-like aroma and a bitter, chocolate-like, intense rich flavor—delicious.

Cascabel Sauce.   Made from a round, dried pepper from Mexico. The seeds sound like a bell when you shake them—hence the name, which means "jingle bell."

Ancho Sauce.   A black color, more intense tobacco aroma than *guajillo*, and slightly bitter flavor.

Mole Sauce.   Sweet and tasty.

continued

Medium Hot

Arbol Sauce.   Tastes like tomato and fire—very zesty.

Mexicana Sauce.   A tasty ranchera with a bite.

Loca Morena Sauce.   Billy Garcia's homemade concoction with seven different peppers in a tart vegetable and lime juice base. Very flavorful; the heat creeps up on you while you're trying to figure out what's in it.

Chipotle Sauce (pronounced chip-OAT-lay). Made with smoked jalapeños—outstanding, but very intense. Jalapeños can't be dried, so they're preserved by smoking.

continued

RUBY'S

512 W. 29th Street (512-477-1651). *Open Sunday–Thursday, 11 a.m.–midnight; Friday and Saturday, 11 a.m.–4 a.m.* NO CREDIT CARDS; BEER AND WINE.

Ruby's is proud of its organic beef brisket. It is the only restaurant in Central Texas to serve certified hormone- and chemical-free barbecued beef. You can also get vegetarian black bean tacos here. But don't let the healthy stuff scare you away—Ruby's puts out a great plate of ribs and outstanding side orders. It is located a few doors away from the legendary Antone's blues club, just off of Guadalupe.

Very Hot Sauces

Morita Sauce.   Involves the same smoking procedure with serranos (dried serranos are called *moritas*). The sauce is even more flavorful and hotter than the chipotle.

Habanero Sauce.   A citrus, sometimes even an apricot-like, unique fruitiness, followed on the tongue by the most exquisitely intense pepper pain known to man.

Xnipec Sauce (pronounced schnee-PECK). A Habanero pico de gallo. *Xnipec* is a Mayan word meaning dog's breath—probably referring to the panting breath of someone who has eaten something too hot.

Arbol Concentrate.   A crushed árbol chile base used to make some of the other sauces, but occasionally requested by Austinites who want something a little hotter.

—ROBB WALSH

SAM'S

2000 E. 12th Street (512-478-0378). *Open Sunday–Thursday, 10 a.m.–3 a.m.; Friday and Saturday, 10 a.m.–5 a.m.* NO CREDIT CARDS; NO LIQUOR.

This old wooden house with a rusty screen door and an outhouse behind the woodpile is located on Austin's east side. Sam's was a favorite of the late Stevie Ray Vaughan and many other blues musicians. The black rural Southern atmosphere is quite authentic, and Sam's is popular with the out-all-night crowd, so it's open very late. Try the ribs and the sausage. This may be the only place you'll ever see that serves barbecued mutton. Sam's serves great barbecue, and although there are lots of places to get great barbecue, there is only one Sam's.

SCHOLZ GARTEN

1607 San Jacinto (512-477-4171). *Open Monday–Saturday, 11 a.m.–11 p.m.* MAJOR CREDIT CARDS; BEER.

A great place to drink pitchers of Shiner Bock on summer nights, the city's oldest public house (since 1866) features an outdoor beer garden where state government officials and university students rub elbows. Oompah music, provided by an irregular bunch of horn players, usually happens on Thursday nights. The restaurant serves student food such as nachos, burgers, and breast of chicken sandwiches. The food isn't very exciting, but the historic charm of the old beer garden, nestled under the huge live oak trees, makes up for it.

SEIS SALSAS

2004 S. 1st Street (512-445-5050). *Open daily, 7 a.m.– 10 p.m.; Friday and Saturday, 7 a.m.–11 p.m.* MAJOR CREDIT CARDS; LIQUOR LICENSE.

Seis Salsas (six salsas), the restaurant dedicated to hot sauce, has been a favorite of governors and paisanos ever since it opened its original hole-in-the-wall location on South 1st Street. Today it is housed in a larger and more attractive building on the same street. Inside, the action centers around a fountain-like column holding a help-yourself display of six salsas, *escabeches,* and freshly chopped cilantro. The salsas are ranchera and tomatillo (the traditional red and green), chipotle (smoked jalapeño), árbol (the hottest by far), verde (hot jalapeño), and pico de gallo. Breakfast is better than lunch or dinner, which is just as well since the sauces are best appreciated with eggs and lots of tortillas. Breakfast is served all day.

THREADGILL'S

6416 N. Lamar (512-476-0728). *Open weekdays, 11 a.m.–
10 p.m.; weekends, 8 a.m.–10 p.m.* VISA, MC; LIQUOR LICENSE.

The late Kenny Threadgill was one of Austin's best-loved
country singers, fiddlers, and yodelers. His beer joint was famous for its non-stop music and for being the place where
Janis Joplin started singing. Today, the building where Kenny
once sold beer has become a popular country cooking restaurant and a shrine to Austin's music scene. Owned by Eddie
Wilson, the founder of Armadillo World Headquarters, Threadgill's features photos and memorabilia of the Austin music
scene and a free jukebox loaded with Austin music. Try the
excellent chicken-fried steak with cream gravy, the chicken
livers, or the fried oysters.

Hill Country Markets and Bakeries

CITY MARKET

109 Kessler, U.S. 77 N in Schulenburg (409-743-3440). *Open
Monday–Friday, 8 a.m.–5:30 p.m.; Sunday, 8 a.m.–
5 p.m.* NO CREDIT CARDS; NO LIQUOR.

Billed as the "best l'il ol' meat market in Texas," City Market,
which is nearly fifty years old, began by giving away weenies
to every kid who came in the door. Owner Roy Smrkovsky
notes: "Weenies are what made us famous." They still make
their own homemade weenies (600 pounds a week!) but also
sell smoked pork loin, pork and beef sausage, and barbecue—
lots of barbecue. On Saturdays, they make 900 pounds of barbecue lathered with their special sauce and sell every bit of
it. Eat in or take it out.

DUTCHMAN'S MARKET

1609 E. Main (U.S. 290 E) (512-997-5693). *Open Monday–Friday, 8 a.m.–5:30 p.m.; Sunday, 8 a.m.–3 p.m. (only during November and December).* VISA, MC; NO LIQUOR.

Dutchman's carries a wide selection of smoked meats, jerky, bacon, and sausages and offers deer processing in season. If you ask nicely, they'll make you a hot, smoked meat sandwich to go.

FREDERICKSBURG BAKERY

141 East Main, Fredericksburg (512-997-3254). *Open Monday–Saturday, 8 a.m.–5:30 p.m.; Sunday, 8 a.m.– 5 p.m.* NO CREDIT CARDS; NO LIQUOR.

Operating continuously since 1917, this aroma-laden establishment is Fredericksburg's most famous bakery. Signature items include sweet German pretzels, apple strudel, homemade breads, potato cake, and coffee. There are seven tables for snacking.

KASPER MEAT MARKET

119 E. Post Office, Weimar (409-725-8227). *Open Monday–Friday, 7 a.m.–6 p.m.; Saturday, 7 a.m.–4:30 p.m.* NO CREDIT CARDS; NO LIQUOR.

Founded in 1917, Kasper Meat Market is most famous for its pork and beef sausage. So famous, in fact, that on an average Saturday (a big day for meat sales in the Hill Country), the market sells an astonishing 1.4 *tons* of sausage! Other delicacies include jalapeño sausage, smoked beef tenderloin, smoked ham and bacon, and their own beef jerky. Be prepared for a picnic as everything is sold for carryout only.

3-4 Jeff Campbell at His Stonewall Chili Pepper Company in the Hill Country

OLD GERMAN BAKERY AND RESTAURANT

225 W. Main Street, Fredericksburg (512-997-9084). *Open Thursday–Monday, 7 a.m.–6 p.m.* NO CREDIT CARDS; NO LIQUOR.

By the sound of the name, you'd expect this establishment to sell and serve German specialties such as bratwurst, knackwurst, schnitzel, sauerkraut, hot potato salad, tortes, and Black Forest cake. They do—and very well, too.

RABKE'S TABLE READY MEATS

Eckert Road, Willow City, on the way to Enchanted Rock (512-685-3266). *Open Monday–Saturday, 8 a.m.–6 p.m.; Sunday, 1:30 p.m.–5 p.m.* VISA, MC; NO LIQUOR.

This is one of Texas' famous carry-out meat markets, with only picnic tables outside. They sell such delicacies as beef jerky, turkey sausage, turkey jerky—as well as turkey breast, ham, beef, and homemade jellies, jams, and pickles. They have a venison processing plant on the premises to process customers' venison.

SOUTHSIDE MARKET

109 Central at Main, Elgin (512-285-3407). *Open Monday– Saturday, 7 a.m.–6 p.m.* NO CREDIT CARDS; NO LIQUOR.

This combination market and restaurant specializes in raw and cooked sausage, fresh all-beef sausage, barbecued pork ribs, barbecued mutton, and barbecued chicken on Saturday.

SUNDAY HOUSE

122 E. Main Street, Fredericksburg (512-997-8292). *Open Monday–Saturday, 9 a.m.–5 p.m.; closed Sundays and holidays.* VISA, MC; NO LIQUOR.

Sunday House specializes in turkey products such as hams and pastrami, but also sells smoked chickens and pastrami. It also sells by mail.

3-5 The Produce Is Piled High at La Pulga, the Austin Flea Market

Hill Country Wineries

BELL MOUNTAIN/OBERHELLMANN VINEYARDS

Just north of Eckert on Highway 16, 14 miles north of Fredericksburg (512-685-3297). *Open Saturdays for tours, tastings, and sales, 10 a.m.–4 p.m. (Easter through Christmas).*

This chateau-like winery and tasting room are surrounded by a hillside vineyard in a lovely Old World setting. The wines produced here include Chardonnay, Riesling, Cabernet Sauvignon, and Pinot Noir, plus private estate varieties.

FALL CREEK VINEYARDS

Highway 2241, off Highway 29, 2.2 miles northeast of Tow (512-476-4116). *Open Sundays for tours, tastings, and sales, noon–5 p.m.*

This winery, on the shores of Lake Buchanan, features 55 acres of vinifera vines and produces Sauvignon Blanc, Chenin Blanc, Emerald Riesling, Cabernet Sauvignon, and Zinfandel. Call for directions.

GRAPE CREEK VINEYARD

U.S. 290, 4 miles west of Stonewall (512-644-2710). *Open for tours, tastings, and sales Tuesday–Sunday, noon–5 p.m. (Easter through Labor Day); Friday–Sunday, 1 p.m.–5 p.m. (Labor Day to Easter).*

The winery produces Chardonnay, Fumé Blanc, and Cabernet Sauvignon; the wines are aged in oak barrels in the cellar. An orchard with peaches and other fruits and a gift shop are on the premises.

PEDERNALES VINEYARDS

On Highway 16 between Fredericksburg and Kerrville (512-997-8326). *Open Monday–Friday for tours, tastings, and sales, 8:30 a.m.–5 p.m.; weekends by appointment.*

Overlooking the Pedernales River and the nearby hills, Pedernales Vineyards produces estate-bottled Cabernet Sauvignon and Sauvignon Blanc made from grapes grown next to the winery.

SISTER CREEK VINEYARDS

Off I-10 at Boerne exit in Sisterdale (512-324-6704). *Tastings and tours at the Sisterdale General Store, by appointment.*

Located in the heart of the Hill Country in tiny Sisterdale (population 25), this winery produces Chardonnay, Pinot Noir, Cabernet Sauvignon, and Merlot. A century-old cotton gin has been restored to house the winery. The vineyards are located between East and West Sister Creeks.

Hill Country Retail Shops

BEST OF TEXAS SPECIALTIES

217½ E. Main, Fredericksburg, (512-997-0123). *Open Monday–Saturday, 10 a.m.–5:30 p.m.; Sunday, noon– 5:30 p.m.* VISA, MC; WINE SALES.

This small shop has a big collection of foods and wines from throughout Texas. If you can't visit all the wineries in the state, at least there's a place to buy all the Texas wines. The shop also carries many salsas, jellies, mustards, hot ketchups, and other chile pepper products.

FREDERICKSBURG HERB FARM

310 E. Main, Fredericksburg (512-997-8615). *Open Monday– Saturday, 9:30 a.m.–5:30 p.m.* MAJOR CREDIT CARDS; NO LIQUOR.

Housed in a limestone Victorian house that dates from 1908, this herb farm and store carries a wide line of garden- and herb-related products such as wine vinegars, pepper garlic, grilling herbs, jams and jellies, herbal salsas, ten potpourris, flower oils, and natural shampoos. Their Days of Wine and Roses vinegar won a first-place award for Outstanding Savory Condiment in the 1991 International Fancy Food and Confection Show. There is a bed and breakfast inn on the premises, and the establishment has a nice mail-order catalog.

PEACH BASKET NATURAL FOODS

334 West Main, Fredericksburg (512-997-4533). *Open Monday–Saturday, 9 a.m.–5:30 p.m.; Sunday, 10 a.m.– 4 p.m.* NO CREDIT CARDS; NO LIQUOR.

Health food enthusiasts flock to the Peach Basket for local fresh produce such as tomatoes, beans, blackberries, nectarines, pecans, peaches, apples, and persimmons—there are 300 persimmon trees in owner Ruby Hallford's orchard. The greenhouse provides fresh, potted herbs; the shelves display pastas, grains, natural cosmetics, local jams and jellies, and variously flavored honeys.

DAS PEACH HOUSE

315 E. Main Street, Fredericksburg (512-997-0124). *Open Monday–Saturday, 9 a.m.–6 p.m.; Sunday, noon–4 p.m.* MAJOR CREDIT CARDS; WINE SALES.

The Peach House has a huge selection of Hill Country delicacies, including Amaretto peach-pecan preserves, jalapeño jams and jellies, onion and garlic jellies, strawberry honey, Texas black peppered mustard, and many salsas. Gift items and cookbooks are also available. During the summer, their Highway 87 S location is open seven days a week, 9 a.m.– 6 p.m., and features fresh peaches.

STONEWALL CHILI PEPPER COMPANY

U.S. 290 in Stonewall (1-800-232-2295). *Open spring, summer, and fall, 9 a.m.–sunset; open sporadically during winter.* VISA, MC; NO LIQUOR.

Stonewall is a combination fruit stand and retail store specializing in chile peppers. Owner Jeff Campbell, who has the largest Habanero plantation in Texas, grows most of the chiles that go into his products—and Stonewall salsas *are* great. Some of the more unusual items for sale include jalapeño and Habanero lollipops (no one we know has ever finished one), Habanero powder and seed, and Stonewall's own Hot and Peachy Preserves, Salsa Diablo, Habanero Ketchup, and Hot and Spicy Pear Relish. The company also sells by mail order.

TEJAS SPECIALTIES

Morales Plumbing Building, U.S. 290 in Fredericksburg (512-997-2583). *Open Monday–Saturday, 8 a.m.–4 p.m.* NO CREDIT CARDS.

Believe it or not, Tejas sells plumbing supplies and jellies. How about a plumber's helper and a jar of jam? They sell twenty varieties of jams and jellies including a special jelly made from flowers and the ever-popular jalapeño jelly.

Hill Country Restaurants

AUSLANDER BIERGARTEN AND RESTAURANT

323 E. Main, Fredericksburg (512-997-7714). *Open Monday– Saturday, 11 a.m.–9 p.m.* NO CREDIT CARDS; BEER AND WINE.

Would you believe a German-Mexican-Italian-Greek restaurant? Well, in Fredericksburg, anything's possible. For thirty-five years, the Auslander (outlander) has been combining cuisines quite effectively, with their most popular entrees being Mexican pizza and wiener schnitzel. They also serve three different sausage plates, *chalupas*, and enchiladas. During the summer, their biergarten outside dining area is quite popular.

BILL'S BARBECUE

1909 Junction Highway, at Highway 27 in Kerrville (512-895-5733). *Open Tuesday–Saturday, 11 a.m.–3 p.m.* NO CREDIT CARDS; BEER.

Bill's offers dine-in or carry-out barbecued brisket, babyback ribs, pork and beef sausage, and homemade potato salad. They sell more than 600 pounds of meat a week and have their own barbecue sauce available by the pint or quart.

COOPER'S BARBECUE

604 W. Young, at Highways 29 and 71 in Llano
(512-247-5713). *Open Monday, Wednesday, and Thursday,*
9 a.m.–7 p.m.; Saturday, 9 a.m.–7 p.m.; Sunday, 8 a.m.–
7 p.m. NO CREDIT CARDS; NO LIQUOR.

For thirty years, Cooper's has been virtually the Hill Country's only source for smoked *cabrito*, slow-cooked over mesquite. Every week, Cooper's produces 1,500 pounds of beef
ribs and jerky, brisket, chicken, pork and beef sausage, and
pork chops. Try their famous red beans and their two basic
condiments, bread and jalapeños.

GUADALUPE SMOKED MEAT COMPANY

1299 Gruene Road in Boerne (512-629-6121). *Open during*
the winter, Monday–Wednesday, 11 a.m.–4 p.m.; Thursday
and Sunday, 11 a.m.–8 p.m.; Friday and Saturday, 11 a.m.–
9 p.m.; during the summer, Monday–Thursday, 11 a.m.–
9 p.m.; Friday and Sunday, 11 a.m.–10 p.m.; Saturday,
11 a.m.–11 p.m. MAJOR CREDIT CARDS; BEER AND WINE.

Most of the seating is outdoors at this combination restaurant
and meat processing plant. Smoked brisket is their best sell-
er, closely followed by the pork ribs and the babyback ribs.
One interesting specialty is smoked chicken tacos. They have
a gift catalog and sell by mail order.

HILLTOP CAFE

Highway 87, 11 miles north of Fredericksburg
(512-997-8922). *Open Wednesday, Thursday, and Sunday,*
11 a.m.–11 p.m.; Friday and Saturday, 11 a.m.–10 p.m.
VISA, MC; WINE AND LIQUOR.

This eclectic establishment serves food from Greece (Tirope-
tas Stuffed with Kasseri Cheese), Louisiana (gumbo and
boudin), and the Hill Country (Pecan-Crusted Chicken with
Spicy Mustard Sauce). They'll even fix chicken-fried steak if
you say "pretty please." Such luminaries as Walter Cronkite

and Carol Channing have feasted here, topping off their dinners with the Tequila Cheesecake.

PLATEAU CAFE

312 W. Main, Fredericksburg (512-997-1853). *Open Tuesday–Thursday, 11 a.m.–9 p.m., Friday and Saturday, 11 a.m.–10 p.m.; Sunday, 11 a.m.–8 p.m.* VISA, MC; LIQUOR LICENSE.

Variety is the spice of life at the Plateau. Start with a specialty margarita, then progress to a catfish dinner or a hand-cut steak. If you'd like some Tex-Mex, they'll serve it hot and spicy with pico de gallo salsa. Since the Plateau is famous for its desserts, you'll have some difficulty deciding among blackberry cobbler, bread pudding with bourbon sauce, and chocolate fudge cake.

Another Hill Country Attraction Vaguely Food-Related

Y. O. RANCH

In Mountain Home (512-640-3222). *Hours vary.*

This combination 40,000-acre game farm and guest ranch has the largest collection of exotic wildlife and features herds of giraffe, ibex, oryx, zebra, ostrich, and eland. Day and overnight tours are available, and the Y. O. serves hearty, ranch-style meals. Call for reservations and directions.

Recipes

SOUTH TEXAS FAJITAS

Fajitas were "discovered" twelve to fifteen years ago. Since then, an awful lot of good meat has been wrecked, and skirt steak—once a grinder item—has risen sharply in price. Because skirt doesn't come from a tender quadrant of the carcass, some care is needed to turn it into good food. First, it needs to be marinated to tenderize and flavor it.

2–4 **jalapeños, canned or fresh, stemmed and pierced**
   3 **tablespoons chili powder**
   1 **teaspoon cayenne powder**
   1 **8-ounce bottle of herb and garlic oil-based salad dressing**
   1 **12-ounce can of beer, preferably Lone Star**
1½ **teaspoons garlic powder**
    Juice of 4 small Mexican *limónes*
   2 **teaspoons cumin seeds, crushed**
   1 **large onion, minced**
   2 **tablespoons cilantro, minced**
   1 **tablespoon Worcestershire sauce**
   1 **bay leaf**
2–3 **pounds beef skirt steak**

Mix together all the ingredients, except the meat, to make a marinade. Put the skirt steak in a non-reactive container. Pour the marinade over the steak and cover. Stir occasionally and marinate for 6 to 8 hours.

Fajitas can be cooked in several ways. If you have the space, smoke the fajitas for about 30 minutes with pure mesquite smoke, and then cook for 4–7 minutes per side over direct heat—mesquite coals being the heat of choice. Baste with the marinade throughout the cooking process. If you need to cook completely over direct heat, use a fairly slow fire, about like you would use when grilling chicken;

cook, covered if possible, for about 10–15 minutes per side, basting with the marinade.

Allow about one-half pound of meat and 3–4 tortillas per person. When slicing fajitas, you'll notice the grain of the skirt steak runs in the same direction. Slice the skirt at a 45-degree angle to the grain, holding the knife on a 45-degree angle as well, and you'll find the fajitas are much more tender! Serve the fajitas with flour tortillas, pico de gallo salsa, guacamole, and cold beer. You'll notice I didn't say anything about chicken fajitas—that's a contradiction in terms.

SERVES: 4 TO 6
HEAT SCALE: MEDIUM

—RED CALDWELL

PORK TENDERLOIN WITH SAGE AND SERRANO LIME CREAM

Here is a good illustration of innovation in New Southwestern cooking. Scott Thompson, chef at Jeffrey's in Austin, combines sage, serrano chiles, and limes for both a marinade and a sauce.

1½ **cups fresh sage leaves**
  3 **serrano chiles, stems removed**
 ½ **bunch green onions**
  2 **cups chicken stock**
  6 **8-ounce pork tenderloins**
 ½ **cup milk**
 ½ **cup vegetable oil**
  1 **cup cream**
   Flour to thicken
  3 **tablespoons lime juice**
   Salt to taste

In a blender, puree the sage, chiles, green onions, and 1 cup of chicken stock. Marinate the pork in half of this mixture, milk, and oil for about 3 hours. Grill the pork tenderloins; then bake in a 500° oven for 10 minutes.

While the pork is baking, combine the remaining chicken stock and cream and cook over low heat for about

25 minutes. Add flour as needed to thicken the sauce. Add the lime juice, salt to taste, and the remaining puree.

Slice the pork and serve topped with the sauce.

SERVES: **6**
HEAT SCALE: **MILD**

XNIPEC (DOG'S BREATH) SALSA

Fresh Habanero chiles are sometimes hard to find, so serranos may be substituted, but double the number used. The salsa, however, won't have the same marvelous aroma.

- **1 onion, diced (red or purple preferred)**
- **4 limes, juiced**
- **4 Habanero chiles, stems and seeds removed, diced**
- **1 tomato, diced**

Soak the diced onion in the lime juice for at least 30 minutes. Add the chiles and tomato and mix. Salt to taste and add a little water if desired.

YIELD: **1½ CUPS**
HEAT SCALE: **EXTREMELY HOT**
SERVING SUGGESTIONS: **USE AS A SALSA WITH GRILLED FISH OR GRILLED CHICKEN. TRY IT WITH EGGS!**

—PINCH-A-POLLO RESTAURANT

GUAJILLO SAUCE

This basic recipe can be used for *guajillos, pasillas, cascabels,* or any other dried chiles. The flavor of the chile is very distinct.

- **5 dried *guajillo* chiles, stemmed, seeded, and de-veined if you wish to make a very mild sauce**
- **Water**
- **½ onion, diced**
- **2 cloves garlic, minced**
- **2 tablespoons olive oil**

2 tomatoes, diced
Salt to taste

Toast the chiles 2 minutes in a dry, hot skillet, flipping often (beware of fumes). Soak the toasted chiles in enough water to barely cover them until soft, about 10 minutes. Sauté the onion and garlic in the olive oil. In a blender, add the tomatoes to the softened chiles and puree. Add the puree to the sauteed onions and peppers and cook for 20 minutes on low heat. Salt to taste.

YIELD: 1½ CUPS
HEAT SCALE: MILD
SERVING SUGGESTIONS: THIS SAUCE IS VERY MILD, SO YOU CAN USE A LOT OF IT. DRIED CHILE SAUCES ARE TRADITIONALLY SERVED WITH PORK.

—PINCH-A-POLLO RESTAURANT

AGUA FRESCA DE TAMARINDO

This is the perfect drink on a really hot summer day in the Southwest. Agua fresca is thirst-quenching, has more nutritive value than tea or water, and, with no caffeine or alcohol, you can drink lots of it without worrying. Kids love it, and it goes great with hot and spicy food, too!

½ pound tamarind beans
¾ cup sugar or honey
1 gallon water

Rinse and drain the beans. Put them in a soup pot and add enough water to cover. Cook at a low boil for 10 minutes or so. Mash the softened beans vigorously with a potato masher. Strain the coffee-colored liquid into a 1-gallon container throwing away the seeds and outer pods. Add the sugar or honey while the liquid is hot. Add water to fill the container. Refrigerate and serve over ice.

YIELD: 1 GALLON

Variation:

Adjust the sugar level to taste. For a diet version, use the specified equivalent amount of artificial sweetener. Serve over more or less ice to make it stronger or weaker, as you like it.

POLLO EN MOLE ALMENDRADO (CHICKEN IN ALMOND MOLE)

This recipe is from Chef Miguel Ravago of Austin's fine Fonda San Miguel restaurant, which specializes in central and coastal Mexican cuisine.

- 10 **cups water**
- 2 **white onions, peeled and quartered**
- 2 **heads garlic; all the cloves peeled**
- 1 **4-inch cinnamon stick**
- 8 **whole cloves**
- 2 **chickens, cut up**
- ¾ **cup vegetable oil**
- 1½ **white onions, peeled and quartered**
- 8 **garlic cloves, peeled**
- 2 **cups almonds, blanched**
- 1 **cup roasted unsalted peanuts**
- 1 **4-inch cinnamon stick**
- 4 **whole cloves**
- 16 **black peppercorns**
- 1 **croissant, torn into pieces**
- 4 **large ripe tomatoes, roasted over an open flame**
- 4 *ancho* **chiles**
- ½ **cup vegetable oil**
- 2 **slices white onion**
- **Salt to taste**

Bring the water to a boil, add the next five ingredients, reduce heat, and simmer 25 minutes until the chicken is partially cooked. Remove the chicken from the broth. Reserve and strain the broth.

Heat the oil in a large saucepan. Add the next eight ingredients and simmer for 25 minutes, adding more oil if the mixture tends to stick. Place the mixture in a blender, add the tomatoes and chiles, and puree.

Heat remaining oil in a saucepan and brown the onion slices. Stir in the pureed mixture and cook until it releases its fat. Salt to taste. Add 2 or 3 cups of reserved chicken stock (or as needed to thin the sauce), add the chicken, and simmer an additional 25 minutes.

SERVES: **6**
HEAT SCALE: MILD

HILL COUNTRY PEACH CRISP

- **10 cups fresh peaches, peeled, pitted, and sliced**
- **2 teaspoons lemon juice**
- **½ teaspoon almond extract**
- **1 cup brown sugar**
- **¾ cup whole wheat flour**
- **3 cups quick oats**
- **1½ cups chopped pecans**
- **¾ cup grated coconut**
- **1 cup melted butter**
- **1 teaspoon almond extract**
- **1 teaspoon nutmeg**

Toss the peaches with the lemon juice and almond extract; place in a 9- by 13-inch baking dish.

Combine the sugar, flour, oats, pecans, and coconut. Stir in the butter and almond extract. Spread this mixture over the peaches and sprinkle with nutmeg.

Bake at 350° for 45 to 60 minutes, or until the top is golden brown.

SERVES: **12**

CHAPTER

⬥

4

SAN ANTONIO

San Antonio may be the tenth largest metropolis in the country, but it doesn't feel like a big city. Its quaint charm lies in its historical significance and the fact that most of the attractions are clustered downtown near the Paseo del Rio, or River Walk. And, because the locals tend to throw a fiesta just because the sun came up, it always seems like there's a party going on. Even when one of the fourteen major festivals is not happening, a stroll along bustling River Walk will convince you one is in progress.

The Paseo del Rio, often described as the "Venice of America" (not quite) is a three-mile walkway built in 1939 as a WPA project along a loop of the San Antonio River. The river has a European feel and is lined with hotels, restaurants, shops, and even a shopping mall, Rivercenter. The river and the Alamo are the major reasons for the vitality of the downtown, which is an inspiration to other cities ("Gee, all we have to do to fix downtown is build a river!"). As an example of the San Antonians' tendency to celebrate, when the river is drained for cleaning and maintenance, the locals celebrate by throwing the River Bottom Festival and Mud Parade.

Near the River Walk are quite a number of attractions. One out of every three visitors makes a pilgrimage to the Alamo (Alamo Street), the historic mission where 189 Texas patriots chose death over surrender in 1836. Nearby is HemisFair Plaza (200 S. Alamo Street), a ninety-acre park with its 750-foot Tower of the Americas, which has an observation deck and a restaurant. Don't miss two interesting museums there, the Institute of Texas Cultures and the Mexican Cultural Institute.

Nearby, along S. Alamo Street is La Villita (the little village), a restored, 200-year-old compound of adobe and stone buildings that now houses specialty shops and galleries. Within a few blocks is San Fernando Cathedral (114 Main Plaza) and the Spanish Governor's Palace (105 Plaza de Armas). Both are open to the public.

Along Mission Road, south of downtown, is San Antonio Missions National Historic Park, with three different missions: Mission Conceptión, Mission San José, and Mission San Juan Capistrano. Just west of the River Walk along Commerce Street is Market Square, three blocks of restaurants, shops, and galleries. Tourists love to cruise the stalls at El Mercado for pottery, baskets, blankets, and piñatas from Mexico. Farther west is the Farmer's Market, where vendors sell fresh fruits and vegetables in season. Market Square is the site of Fiesta of San Jacinto in April, Cinco de Mayo in May, Diez y Seis in September, and Fiesta Navidena in December.

Other sights not to miss in San Antonio are the Museum of Art (200 W. Jones), housed in the former Lone Star Brewery; the striking Botanical Center (555 Funston Place), with 1,800 plants on thirty-three acres; the San Antonio Zoo and its 3,000 animals (3903 N. St. Mary's); Sea World of Texas (northwest on Loop 1604) and Baby Shamu in her 7-million-gallon aquarium; and Fiesta Texas (I-10 and Loop 1604), a theme and music park.

For more information on visiting San Antonio, contact the San Antonio Convention and Visitors Bureau, P.O. Box 2277, San Antonio, TX 78298 (800-447-3372).

The Food Scene

If there is such a thing as a normal Southwestern city, San Antonio is certainly not it—particularly concerning food. San Antonians, like most Texans, have a strong individualistic bent, and this characteristic traditionally has been reflected in the offbeat nature of the city's eating establishments. This quirkiness has been enhanced by several facts: first, incomes in San Antonio have always been moderate to low; and second, until the early 1970s, liquor was forbidden in Texas restaurants.

Lacking the profits from mixed drinks, restaurateurs could not afford much in the way of decor. Depending just on food sales meant menu items had to be both delicious and inexpensive. From this background grew a profusion of funky eateries reflecting the idiosyncrasies of their owners rather than market research, but such a situation has made San Antonio one of the most enjoyable and fun places to eat out in the Southwest—particularly for the adventurous and unpretentious diner.

In recent years, San Antonio has grown tremendously and, at least on the north side, is much like any other U.S. city with its complement of franchise fast-food outlets and neon-lit restaurants. It is the old-style, eclectic restaurants (many of which still exist), however, that are dear to old San Antonians.

San Antonio's first and possibly funkiest food purveyors were the chili queens. Beginning around 1880, these colorful women set up carts at dusk in Military Plaza, where they cooked chili con carne in iron pots over mesquite coals. Their flirtatiousness and the aroma of chili were their sales tools. Frank X. Tolbert, writing in his famous paen to chili, *A Bowl of Red*, described them: "The chili queens dressed gaily and, according to one account, pinned bunches of roses, in season, to their bosoms. Street musicians serenaded the chili eaters."

Unfortunately, health regulations drove the chili queens away in the late 1930s, though they do make a comeback every year during the Return of the Chili Queens celebration during Memorial Day weekend. Unfortunately, most San Antonio restaurants have not carried on the tradition of Texas-style chili, preferring instead to serve a chile-based enchilada sauce.

One typical San Antonio haunt that still serves chili con carne is the Original Donut Shop. Although it prepares fine donuts, its main attractions are the *gorditas*, flour tortillas, tacos, and *barbacoa*. Other spots that deliver fun and a nostalgic slice of San Antonio's past (and interesting food to boot) include Little Hipp's Gimmedraw Parlour, Henry's Puffy Taco, Bob's Smokehouse, the Tip Top Cafe, and the Esquire Tavern. There is nothing fancy (quite the opposite) about these eateries, but they provide a lot of fun for visitors who like offbeat spots and good food.

But to prove San Antonio can also play with the cosmopolitan set, there are many new restaurants with brilliant chefs, such as the Zuni Grill, Biga, and La Buca. And these are not just good, upscale restaurants—they are places gaining national attention.

San Antonio's largest ethnic heritage is Spanish, followed by German; both cultures are known for injecting heavy doses of food and merriment into their celebrations. The largest festival in San Antonio is the Fiesta of San Jacinto (also called Fiesta San Antonio), which officially commemorates Texas' independence from Mexico. The highlight is a Night in Old San Antonio, or NIOSA as it is now called, which combines the joyousness of a Mexican fiesta with the raucous bonhomie of Oktoberfest. For a full week, San Antonio reverts to its colorful past, including food stalls that serve everything from Peruvian *anticuchos* to sausages from the nearby German towns in the Hill Country.

So, if you're coming to San Antonio, be prepared to party.

—JIM PEYTON

4-1 There's Always a Party Going On Along the River Walk

Markets

FARM TO MARKET

133 Austin Highway (512-822-4450). *Open Monday–Saturday, 8:30 a.m.–7 p.m.* NO CREDIT CARDS; BEER AND WINE TAKEOUT.

This market specializes in both ordinary and gourmet produce, cheeses, meats, deli items, and Italian baked goods. Texas and Southwestern items include dried and fresh chiles. A boxcar addition to the market features the market's chef, who prepares gourmet meals for carryout.

FARMER'S MARKET

Commerce Street, adjacent to Market Square. *Open daily, 9 a.m.–5 p.m.* NO CREDIT CARDS; BEER AVAILABLE AT MARKET SQUARE.

An ever-shifting number of vendors sell fresh vegetables and fruit in season. Other vendors sell gift items and Mexican imports.

HEB MARKETPLACE

5601 Bandera Road (and other locations) (512-647-2700). *Open daily, 9 a.m.–10 p.m.* NO CREDIT CARDS; LIQUOR AVAILABLE.

The marketplace-concept store is, to food lovers, one of San Antonio's main attractions. Customers enter through a produce section containing items from around the world. At last count, the store carried twenty-two different fresh and dried chiles. From the produce section, customers wander into the Italian deli section, which boasts a wood-burning oven for cooking fresh pizza. The Mexican section of the Marketplace has a small tortilla factory, which continuously produces corn and flour tortillas. The bakery features more than thirty ethnic breads that are baked daily. The meat department features sausage from around the world, hormone- and additive-free meats, and hard-to-find specialty meats such as *cabrito*.

The cheese department offers international cheeses with a particularly fine selection from Italy. The seafood section carries a huge offering of fresh fish flown in daily. There are also a fresh-roasted coffee department, a sushi department, food stalls, fresh herbs by the ounce, and much more.

INTERNATIONAL FOOD MARKET

2449 Nacodoches Road (512-821-6451). *Open Monday–Saturday, 9:30 a.m.–7 p.m.* NO CREDIT CARDS; BEER AVAILABLE.

This small Hispanic grocery specializes in Central and South American products including canned goods, produce, and beer—as well as cooking utensils. It's worth a trip just for the Jamaican ginger beer.

VERSTUYFT FARMS

14819 I-35 S, Von Ormy, Loop 1604 exit on the access road (512-622-3423). *Open Monday–Saturday, 8:30 a.m.–6 p.m.* NO CREDIT CARDS.

This family farm sells wholesale and retail to the public. It specializes in tomatoes and other seasonal crops such as jalapeños, serranos, and New Mexican chiles.

Brewery and Wineries

LONE STAR BREWERY

600 Lone Star Boulevard, off Mission Road (512-270-9460). *Open daily, 9:30 a.m.–5 p.m. Admission $3.50.* NO CREDIT CARDS; BEER AVAILABLE (OBVIOUSLY).

The admission charge covers a tour, two beers, and entrance to the Buckhorn Saloon hallowed Hall of Horns (five halls with every animal horn know to man, including a 78-point set of deer antlers); the Hall of Fins (see the 1,056-pound black marlin!); the Hall of Feathers (complete with two extinct passenger pigeons, circa 1914); and the Texas Wax Museum ("Look, Mom, it's Sam Houston!"). As Peyton notes, "This is a pleasant visit, particularly if you are in the mood for some kitschy entertainment."

ALAMO FARMS WINERY AND VINEYARD

25 miles southeast of San Antonio on Fuller, off Live Oak via FM 3432 (512-947-3331). *Open Saturday and Sunday, 1 p.m.–4 p.m. (March to December). Admission charge.*

Nestled behind a hill overlooking San Antonio, Alamo has a quaint underground wine cellar. The tour traces the path a grape takes from the vine through the cellar to the bottle.

GUADALUPE VALLEY WINERY

1720 Hunter Road in New Braunfels (512-629-2351). *Open Monday–Friday, 10 a.m.–5 p.m.; Saturday, 10 a.m.–6 p.m.; Sunday, noon–5 p.m. Tours on weekends, noon–5 p.m., during the summer.*

There are no vineyards here as the owners buy grapes throughout Texas and encourage local grape production. The winemaking is done in a restored cotton gin that's listed on the National Register of Historic Sites.

MOYER CHAMPAGNE COMPANY

1941 I-35 E, New Braunfels (512-625-5181). *Open daily, 9 a.m.–5 p.m.; tours Saturday, 11 a.m.–5 p.m., and Sunday, 1 p.m.–5 p.m.*

The champagnes are produced in the traditional Methode Champenoise (the wine is fermented in the bottle and aged eighteen months to two years). This modern facility has a tasting room and a gift shop.

Retail Shops

OLD SAN ANTONIO STYLE GOURMET SAUCES

Market Square on Congress Street, across from Mi Tierra (512-340-6615). *Open daily, 10 a.m.–8 p.m. (summer); 10 a.m.–6 p.m. (winter).* MAJOR CREDIT CARDS; NO LIQUOR.

This small shop inside Market Square has a large selection of its own, as well as many other, brands of salsas, dried chiles, jellies, and other Southwestern and Mexican food items. It also has a nice selection of *comales* and other Mexican cooking utensils. They accept mail orders (800-972-3049).

THE NEW-AGE VERSION OF THE ORIGIN OF CHILI

Some chili con carne fanatics are not satisfied with mundane explanations—such as cattle-drive cooking—for the origin of chili. In his book, *Bull Cook and Authentic Historical Recipes and Practices*, George Herter weaves a strange tale indeed about the possible origin of chili.

The story of the "lady in blue" tells of Sister Mary of Agreda, a Spanish nun in the early 1600s. Although she never left her convent in Spain, she nonetheless had out-of-body experiences during which her spirit was transported across the Atlantic to preach Christianity to the peoples of the New World.

After one of the return trips, her spirit wrote down the first primitive recipe for chili con carne, which the now-converted Indians had given her out of gratitude: chile peppers, venison, onions, and tomatoes. Believe that one, and we have a deal for you on some swamp land in New Mexico.

Incidentally, there is a chili museum that collects stories such as this, but it's located in Houston, of all places. Contact Chuck Thompson, Director, National Chili Museum, P.O. Box 11652, Houston, TX 77293.

Los Patios

2015 Northeast Loop 410 (512-655-6171). *Open daily,*
10 a.m.–6 p.m. (restaurants open later). MAJOR CREDIT CARDS;
LIQUOR LICENSE.

On twenty acres along historic Salado Creek, Los Patios is
quite a shopping and dining experience. There is a garden
center here; early Spanish colonial architecture; galleries;
three indoor/outdoor restaurants; and a nice retail shop, Tejas Gifts, that sells food, wine, and books about Texas.

Rivera's Chile Shop

109½ Concho Street in Market Square (512-226-9106). *Open*
daily, 10 a.m.–6 p.m. MAJOR CREDIT CARDS; NO LIQUOR.

Aha, a shop for the true chile lover! Not only are all the pods
here, but just about every other chile product you can imagine, including clothing, jewelry, posters, salsas, jams, jellies,
candies, and many other food items. Additionally, Rivera's has
a fine collection of Mexican and Southwestern cookbooks.

Taste of Texas Market

3939 I-35 S in San Marcos (512-396-7055). *Open Monday–*
Saturday, 9 a.m.–9 p.m.; Sunday, 11 a.m.–6 p.m. VISA, MC;
BEER AND WINE SALES.

This shop carries only Texas products: wines, beers, hot
sauces, salsas, spices, seasonings, and a special Cajun seasoning. They specialize in gift baskets, Fall Creek wines, and
unusual gift items.

Restaurants

Los Barrios Mexican Restaurant

4223 Blanco (512-732-6017). *Open Monday–Thursday,*
10 a.m.–10 p.m.; Friday and Saturday, 10 a.m.–midnight;
Sunday, 9 a.m.–10 p.m. MAJOR CREDIT CARDS; LIQUOR LICENSE.

This family restaurant, in business since 1979, serves, in addition to their Tex-Mex specialties, such signature items as: their "mofofo" grill, churrasco steak, *cabrito* dinner, and *milaneza papas.*

BIGA

206 E. Locust Street (512-225-0722). *Open Tuesday– Friday, 11 a.m.–2 p.m. (lunch); Monday–Thursday, 6 p.m.– 10:30 p.m.; Friday and Saturday, 6 p.m.–11:30 p.m. (dinner).* MAJOR CREDIT CARDS; BEER AND WINE.

Lodged in a beautiful mansion, Biga is the creation of chef/ owner Bruce Auden, who changes his menu often. The food varies from Southwestern to Asian to Mediterranean. He creates elegant and interesting dishes such as Chilled Sour Apricot Soup with Champagne, but believe it or not, his specialty is Beer Batter Onion Rings Served with Habanero Ketchup and Pickled Serranos. Whew.

BOB'S SMOKEHOUSE

3306 Roland (512-333-9611). *Open Sunday–Thursday, 10:30 a.m.–8 p.m.; Friday and Saturday, 10:30 a.m.–9 p.m.* NO CREDIT CARDS; NO LIQUOR.

The hole-in-the-wall atmosphere, what every barbecue joint should have, is perfect for Bob's carefully smoked lamb and beef and pork ribs, sausage, and brisket.

LA BUCA DI SAINT ANTONIO

7720 Jones-Maltsberger (512-826-2397). *Open Monday– Friday, 11:30 a.m.–2 p.m. (lunch); Monday–Thursday, 6 p.m.–10 p.m.; Saturday, 6 p.m.–11 p.m.; Sunday, 6 p.m.– 9 p.m. (dinner).* MAJOR CREDIT CARDS; LIQUOR LICENSE.

Another escape from the Southwest, "the mouth of San Antonio" features northern Italian specialties like Fried Ravioli Stuffed with Cheese and Crab, "Handkerchief" Pasta with Porcini, Creamy Spinach Lasagne, and a killer tortellini soup. For lunch, try the Butterflied Grilled Chicken Breasts on a Bed of Greens.

4-2 A Feast of the New Southwest at
the Zuni Grill

LA CALESA

2103 E. Hildebrand (512-822-4475). *Open Monday–*
Thursday, 11 a.m.–9:30 p.m.; Friday and Saturday,
11 a.m.–11:30 p.m.; Sunday, noon–10 p.m. MAJOR CREDIT
CARDS; LIQUOR LICENSE.

Central Mexican dishes from as far south as Mérida in Yucatán are the specialties of the house at the expanded La
Calesa (a horse-drawn carriage). The *Cochinita Pibil* (pork
stew), Enchiladas *Potosinas* (with potatoes and chorizo!), and
the *Rajas Poblanas* (*poblano* chile strips) in cream sauce are
highly recommended.

EL CHAPARRAL

15103 Bandera Road, Helotes (512-695-8302). *Open*
Monday–Saturday, 7 a.m.–10 p.m.; Sunday, 7 a.m.–9 p.m.
MAJOR CREDIT CARDS; LIQUOR LICENSE.

Located in picturesque Helotes, just north of San Antonio, El
Chaparral has been serving fine Tex-Mex food for more than

twenty years. The most popular items are the basic Tex-Mex enchiladas, green enchiladas, and their unusual Creole Tacos. The restaurant is a popular stop on the way to or from the racetrack at Bandera.

COCULA

329 Alamo Plaza (512-223-2281). *Open daily, 11 a.m.– 10 p.m.; Sundays during the winter, 11 a.m.–3 p.m.* MAJOR CREDIT CARDS; LIQUOR LICENSE.

A fine collection of photographs from the Mexican revolution highlights Cocula, which specializes in recipes from the interior of Mexico. One favorite dish is Acapulco Rajas, a combination of broiled chicken in *adobo* sauce, chile strips in cream, a *quesadilla*, refried beans, and broiled scallions. Others are Tortilla Soup and Meatballs with Chipotle Sauce.

DEWESE'S TIP TOP CAFE

2814 Fredericksburg Road (512-732-0191). *Open Monday– Thursday, 11 a.m.–8 p.m.; Friday and Saturday, 11 a.m.– 9 p.m.* NO CREDIT CARDS; NO LIQUOR.

Here it is: San Antonio's mecca for made-from-scratch, home-style country cookin'. Ownership of this institution is somewhere between the third and fourth generations of the DeWese family, and many of the employees have worked there for decades. Hint: The chicken-fried steak is to die for, according to Peyton.

ERNESTO'S

2559 Jackson-Keller (512-377-1248). *Open Monday–Friday, 11:30 a.m.–2 p.m. (lunch); Monday–Thursday, 5:30 p.m.– 10 p.m.; Friday and Saturday, 5:30 p.m.–10:30 p.m. (dinner).* MAJOR CREDIT CARDS; LIQUOR LICENSE.

Ernesto's is one of those collision-of-cultures restaurants that dazzles with a combination of Mexican traditions, fresh seafood, and French influences. Signature dishes include Snapper with Salsa Veracruzana, Enchiladas à la Ernesto, Ceviche, Green Chicken Enchiladas, and Fish with Garlic Sauce. Ernesto's has a fanatically loyal clientele.

4-3 Outside Dining at Market Square (*Credit:* Jim Peyton)

ESQUIRE TAVERN

155 E. Commerce (512-222-2521). *Open Monday–Friday, 7 a.m.–1 a.m.; Saturday and Sunday, 7 a.m.–2 a.m.* NO CREDIT CARDS; LIQUOR LICENSE.

Care for a cold one? Need a little pick-me-up after wandering around and around the River Walk? Then the Esquire Tavern is the bar for you. It's a must for anyone who desires the feel of old San Antonio combined with the excitement of new San Antonio.

LA FOGATA

2427 Vance Jackson (512-340-0636). *Open daily, 7:30 a.m.– 10 p.m., except Monday when it opens at 11 a.m.* MAJOR CREDIT CARDS; LIQUOR LICENSE.

Once an abandoned filling station, La Fogata (the flame) is now regarded as San Antonio's premier Mexican restaurant with its complex of spreading terraces. The food, in the style of north-central Mexico, includes such temptations as Queso Flameado (flaming cheese); Guayaba Enchiladas (with guava); and *Carne Adobada*, with rich chiles and a hint of cinnamon. Be prepared for a wait at this very popular restaurant.

LA FONDA

2415 N. Main (512-733-0621). *Open Monday–Saturday, 11 a.m.–2 p.m. (lunch); Monday–Wednesday, 5:30 p.m.– 8:30 p.m.; Thursday–Saturday, 5:30 p.m.–9 p.m. (dinner).* VISA, MC; LIQUOR LICENSE.

"The Inn" has been serving Tex-Mex favorites since 1932 and is considered to have mastered the style. It is probably the oldest continually operated Mexican restaurant in San Antonio and one of the oldest in the country. Recommended dishes are Chiles Rellenos Stuffed with Meat and Raisins, Chicken Tortilla Soup, and Chilled Avocado Soup.

GOLFO DE MEXICO

603 Bandera (512-434-8662) and 5128 Blanco Road (512-344-4439). *Open Sunday–Thursday, 10 a.m.–11 p.m.; Friday and Saturday, 10 a.m.–1 a.m.* VISA, MC (BLANCO LOCATION ONLY); BEER.

Both locations are plain but clean hole-in-the-wall restaurants that resemble the South-of-the-border *ostiónerias* (oyster bars) found throughout Mexico. Golfo de Mexico specializes in serving Mexican-style seafood at low prices in a friendly atmosphere. Try the seafood cocktails, any of the soups, and the fried and broiled fish.

HENRY'S PUFFY TACO

3202 W. Woodlawn (512-432-7341). *Open Monday–Saturday, 8 a.m.–8 p.m.* VISA, MC; BEER AND WINE.

Puffy tacos are a Tex-Mex specialty not usually found outside of San Antonio, and Henry's are some of the best. This restaurant is a family affair, reflected by the warmth and friendliness that accompany the Tex-Mex combination plates.

JANITZIO

4404 Walzem Road, Suite A (512-657-7363). *Open daily,
8 a.m.–10 p.m.* MAJOR CREDIT CARDS; BEER AND WINE.

Janitzio serves an interesting combination of Mexican regional, South American, Caribbean, and Continental dishes.

A MOVEABLE FEAST:
THE TEXAN DINING TRAIN

All aboard! All aboard! The Texan Dining Train is now departing for a three-and-one-half-hour tour of the Southwestern Texas plains—in the dark. Okay, okay, the purpose of the train ride is not sightseeing, but rather dining—and experiencing elegant train travel aboard a fleet of authentically restored lounge and dining cars.

Enjoy a cocktail in the 1937 Santa Fe lounge car, Nambe, with its Southwestern designs. Or dine in the 1947 New York Central Diner No. 406, or in the floral-motifed diner, Botsford Tavern, which used to run on the Chesapeake and Ohio Railroad. Another choice is to be served in the domed California Zephyr.

The venue is elegant and exciting, especially for railroad buffs. *Texas Monthly* commented: "The service is good, the limited menu a notch below that." The Texan Dining Train boards at the Southern Pacific Depot at 1174 E. Commerce in San Antonio. Call for more information (512-225-RAIL). (The train does not run during January and February.)

KARAM'S MEXICAN DINING ROOM

121 N. Zarzamora (512-433-0111). *Open daily, 11 a.m.–*
10 p.m. VISA, MC; LIQUOR LICENSE.

One of San Antonio's oldest and finest Tex-Mex restaurants,
Karam's serves delicious Tex-Mex favorites but specializes in
cabrito.

LITTLE HIPP'S GIMMEDRAW PARLOUR

1423 McCullough (512-222-8114). *Open Monday–Friday,*
11 a.m.–9 p.m.; closed weekends. NO CREDIT CARDS; BEER AND
WINE.

Little Hipp's came to prominence following the loss of the
revered Hipp's Bubble Room, which unfortunately was converted into a parking lot. Specialties are the "gimmedraw"
draft beer served in a milkshake glass, Shypoke Eggs (round
nachos decorated with yellow and white cheese to resemble a
fried egg), and huge, Texas-style hamburgers.

LA MARGARITA MEXICAN RESTAURANT AND OYSTER BAR

120 Produce Row in Market Square (512-227-7140). *Open*
Sunday–Thursday, 11 a.m.–10 p.m.; Friday and Saturday,
11 a.m.–midnight. MAJOR CREDIT CARDS; LIQUOR LICENSE.

Although definitely a tourist restaurant, it's pleasant to sit
on the outdoor patio, feast on fajitas, and watch life go by. A
specialty here is the Mexican *parrillada*, a dish that includes
short ribs, sausage, *chiles rellenos*, fajitas, tortillas, and
frijoles.

MI TIERRA CAFE AND BAKERY

218 Produce Row in Market Square (512-225-1262). *Open*
daily, 24 hours. VISA, MC; LIQUOR LICENSE.

Now, this is quite a hangout. The restaurant has been in the
same location for more than fifty years, but originally the
area was a red-light district. Although it was located in a
rough neighborhood, people from all walks of life and all

parts of town found their way to Mi Tierra. In 1974 the area was developed into a tourist-oriented marketplace with a Mexican atmosphere, and Mi Tierra expanded to its current large size, including an adjacent bakery. Specialties include *cabrito*, *chilaquiles*, beef *chiles rellenos*, and the ubiquitous Tex-Mex favorites.

EL MIRADOR

722 S. St. Mary's (512-225-9444). *Open Monday–Friday, 6:30 a.m.–4 p.m.; Saturday, 6:30 a.m.–3 p.m.* NO CREDIT CARDS; BEER AND WINE.

During a reasonable amount of time, you will see just about anybody who counts in San Antonio at El Mirador. The best time to arrive at this tiny cafe is Saturday after 11 a.m., when the restaurant serves the soups for which it is justly famous. Recommended are the *caldo xocitil*, *huevos rancheros*, enchiladas, and the mind-boggling *caldo azteca*, which contains chunks of chicken, fresh spinach, strips of corn tortilla, chiles, sliced avocado, melted cheese, zucchini, carrots, and potatoes!

ORIGINAL DONUT SHOP

3307 Fredericksburg (512-734-5661). *Open Monday– Saturday, 6 a.m.–8 p.m.; Sunday, 7 a.m.–8 p.m.* NO CREDIT CARDS; NO LIQUOR.

Aside from donuts, this cafe-style eatery specializes in basic Tex-Mex favorites made from scratch. The shop serves tacos in fantastic, hand-made flour tortillas; chili con carne; *menudo*; and, on weekends, *barbacoa*.

PICO DE GALLO

111 S. Leona (512-225-6060). *Open Monday–Thursday, 7 a.m.–10 p.m.; Friday and Saturday, 7 a.m.–2 a.m.; Sunday, 8 a.m.–9 p.m.* MAJOR CREDIT CARDS; LIQUOR LICENSE.

Under the same ownership as Mi Tierra and La Margarita, Pico de Gallo serves the same *parrillada* as La Margarita. Typical of *norteño* cooking, this dish is served for two and contains char-broiled chicken, beef fajitas, sausage, grilled onions and potatoes, *frijoles ñ la charra*, tortillas, and, of course, pico de gallo salsa. The restaurant is decorated with stone sculptures and a hand-carved bar by Jesus Garza.

PIEDRAS NEGRAS DE NOCHE

1312 S. Laredo (512-227-7777). *Open Monday–Thursday, 11 a.m.–10 p.m.; Friday and Saturday, 11 a.m.–3 a.m.*
NO CREDIT CARDS; NO LIQUOR.

This interestingly named restaurant (black rocks at night) serves authentic northern Mexican food. A specialty is steak with *chiles rellenos*.

LA PLAYA

2702 N. St. Mary's (512-737-1005). *Open Monday–Wednesday, 11 a.m.–11 p.m.; Thursday–Sunday, 11 a.m.–2 a.m.* MAJOR CREDIT CARDS; LIQUOR LICENSE.

"The beach," located on the St. Mary's strip, is an interesting, off-beat place. Sunday brunch is particularly popular, when diners come to enjoy live music as well as the food—which is creative, Mexican-style seafood. Popular offerings include crab enchiladas, shrimp and spinach salad, and crab nachos.

ROSARIO'S AUTHENTIC MEXICAN CUISINE

1014 S. Alamo (512-223-1806). *Open Sunday–Tuesday, 10 a.m.–10 p.m.; Wednesday–Saturday, 10 a.m.–midnight.* MAJOR CREDIT CARDS; LIQUOR LICENSE.

Rosario's is one of the only restaurants in San Antonio that makes its own corn tortillas. The food served here comes from all states of Mexico and favorites are *rajas con queso blanco*, black bean soup, and tortilla soup.

RUDY'S COUNTRY STORE AND BARBECUE

North of San Antonio off I-10 W in downtown Leon Springs (512-698-0418). *Open Sunday–Thursday, 10 a.m.–9 p.m.;*

Friday and Saturday, 10 a.m.–10 p.m. NO CREDIT CARDS;
BEER.

Imagine a restaurant that advertises itself as serving "the
worst barbecue in Texas" and you've conjured up Rudy's.
The reverse psychology seems to work because the place is
jammed. In addition to the usual brisket, spare ribs, and sausage, Rudy's serves barbecued prime rib, rainbow trout, babyback ribs, and pork loin. All these items are served on butcher
paper, the old-fashioned way. A unique aspect of Rudy's is the
pit, which is designed so the burning oak logs heat the outside
dining area while providing heat and smoke for cooking. Incidentally, tiny Leon Springs is becoming quite a gourmet
compound. In addition to Rudy's, it offers the Leon Springs
Cafe with great hamburgers and French fries; Macaroni Grill
with gargantuan portions of Italian food; and Ping's, which
serves excellent and spicy Hunan-style Chinese food.

TOMATILLOS CAFE Y CANTINA

3210 Broadway (512-824-3005). *Open Sunday–Thursday,*
11 a.m.–10 p.m.; Friday and Saturday, 11 a.m.–11 p.m.
MAJOR CREDIT CARDS; LIQUOR LICENSE.

Tomatillos, a new and spacious restaurant in the Alamo
Heights area, is attracting a lot of business. It serves Tex-
Mex standards, Chicken Acapulco, and the interesting *tres
colores* (three colors) plate, which combines three different
enchiladas.

ZITO'S SANDWICH SHOP

8800 Broadway (512-826-4723) and 6007 Callaghan
(512-684-6555). *Open Monday–Saturday, 9 a.m.–5 p.m.*
NO CREDIT CARDS; NO LIQUOR.

Escaping from Tex-Mex? Try the incredible Serious Sandwich, which is 10 inches in diameter and uses pizza crusts
instead of bread. Also, not to be missed are the Roast Beef
Italia and Italian Combo. Yearn for a non-Texas dessert? Try
the baklava.

ZUNI GRILL

511 River Walk (221 Lasoya), just south of the Hyatt Regency (512-227-0864). Open Monday–Friday, 10 a.m.–midnight; Saturday and Sunday, 8:30 a.m.–midnight. MAJOR CREDIT CARDS; LIQUOR LICENSE.

The huge jars full of pickled chiles are a tip that you're in serious New Southwest country here. Jay McCarthy, the talented young chef at this trendy River Walk establishment, takes pains to see that everything on the menu is fresh and perfectly prepared. Start with a Cactus Margarita, made with *tunas* marinated in Cuervo Gold. Then try the Duck Quesadillas for an appetizer and the Shiner Bock Black Bean Soup. Proceed to Pecan-Crusted Chicken on Mixed Greens with Pepper Raspberry Vinaigrette and an entree of Grilled Cider-Cured Pork Loin with Adobo Sauce. Finish with Chilled Rice Flan with Lime Caramel for dessert, and you're in foodie heaven. Incidentally, all this happiness won't break your bank; the entrees are under $10, a remarkable price for the quality of the food. Be careful not to fall in the river when you leave.

Recipes

CHILI QUEEN'S CHILI

According to legend, this is one of the original chili queens' recipes. Some changes have been made to take advantage of modern ingredients.

Flour for dredging
2 pounds beef shoulder, cut into ½-inch cubes
1 pound pork shoulder, cut into ½-inch cubes
¼ cup suet
¼ cup pork fat
3 medium onions, chopped
6 cloves garlic, minced
1 quart water
4 ancho chiles, stems and seeds removed, chopped fine
1 serrano chile, stems and seeds removed, chopped fine
6 dried red chiles, stems and seeds removed, chopped fine
1 tablespoon cumin seeds, freshly ground
2 tablespoons Mexican oregano
Salt to taste

Lightly flour the beef and pork cubes. Quickly cook them in the suet and pork fat, stirring often. Add the onions and garlic and sauté until they are tender and limp. Add water to the mixture and simmer for 1 hour.

Grind the chiles in a *molcajete* or blender. Add to the meat mixture. Add the remaining ingredients and simmer for another 2 hours.

Remove suet casing and skim off some fat. Never cook beans with chiles and meat! Serve them as a separate dish.

SERVES: 6 TO 8
HEAT SCALE: MEDIUM

SALSA DE JALAPEÑO O SERRANO ASADO

The simplicity of this salsa, imported from northern Mexico, is deceiving, for it is one of the best all-around table sauces in either of its final forms: ground or blended and strained. The charred tomatoes and chiles add a robust flavor, and you can control the texture.

2 **medium-large tomatoes**
2 **jalapeño or serrano chiles, stems removed**
¼ **teaspoon salt, or to taste**

Grill the tomatoes and chiles by placing them 3 to 6 inches above hot coals. Turn often; they should be soft and the skins should be charred.

The seeds can be removed from the chiles and tomatoes, and they can be ground in a *molcajete* with salt. Or, the grilled tomatoes and chiles can be blended for 30 seconds in a blender, strained, and lightly salted. The texture is smooth and the sauce is flecked with tiny bits of the charred chile and tomato skins, which adds an interesting taste.

SERVES: **2 TO 4**
HEAT SCALE: **MEDIUM**

—JIM PEYTON

4-4 The Big Restaurant Biga

VENISON STEAKS WITH CHILE WINE SAUCE

Game is very popular in Texas, despite the fact that there is no public land open for hunting in the state. To fill this void, hunters pay ranchers and other private landholders for the right to hunt on their property. If venison is not available, beef or lamb can be substituted.

8 crushed chiltepins, or other small hot chile
½ cup dry red or port wine
¼ cup vinegar
¼ cup vegetable oil
2 cloves garlic, minced
1 tablespoon crushed fresh rosemary
Freshly ground black pepper
2 venison steaks, 1½ to 2 inches thick
Vegetable oil

Combine all the ingredients, except the venison. Add the meat and marinate in the mixture for at least 24 hours; remove and drain, reserving the marinade.

Rub the steaks with vegetable oil and sear quickly to hold in the juices. Grill the steaks, basting frequently with the marinade until just done.

SERVES: **2**
HEAT SCALE: MEDIUM

—NANCY GERLACH

TEXAS CAVIAR

No collection of recipes from the Lone Star State would be complete without a recipe for "Texas caviar" or black-eyed peas, a major crop in Texas. Black-eyed peas are traditionally served on New Year's Day for good luck in Texas and throughout the South.

6 jalapeño chiles, stems and seeds removed, chopped
½ cup vegetable oil, olive preferred

¼ **cup vinegar**
 2 **cloves garlic, minced**
¼ **teaspoon dry mustard**
   Freshly ground black pepper
 2 **cups cooked black-eyed peas**
 4 **green onions, sliced, including the greens**
 1 **stalk celery, chopped**

Combine the chiles, oil, vinegar, garlic, mustard, and pepper to form a dressing. Toss the peas, onions, and celery with the dressing and marinate in the refrigerator overnight. Serve as a salad.

SERVES: **4 TO 6**
HEAT SCALE: **MEDIUM**

—NANCY GERLACH

4-5 Mexican Specialties Fill Market Square Shops (*Credit:* Jim Peyton)

PICO DE GALLO SALSA

This universal salsa is served everywhere in the Southwest and often appears with non-traditional ingredients such as canned tomatoes, bell peppers, or spices like oregano. Here is the most authentic version. Remember all the ingredients should be as fresh as possible, and the vegetables must be hand-chopped. Never, never use a blender or food processor. Pico de gallo is best when the tomatoes come from the garden rather than the supermarket. It can be used as a dip for chips or for spicing up fajitas and other northern Mexican specialties such as soft tacos filled with *carne asada*.

> 4 **serrano or jalapeño chiles, stems removed, chopped fine (more for a hotter salsa)**
> 2 **large, ripe tomatoes, chopped fine**
> 1 **medium onion, chopped fine**
> 2 **cloves garlic, minced**
> ¼ **cup minced fresh cilantro**
> 2 **tablespoons vinegar**
> 2 **tablespoons vegetable oil**
>
> Combine all ingredients, mix well. Let the salsa sit, covered, for at least 1 hour to blend the flavors. It will keep only about a day in the refrigerator.
>
> YIELD: **3 CUPS**
> HEAT SCALE: **HOT**

SHORT RIB CHILE STEW

This hearty Texas beef dish is perfect for serving on a cold winter Sunday when the Cowboys play the Redskins for the NFC championship.

4 pounds beef short ribs
1 onion, chopped
1 bell pepper, seeded and chopped
2 cloves garlic, chopped
2 tablespoons red chile powder
½ teaspoon ground cumin
¼ teaspoon oregano
1 can stewed tomatoes
½ cup chopped green chile
1 cube beef bouillon dissolved in 1 cup water
Salt to taste
1 can corn, drained
1 can cooked kidney beans, drained
1 cup cooked pinto beans

Trim the fat from the ribs, reserving 2 tablespoons. Render the fat, brown the ribs, and remove. Sauté the onion, bell pepper, and garlic. Add the chile powder, cumin, oregano, tomatoes, and green chile. Return the ribs to the pot, add the water-bouillon mixture, and simmer for 2 hours. Stir occasionally, adding more water if necessary.

Adjust the salt, add the corn and beans, stir, and heat for 10 minutes before serving.

SERVES: 8
HEAT SCALE: MILD

CHAPTER

———————◆———————

5

EL PASO AND CIUDAD JUÁREZ

Culturally, scenically, economically, and gastronomically, El Paso belongs more to New Mexico than Texas. El Pasoans, who despite living in the fourth-largest city in the state, often feel isolated from and slighted by the rest of Texas, love New Mexico and visit the state frequently. Thus, the trade between the city and the region to the north that began with treks up and down the Camino Real continues today along Interstate 25.

The modern history of the region began in 1659 when Fray Garcia de San Francisco y Zuniga constructed a small sanctuary and named it the Mission of Our Lady of Guadalupe of Paso del Norte, which later became the Mission of Guadalupe. The settlement that slowly grew around the mission was named El Paso del Norte, the Pass of the North.

El Paso became a major stop on the Camino Real, which connected Mexico City with Santa Fe. From El Paso, travelers and explorers had the option of moving farther north to Santa Fe or heading east to San Antonio.

During the Pueblo Revolt of 1680 in New Mexico, El Paso del Norte gave asylum to the governor of the Province of New Mexico, Don Antonio de Otermín, who improved the city and organized an army to defend it. Along with Otermín came friendly Indians from Isleta Pueblo, who did not participate in the revolt. They founded a new pueblo, spelled it Ysleta, and have survived to this day.

In 1847, Susan Magoffin, visiting El Paso del Norte, noted: "Our dishes [here] are all Mexican, but good ones, some are delightful; one great importance, they are well cooked; their meats are all boiled, the healthiest way of preparing them, and are in most instances cooked with vegetables, which are onions, cabbage, and tomatoes; with the addition of apples and grapes."

During Prohibition, Ciudad Juárez became a mecca for Americans eager to enjoy pleasures that were illegal in the United States, especially drinking. Distilleries were constructed that supplied bootlegged liquor to cities as far north as St. Louis, and Avenida Juárez had more saloons that any other street in the world, a bar every twenty feet for six blocks!

"Juárez is the most immoral, degenerate, and utterly wicked place I have ever seen or heard of in my travels," raged U.S. Consul John Dye in 1921. "Murder and robbery are everyday occurrences and gambling, dope selling and using, drinking to excess and sexual vices are continuous." An American evangelist of the time added: "I would rather shoot my son and throw his body in the river than have him spend one hour in the raging inferno of Juárez."

5-1 Ristras Are Sold at Roadside Stands in El Paso

Juárez has cooled off and mellowed considerably during the past seventy years. We have visited the city perhaps fifty times since 1965 and have never experienced any problems at all. On the contrary, the people there—as in all of Mexico—are gracious and helpful. Juárez has also boomed since the days of vice and bootlegging. More than 1.2 million people live there now, in addition to the 600,000 who live across the river in El Paso. No passports or visas are needed; you can bring back $400 of merchandise per person duty free.

A lot of food and fun and some interesting non-culinary sightseeing can be found in El Paso and Juárez. Three of the most fascinating museums we've ever visited are in the area. One is devoted to the history of smuggling interception (Border Patrol Museum, 310 North Mesa); another is devoted to boots (Tony Lama Boot Museum, 109 East Overland Street); and the third has Pancho Villa's death mask (Old Custom House Museum of History, Avenida Juárez, Avenida 16 de Septiembre).

The Wilderness Park Museum, 2000 Transmountain Road, has displays of early man and Native Americans before the arrival of Europeans; and the El Paso Museum of History, 12901 Gateway West at Avenue of the Americas, tells the story of the region from the coming of the Spaniards to the present day. In Juárez, the Juárez Museum of History and Art (near Pronaf Center) has ancient artifacts from Mexico's earliest inhabitants as well as striking works from modern Mexican artists.

Also telling the history of the region are the Spanish missions, which still stand today. Socorro Mission (Socorro Road, lower valley) is the oldest continuously occupied active parish in the United States, first built in 1681. Even older is Guadalupe Mission (two blocks west of Avenida Juárez in downtown Juárez), which was built between 1658 and 1668. Ysleta Mission (Zaragosa Drive, lower valley), is adjacent to the Tigua Indian Reservation (Chapter 1, p. 14).

For less ethereal pleasures, the region has a horse racing track (Sunland Park in west El Paso); a dog racing track (Juárez Racetrack on the Pan-American Highway); and a bull ring (Plaza Monumentál, also on the Pan-American Highway), which is the fourth-largest in the world, seating 17,000.

For further information on El Paso and Juárez, contact the El Paso Convention and Visitors Bureau, One Civic Center Plaza, El Paso, TX 79901 (800-351-6024).

Markets and Wineries

BIEGANOWSKI CELLARS

5923 Gateway West, El Paso (915-775-0842). *Open Monday–Friday, 8 a.m.–5 p.m.* MAJOR CREDIT CARDS.

This winery produces about 8,000 cases of wine annually from Texas-grown grapes, including an award-winning Merlot, a Blanc de Noir champagne from Pinot Noir grapes, and a white Zin. The facility has a tasting room and a large room for parties.

CENTRO MERCADO

Avenida 16 de Septiembre at Melgar in Juárez. *Open daily, 9 a.m.–5 p.m.* NO CREDIT CARDS; BEER AVAILABLE.

This classic, two-story Mexican market is one of the highlights of a visit to Juárez. In addition to every imaginable piece of clothing, art or craft, or gift, the market has a fabulous collection of Mexican packaged foods, plus produce like dried and fresh chiles. A small restaurant serves traditional specialties. Food lovers should not miss this place.

LA VIÑA WINERY

P.O. Box 121, Chamberino, N.M. on El Paso's west side, on Route 28, about 3 miles beyond Gadsden High School (915-882-2092). *Open Saturdays only, 1 p.m.–4 p.m.* LIQUOR LICENSE.

La Viña's Chamberino Riesling is the top-selling wine produced from grapes grown in New Mexico. There is a small shop and wine tasting room on the premises, and the winery is used as an events site.

5-2 The Centro Mercado in Ciudad Juárez

Retail Shops

AZAR NUT FACTORY

1800 Northwestern (I-25 W, exit Transmountain, right on Northwestern) (915-877-4079). *Open Monday–Friday, 10 a.m.–6 p.m.; Saturday, 10 a.m.–2 p.m.* VISA, MC.

Azar sells locally grown pecans and pistachios and imported nuts such as cashews. Sampling is offered on the premises to educate the palate and teach more about the exciting world of nuts. Products include gift baskets, a jalapeño snack mix, perfect pecans for show-off baking, and deluxe almonds.

THE COOKING PLACE

750 Sunland Park Dr. in Sunland Mall (915-833-0222). *Open during mall hours.* MAJOR CREDIT CARDS.

Highlights of this cookware shop include "El Pasobilia" such as chile-shaped ceramic salsa dishes, locally made refrigerator magnets in the shape of tacos and miniature *ristras*, Southwestern tiles, regional cookbooks, and an array of conventional cookware.

COPPERFIELD'S COFFEE SHOP AND BOOKSTORE

1840 N. Lee Treviño (915-590-0602). *Open Monday–Thursday, 10 a.m.–8 p.m.; Friday and Saturday, 10 a.m.–9 p.m.; Sunday, 1 p.m.–7 p.m.*

Copperfield's carries many coffees, specialty cakes and sandwiches, kitchen items, coffee supplies, books, and magazines.

EL PASO CHILE COMPANY √

909 Texas St. (915-544-3434). *Open Monday–Friday, 9 a.m.–5:30 p.m.; Saturday, 10 a.m.–2 p.m.* MAJOR CREDIT CARDS.

In addition to wreaths and Indian folk art, this hot shop carries an extensive supply of chiles, chile topiaries, and chile products. Some of their products include Snakebite Salsa, Cowboy Catsup, Coyote Nuts, and pastas and vinegars.

GUSSIE'S TAMALES AND MEXICAN BAKERY

2218 N. Piedras (915-566-8209). *Open daily, 7 a.m.–8 p.m.* NO CREDIT CARDS.

Gussie's is considered to have the best tamales in town, with a sauce made from scratch. It also has cocktail tamales for parties. The storefront is a *panadería* with classic Mexican wedding cookies, *pan dulce*, and multicolored cookies.

THE KNIFE SHOP

Placita Shopping Arcade, El Paso International Airport (915-772-5894). *Open daily, 8 a.m.–7 p.m.* MAJOR CREDIT CARDS.

In addition to cutlery for experts and all types of knives, this shop has red chile *ristras*, garlic ropes, and lots of local cookbooks.

Restaurants

BEST BUY TORTILLA FACTORY

1110 Pendale Rd. (915-595-6555). *Store open daily, 7 a.m.–5 p.m.; Saturday, 6 a.m.–2 p.m. Kitchen open daily, 7 a.m.–3 p.m.; Saturday, 6 a.m.–1 p.m.* NO CREDIT CARDS; NO LIQUOR LICENSE.

Nine members of the Valadez family work here to produce tortilla products for retail sale (4,500 corn tortillas per hour and 8,400 pounds of tortilla chips a day!) and border specialties for hungry diners. Try the soft chicken tacos, the *chiles rellenos, carnitas, albóndigas* soup, and tamales. A specialty is their *gorditas*—fried, thick corn tortillas stuffed with ground beef and topped with chile sauce. They will send tortilla products by UPS; call for information.

CAFE CENTRÁL

One Texas Court (915-545-2233). *Open Monday–Thursday, 11 a.m.–10 p.m.; Friday and Saturday, 11 a.m.–11 p.m.* MAJOR CREDIT CARDS; LIQUOR LICENSE.

Here's where El Pasoans "play society," with appearances by politicians, designers, photographers, and travel guide writers. "It's like a '30s movie," says Elaine Corn. Some of their eclectic specialties include *asadero quesadillas* with Hatch green chiles, red chile pasta, steak Tampiqueña with chiles and jack cheese, and pepper steak with extremely spicy Moroccan *harissa* with seven peppers.

CANUTILLO TORTILLA FACTORY AND LITTLE DINER

7209 Seventh St., Canutillo, Tex. (915-877-2176). *Open daily except Wednesday, 11 a.m.–6:30 p.m.* NO CREDIT CARDS; BEER.

Since 1976, this establishment in nearby Canutillo (east on I-10), has served great chicken tamales with cheese; and huge, fat *gorditas* in browned tortillas, which are the color of cheddar cheese. Elaine Corn observes: "This food is without a doubt the classiest ode to an ancient cuisine, with sparkling fresh ingredients and profound flavor. Okay, so what if the place looks like a bus depot?"

Casa Jurado

226 Cincinnati (915-532-6429). *Open Monday–Thursday, 11 a.m.–8 p.m.; Friday and Saturday, 11 a.m.–9 p.m.* 4772 Doniphan Drive (915-833-1151). *Open Tuesday– Thursday, 11 a.m.–9 p.m.; Friday and Saturday, 11 a.m.– 10 p.m.; Sunday, noon–8 p.m.* MAJOR CREDIT CARDS; LIQUOR ONLY AT DONIPHAN LOCATION.

Henry Jurado credits his mother, Estela, with the recipes for his restaurants, which he first opened in 1972. Some of her favorites include chicken *mole* (made from scratch from pecans, chile *ancho*, almonds, and chocolate); *salpicón*; and fillet Casa Jurado with *asadero* roasted tomatoes and green chiles. Their to-die-for smooth salsa contains three different chiles, plus tomatillos.

La Fogata

2323 Paseo Triunfo de la Republica (parallel to Avenida 16 de Septiembre), Juárez (011-52-16 13-00-40). *Open daily, 7 a.m.–11 p.m.* MAJOR CREDIT CARDS; LIQUOR LICENSE.

Steaks and *norteño* specialties are the order of the day at this long-time favorite watering hole and restaurant. Try the *carne asada*.

MARGARITA MAN

The fiftieth anniversary of the margarita was the Fourth of July 1992, according to Francisco "Pancho" Morales' calculations. Pancho should know. He invented the drink—no matter what anyone else says.

Claims to the origin of the margarita are as common as Elvis sightings. Some stories say the margarita was created by a bartender at the Tail o' the Cock in Los Angeles in the early 1950s. This margarita was named for a customer (a Margaret Whatsherface, of course). The bartender used the macho-man tequila José Cuervo; and when the word spread, the drink became for Heublein the financial equivalent of an endless night on the town. Anyway, that's how the advertising copywriters tell it.

Another yarn holds that a San Antonio socialite named Mrs. William Sames devised the drink in 1948 when she hastily combined tequila and Cointreau to serve to her wealthy friends. Her family called it "the drink" until her husband gave it his wife's first name—you got it—Margarita. Wrong again.

A lot of people probably think singer/songwriter Jimmy Buffet first concocted the margarita because of all the publicity he gave the drink while wasting away in his fictional Margaritaville. But Buffet was merely the musical pitchman for a lively libation that was created because of miscommunication and bartender hustle. And it was all Pancho Morales' fault.

It was Independence Day 1942. The heat was sweltering, and the scene was Juárez, Mexico. Not that you couldn't celebrate the independence of America in Mexico. During those days, just over the bridge in Juárez's busiest commercial district, you could celebrate anything you wanted.

Pancho was tending bar at Tommy's Place, a favorite hangout for GIs from Fort Bliss. A lady walked in, sat at the bar, and ordered a magnolia. The only thing Pancho knew about a magnolia was that it had lemon or lime in it and some kind of liquor. So he did what any good bartender would do—he winged it and used the most popular liquor served in Juárez: tequila.

With a single taste, the woman, who knew a magnolia was made of gin, cream, lemon juice, and grenadine, realized that the drink was an impostor but liked it anyway because Pancho had loaded it with enough tequila to make anyone smile. When she asked what the new drink was called, Pancho's brain was thinking flowers and "m"s and leaped from magnolia to *margarita*—Spanish for daisy.

And so mixology history was made, and Pancho later immortalized the drink when he taught at the bartender's school in Juárez before immigrating to El Paso in 1974. Pancho, now a retired milk truck driver, still gets calls from reporters all over the country who ask him questions about the invention of the margarita.

What about the bartender in Los Angeles?

"A kook," replies Pancho.

How about that Margarita in San Antonio?

"I don't even want to know her."

What about the claims of the management of La Florida, another popular Juárez bar, that they created the drink?

"They're kooks, too."

Pancho says today's margaritas are breaches of trust. "All these guys, they put bananas in

continued

the margaritas. They put in cactus, onions, and pink color and serve it in champagne glasses. And they use too much salt. Kooks, all of them."

His recipe is simple and given in the language of a true barkeep. Here it is.

FRANCISCO "PANCHO" MORALES' PERFECT, ORIGINAL MARGARITA

Juice of ½ lime
2 parts white tequila
1 part Cointreau

Now, here's the translation. Squeeze the juice from half a Mexican *limón* (not a Persian lime) into a shaker glass filled with chunks (not cubes) of ice (never shaved). Take the squeezed *limón* and run it around the rim of a cocktail glass. Put the glass on a towel, sprinkle it lightly with salt, and then shake off *all* the excess salt. Now, allowing for the juice already in the glass, and any ice that may have melted to contribute to the 4-ounce final tally of liquid, the remainder of the formula requires enough tequila (please, a great tequila like Herradura) and Cointreau (never Triple Sec), two parts to one, to equal exactly 4 ounces of drink to be shaken, strained, and poured into a 4-ounce cocktail glass. This takes some skill, but it's not brain surgery.

"The two parts doesn't mean jigger, and it doesn't mean bottles," warns Pancho. "I've seen this all mixed up."

—ELAINE CORN

FORTI'S MEXICAN ELDER

321 Chelsea (915-772-0066) and 7410 Remcon Circle,
Suite V (915-585-0086). *Open Monday–Thursday,*
11 a.m.–10 p.m.; Friday and Saturday, 11 a.m.–11 p.m.
MAJOR CREDIT CARDS; LIQUOR LICENSE.

Named for the elder tree in front, this restaurant features
tacos *al carbón*, *salpicón*, fish Veracruzano, Mexican shrimp,
a searing table salsa full of texture, and magically greaseless
flautas. "Forti's combines border food with the food of the interior of Mexico," notes Elaine Corn, "and its heat level is a
few notches above average."

GRIGG'S RESTAURANT

5800 Doniphan (915-584-0451) and 9007 Montana
(915-598-3451). *Open daily, 11 a.m.–9 p.m.* VISA, MC; LIQUOR
LICENSE.

Since 1939, El Pasoans have feasted on Grigg's generous New
Mexico–style dishes. Try the green chile chicken enchiladas,
red enchiladas with an egg cracked on top just before removing them from the oven, or guacamole tacos. The stuffed *sopaipillas* look like they're covered with red chile sauce, but
the sauce is really green-based, with the addition of tomatoes.

H & H CAR WASH & COFFEE SHOP

701 East Yandell (915-533-1144). *Open Monday–Saturday,*
7:30 a.m.–3 p.m. NO CREDIT CARDS; NO LIQUOR.

It is written that when you come to H & H, you'll either run
into someone you know or meet someone you'll never forget.
At least, it's the best "Mexican" food you'll ever get at a car
wash. Try their signature *huevos rancheros*, or the "concealed
weapon" of El Paso's food: green salsa made with microscop-
ically cut jalapeños. The breakfast taco can be filled with a
tasty *picadillo*, and H & H serves *menudo* on Saturday.

LA HACIENDA

1729 W. Paisano (915-456-9197). *Open Tuesday–Sunday,
10 a.m.–10 p.m.* VISA, MC; LIQUOR LICENSE.

This amazing and historical restaurant was built in 1851 and
is now on the National Register of Historic Sites. It was part
of the original Fort Bliss, and the Rio Grande still flows just
behind the building. Specialties include Green Chile Chicken
Enchiladas (with an egg on top), Steak Tampiqueña, *Chile
Colorado con Carne*, and Charlie Brown Beans (more of a
soup topped with chopped onions than beans).

JAXON'S

4799 N. Mesa (915-544-1188) and 1135 Airway (915-
778-9696). *Open daily, 11 a.m.–10 p.m.* MAJOR CREDIT
CARDS; LIQUOR LICENSE.

Owner Jack Maxon has fashioned his two restaurants into
local watering holes that also serve good border specialties—
with some interesting twists. For example, Jaxon's has a
green chile potato soup (sort of a killer *vichyssoise*) that is
quite hot. Also recommended are the Chicken Santa Fe (with
green chiles and jack cheese melted all over it) and Steak
Tampico (also smothered in chile). Their desserts—like Adobe
Mud Pie—are scrumptious.

JULIO'S CAFE CORONA

8050 Gateway East, El Paso (915-591-7676). *Open Monday–
Saturday, 11 a.m.–10 p.m.; Sunday, 8 a.m.–8 p.m.* MAJOR
CREDIT CARDS; LIQUOR LICENSE.

Since its founding in Juárez in 1944, Julio's has been a major
force in border cookery. It is justly famous for its *salpicón*
(see recipe) and green *mole* made from sunflower seeds, peanuts, chiles, radish leaves, and three pounds of bananas. Also
great is the *cochinta pibíl*, the "state dish" of Yucatán: pork
shredded in orange juice and *achiote*.

MARTINO'S (NUEVO RESTAURANTE MARTINO)

417 Avenida Juárez, Juárez (011-52-16 12-33-70). *Open daily, 11 a.m.–11 p.m.* MAJOR CREDIT CARDS; LIQUOR LICENSE.

Martino's is the most Continental restaurant in Juárez, featuring a huge menu offering many variations on classic dishes. Regional specialties include Boquilla black bass, *caldillo*, and entrecote Mexican-style. On our bulletin board is a snapshot of authors DeWitt and Wilan cuddling in Martino's, on one of our first dates. The service—provided by waiters who've been there since the Jurassic period—is impeccable.

PASO DEL NORTE

3650 Avenida Hermanos Escobar, Juárez (011-52-16 13-40-34). *Open daily, 11 a.m.–11 p.m.* MAJOR CREDIT CARDS; LIQUOR LICENSE.

This beautiful restaurant has the true feeling of Spanish colonial Old Mexico, excellent wait service, and delicious regional specialties. Try their Pierna de Cordera Adobada, an entire lamb shank smothered in red chile sauce, or any other meat dish on the menu.

THE STATE LINE BARBECUE

1222 Sunland Park Dr. (915-581-3371). *Open Monday–Saturday, 11:30 a.m.–2 p.m. and 5 p.m.–9:30 p.m.; Sunday, 11:30 a.m.–2 p.m. and 4 p.m.–9 p.m.* MAJOR CREDIT CARDS; LIQUOR LICENSE.

The State Line is a large restaurant (with a long wait) decorated in Wild West/Gay '90s saloon style. They serve enormous prime beef ribs, slowly cooked in a pit, and an 18-hour smoked prime rib. Other south Texas specialties include tons of slaw, potato salad, beans, and barbecue brisket. Corn comments: "The best barbecue I've ever had."

VILLA DEL MAR

1400 Avenida de las Américas, Juárez (011-52-16 13-87-20).
Open daily, noon–11 p.m. MAJOR CREDIT CARDS; LIQUOR
LICENSE.

This remodeled, expanded restaurant has long been a favorite
seafood restaurant in Juárez. Two suggestions: *Pulpo* (octopus in its ink) and Shrimp Villa del Mar.

5-3 The Historic La Hacienda Restaurant

Ristra Bargains

Supple strings of dark red chiles sparkle in the sun, strung together with needle and thread and hanging from hooks on a pickup truck—and you can't find a better buy on these decorator/gourmet items anywhere but El Paso.

These are *ristras*, cascades of chiles that elsewhere in the country can cost as much as $30 per string. But here on the border, after the chiles turn red in the fall and have dried in the crisp air, a hefty 3-foot, crunchy-fresh *ristra* can run you—oh—about $3. Add another foot and the price doubles for some reason. Chile wreaths run about $10.

This area is the source, after all. With a growing valley on each side of town—the upper and lower valleys beside the Rio Grande—El Paso is easily the best bargain town for "chile-bilia." ✓

Non–El Pasoans can't believe their eyes as they drive past the typical street vendor who has parked a truck on the shoulder of a busy street, scrawled some prices on a cardboard sign and leaned it against a tire, and hung a virtual red curtain of chiles around the truck bed.

The prices are kept low by local homeowners and restaurateurs rather than by tourists. Also, competition is fierce among vendors, who seem to multiply every year. One such vendor is Ristras by Rosa, a tiny company run by Rosa and Refugio Garcia from their place east of town in Socorro, Texas.

continued

Rosa strings the *ristra*s by hand. She is nimble, spending about two minutes threading the needle through all the stems needed for a medium-length *ristra*.

Refugio, a firefighter, got into the *ristra* business after a day off spent picking chiles for an extra $50 a day.

"I saw a truck vendor selling *ristra*s and decided this was easier than picking chiles," he reasoned. For the next three years, he and Rosa collected chiles from El Paso's growing valleys.

Once strung, the chiles remain completely edible as long as they're not sprayed with preservatives. No. 6–4 chiles and Sandia varieties of New Mexican chiles developed by New Mexico State University are used.

Should you have an opportunity to purchase a *ristra* in El Paso or New Mexico, Refugio shares these tips for its care and preservation:

- Once the freshly strung chiles are completely dried and you have decided to use them for decoration instead of cooking, dip them in Johnson's wax or spray them with polyurethane to seal in the moisture. They should last several years.
- Never ship fresh *ristra*s in plastic. The *ristra* may rot or arrive infested with insects. And they will stink!
- Allow the *ristra* to dry in El Paso before shipping (this may take weeks) because it will weigh less.

—ELAINE CORN

Recipes

El Paso Green Chile Casserole

No other dish says "party" in El Paso like the green chile casserole, which is served at luncheons, cocktail parties, and even bar mitzvahs. This is the dish that's the cheater's *chiles rellenos* and avoids the tedious stuffing of the chiles. It is assumed you will use fresh green chiles, roasted and peeled by hand. If you must, you may sneak in canned chiles.

10 to 12 whole fresh green chiles, roasted, peeled, stems removed, seeded
8 ounces Monterey jack cheese, grated
8 ounces longhorn or cheddar cheese, grated
4 eggs, separated
⅔ cup evaporated milk
1 tablespoon flour
Salt and pepper to taste

Butter the bottom of a medium-sized ovenproof casserole dish. Place the chiles in the bottom of the dish and sprinkle with the jack cheese, then the longhorn or cheddar.

Beat the egg yolks with the evaporated milk, flour, salt, and pepper until thick and light-colored. Beat the whites until stiff peaks form. Fold the whites into the yolk mixture and spread over the casserole. Run a spatula through the eggs to fill the air pockets.

Bake at 350° for 1 hour or until a toothpick comes out clean.

SERVES: **8 to 10**
HEAT SCALE: **MILD**

—Elaine Corn

JULIO'S SALPICÓN

It is generally believed that one of El Paso's most popular and unique dishes—the shredded meat salad called *salpicón*—crossed the border because of Julio Ramirez. Julio opened his first restaurant in 1944 in Juárez on Avenida 16 de Septiembre and a second location in El Paso in 1985. The recipe for *salpicón* has been imitated and begged for, and local restaurateurs have paid hundreds of dollars to professional recipe testers to see if they could approximate the recipe. Finally, the Ramirez family has released it. Here it is.

- 3 **pounds beef brisket**
- 2 **cloves garlic, minced**
  Salt to taste
  Water
- 1 **cup diced white cheddar cheese**
- ½ **cup chopped cilantro**
- ½ **cup diced, seeded tomatoes**
- ½ **cup vegetable oil**
- ½ **cup wine vinegar**
- 4 **chipotle chiles in adobo, minced**
  Diced avocado for garnish

Bring the brisket to a boil with garlic and salt in water to cover. Reduce heat and simmer for about 1½ hours, uncovered, until the meat is tender enough to be shredded. Cool the meat in the broth and then shred finely by hand. Reserve the broth to make a stew or soup.

Toss the shredded brisket with the remaining ingredients (except the avocado). Chill the mixture and allow it to marinate for several hours or preferably overnight.

Line a platter with lettuce leaves, place the *salpicón* on the leaves, and garnish with the avocado. Serve with hot, buttered flour tortillas.

SERVES: **12**
HEAT SCALE: **MEDIUM**

—ELAINE CORN

CALDILLO PASO DEL NORTE

This variation on green chile stew is often served in El Paso restaurants. It is unique because of the addition of potatoes—imported from South America into the American Southwest.

3 pounds stew beef, cubed
1 large onion, chopped fine
2 cloves garlic, minced
   Bacon fat
2 large tomatoes, chopped fine
2 cups New Mexican green chile, chopped
2 cups beef stock
1 teaspoon cumin
2 pounds potatoes, peeled and diced
   Salt and pepper to taste

Sauté the beef, onion, and garlic in bacon fat. Add the remaining ingredients except the potatoes and simmer until the meat is tender, about 2 hours. Add more stock if the stew gets too thick. Add the potatoes during the last 40 minutes and season to taste.

YIELD: **1 GALLON**
HEAT SCALE: **MEDIUM**

5-4 Casa Jurado—Open for Great Border Food

CHORIZO

This traditional Mexican sausage is often served with *huevos rancheros* for breakfast. Unlike other sausages, it is usually not placed in a casing but rather served loose or formed into patties.

 1 **clove garlic**
 ½ **cup hot red chile powder**
 ½ **teaspoon freshly ground black pepper**
 ¼ **teaspoon each ground cloves, cinnamon, oregano, and cumin**
 ½ **teaspoon salt**
 1 **teaspoon oregano**
 ½ **cup vinegar**
 2 **pounds ground pork**

In a blender, combine the first seven ingredients and puree. Knead this mixture into the pork until it is thoroughly mixed. Cover and let sit at room temperature for at least 24 hours; then refrigerate or freeze.

 To cook, crumble in a skillet and fry. Drain before serving.

SERVES: **8**
HEAT SCALE: MEDIUM

5-5 Jaxon's Restaurant in El Paso

PART

THREE

NEW MEXICO

The extravagant use of red pepper among the [New] Mexicans has become truly proverbial. It enters into nearly every dish at every meal, and often so predominates as entirely to conceal the character of the viands.

—JOSIAH GREGG,
THE COMMERCE OF THE PRAIRIES (1844)

CHAPTER

6

AN ENCHANTED FEAST

Chile sauces were already being served over tortilla-wrapped game with sides of beans and squash in the Land of Enchantment, as New Mexico is called now, when the Europeans landed in the New World. The Spanish, however, brought a new dimension to this ancient cuisine because the native peoples had never before experienced food sources such as cattle and wheat. The new foodstuffs merged with the old, but did not overwhelm them. Rather, they were incorporated into the ancient techniques, and the result was a unique and highly spiced cuisine.

We can only hope Josiah Gregg eventually built up a tolerance to spicy food and learned that rather than concealing the character of a meal, chile greatly enhances it—eliminating blandness while adding flavor. His comments illustrate the typical collision of cultures that resulted from exploration and settlement of the Southwest by the Spanish and Anglo cultures.

The Early Invasion of Old World Foods

Imagine Southwestern cuisine without beef, lamb, pork, chicken, cilantro, cumin, limes, onions, wheat bread, rice, beer, and wine. That's where New World cooking would be without the Old World, and it's particularly true of New Mexico.

The first and most obvious Old World influences on the cooking of the New were meats and grains. "Wherever Spaniards went, they took their livestock with them," notes John C. Super, an expert on colonial Latin American history. "Pigs, sheep, and cattle were as much a part of the conquest as Toledo steel and fighting mastiffs."

Indeed they were. In fact, the introduction of livestock was so successful that the animals thrived even when they escaped into the wild. Within a century after the arrival of Columbus, the estimated New World cattle population was 800,000, along with an astonishing 4.6 million sheep. With all that additional meat available, no wonder the cuisines of the Americas changed radically.

Wheat was also instrumental in changing the ways the Americas cooked. It was planted in such abundance throughout Mexico that by the middle of the fifteenth century, it was more common in the New World than in Spain, where wheat supplies had dropped, and the people were eating rye bread. The same patterns were repeated in New Mexico. Sheep were introduced by Juan de Oñate in 1598, and, by the 1880s, there were millions of sheep in New Mexico and about 500,000 a year were exported. The number of sheep produced today remains at about half a million.

It is not generally known that New Mexico and El Paso are the two oldest wine-producing regions in the United States. A Franciscan friar, Augustín Rodríguez, is credited with bringing grape vines to southern New Mexico in 1580, about 100 years before the friars in California planted their vineyards. By 1662, priests in the Mesilla Valley were regularly producing sacramental wine for Mass.

Winemaking gradually spread north; grapes, wine, and brandy were common subjects in the reports of explorers and travelers to New Mexico. In 1846, a traveler and author W. W. H. Davis (*El Gringo, or New Mexico and Her People*) commented about the Mesilla Valley to El Paso: "The most important production of the valley is grapes, from which are annually manufactured not less than 200,000 gallons of perhaps the richest and best wine in the world. This wine is worth $2 per gallon, and constitutes the principal revenue of the city. Also, a great quantity of grapes of this valley are dried in clusters and preserved for use through the winter. . . . I regard them far superior to the best raisins that are imported into the United States. . . . "

But grapes were not the most important New Mexican crop. That honor goes to one of New Mexico's state "vegetables."

The Ubiquitous Chile

According to most accounts, chile peppers were introduced into what is now the United States by Capitán General Juan de Oñate, who founded Santa Fe in 1598. But this generally accepted theory could be completely wrong, and it is possible that the ancestors of the Pueblo Indians may have been collecting or even growing chiles prior to the Spanish colonization of the Southwest.

Chile peppers were well established in Mexico by the time of the Spanish invasion in the early 1500s. But how far north were they cultivated? And when did they reach the present Southwest? These are two of the biggest mysteries about Southwestern food, and they may never be solved.

Standing in the way of a solution are two negative facts. First, no chile pepper seeds have ever been found in pre-Columbian archaeological sites in the Southwest—lending credence to the theory that the Spanish introduced chiles. But, contrary to popular belief, extensive searches of early colonial journals reveal no evidence that the Spanish brought chile seeds with them from central Mexico. The attribution of chiles to Oñate has no basis in fact.

Negative facts, however, do not constitute proof. Maybe the chile seeds simply have not been found yet, or perhaps Oñate (or a contemporary) brought chiles north but never mentioned it in

6-1 Harvesting Chiles near Las Cruces

his journal. We may lack hard evidence, but there is no dearth of theories.

Many Southwest Indian chile dishes have been passed down through the oral tradition, which indicates some pre-Hispanic culinary usage. Perhaps the simplest of these recipes is one from the Pimas of Arizona: *chile pasado*, green chile pulp made into pancake shapes and dried in the sun. Another basic recipe calls for red chile pods to be crumbled and cooked in oil or lard, which is what the Rio Grande Pueblo people call Indian bacon. But if chiles were present in the Southwest before the Spanish arrived, how did they get there?

By studying ancient American trade routes, a theory can be proposed for how chile peppers moved north from Mexico. From the height of the Mayan civilization (first century A.D.) until the Aztecs were conquered by the Spanish (c. 1500), long-distance traders (*pochteca*) traveled far and wide from southern Mexico. The *pochteca* were a hereditary class, similar to a guild, who had their own rites, insignia, and gods. The *pochteca* established what anthropologists call a down-the-line trading system that connected Mexican civilizations with what is now the American Southwest. In this system, the Toltecs, for example, would not have had a great amount of direct trade with the Anasazi, but rather the commerce, overseen by the *pochteca*, would proceed "down the line" from one culture to another.

The connection between Southwest civilizations and the Mexicans was through the ancient city of Casas Grandes in Chihuahua. From about A.D. 1050, regular trade routes were established between Casas Grandes and the ancestors of the Rio Grande Pueblo people, the Hohokam and Anasazi. The people of the Southwest traded turquoise and salt for copper bells, seashells, parrots, macaws, cotton, and presumably at some time, dried chiles containing seeds.

This hypothetical scenario does not assume chiles were commonly grown in the Southwest before the arrival of the Spanish because it is likely chiles and their seeds would be less common the farther north they traveled. The colder climate of the Southwest would necessitate growing the chiles as annuals rather than as perennials—except for the wild chiltepin (see Chapter 1).

Even if the Spanish did not introduce chiles into the Southwest, they certainly assisted in their spread and use during colonization. The Spanish settlers embraced the fiery fruits with a

6-2 New Mexico's State Tree, the Piñon, in a
Snowstorm

proper passion, and that love led to the development of the unique
cuisines of the Southwest.

After the Spanish settled in the Southwest, the cultivation of
chile peppers exploded, and they were grown throughout New
Mexico. Probably many different varieties were cultivated, including early forms of jalapeños, serranos, *anchos*, and *pasillas*. But
one variety that adapted particularly well to New Mexico was a
long green chile that turned red in the fall. Formerly called Anaheim because of its transfer to California around 1900, the New
Mexican chiles were cultivated for hundreds of years in the region
with such dedication that several varieties known as "land races"
emerged. Chimayo and Española are land races that adapted to
particular environments and are still planted today in the same
fields they were grown in centuries ago; they constitute a small
but distinct part of the tons of pods produced each year in New
Mexico.

In 1846, William Emory, chief engineer of the U.S. Army Top-
ographic Unit, was surveying the New Mexico landscape and its
customs. He described a meal eaten by people in Bernalillo, just
north of Albuquerque: "Roast chicken, stuffed with onions; then
mutton, boiled with onions; then followed various other dishes, all
dressed with the everlasting onion; and the whole terminated by
chile, the glory of New Mexico."

Emory went on to relate his experience with chiles: "Chile the Mexicans consider the chef-d'oeuvre of the cuisine, and seem really to revel in it; but the first mouthful brought the tears trickling down my cheeks, very much to the amusement of the spectators with their leather-lined throats. It was red pepper, stuffed with minced meat."

The earliest cultivated chiles in New Mexico were smaller than those of today; indeed, they were (and still are, in some cases) considered a spice. But as the land races developed and the size of the pods increased, the food value of chiles became evident. There was just one problem—the bewildering sizes and shapes of the chile peppers made it very difficult for farmers to determine which variety of chile they were growing from year to year. And there was no way to tell how large the pods might be or how hot. But modern horticultural techniques finally produced fairly standardized chiles (see Chapter 7).

Today, New Mexico is by far the largest commercial producer of chile peppers in the United States—about 25,000 acres under cultivation produce about 36,000 dry tons of chile peppers each year. California is in second place, Texas is third, and Arizona is fourth in chile pepper production. Also, about 10,000 metric tons of chiles are imported into the United States from major foreign producers such as Mexico, Pakistan, People's Republic of China, Korea, India, and Costa Rica.

All the primary dishes in New Mexico cuisine contain chile peppers: sauces, stews, *carne adovada*, enchiladas, *posole*, tamales, *huevos rancheros*, and many combination vegetable dishes. The intense use of chiles as a food rather than just as a spice or condiment is what differentiates New Mexican cuisine from that of Texas or Arizona. In neighboring states, chile powders are used as a seasoning for beef or chicken broth–based chile gravies, which are thickened with flour or cornstarch before they are added to, say, enchiladas. In New Mexico, the sauces are made from pure chiles and are thickened by reducing the crushed or pureed pods.

New Mexico chile *sauces* are cooked and pureed, while *salsas* use fresh ingredients and are uncooked. Debates rage over whether tomatoes should be used in cooked sauces such as red chile sauce for enchiladas. Despite recipes in numerous cookbooks (none of whose authors live in New Mexico), traditional cooked red sauces do *not* contain tomatoes, though uncooked salsas do.

NEW MEXICO FOOD EVENTS

National Fiery Foods Show, Albuquerque, mid-February (505-873-2187)

Corporate Chili Challenge, Albuquerque, mid-August (505-821-3333)

New Mexico Wine Festival, Bernalillo, late August (505-646-4543)

Hatch Chile Festival, Hatch, Labor Day week- ✓ end (505-267-4847)

Apple Festival, Hillsboro, early September (505-895-5328)

New Mexico State Fair, Albuquerque, early September (505-265-1791)

Old Taos Trade Fair, a re-creation of the past in Taos, late September (505-758-0505)

Santa Fe Chile and Wine Fiesta, late September (505-988-7124) ✓

Whole Enchilada Fiesta, Las Cruces, early October (505-524-1968)

Harvest Festival, El Rancho de Las Golondrinas at La Cienega, early October (505-471-2261)

New Mexico Chile Cookoff, Ruidoso, early October (505-257-7395)

Lincoln County Barbecue War, Ruidoso, late October (505-378-5466)

Carne adovada is one of the most popular New Mexican entrees. Another is enchiladas; in fact, there are so many enchilada variations that cooks soon determine their favorites through experimentation.

New Mexicans love chile peppers so much that chiles have become the de facto state symbol. Houses are adorned with *ristras*. Images of the pods are emblazoned on signs, T-shirts, coffee mugs, posters, windsocks, and even underwear. In late summer and early fall, the aroma of roasting chiles fills the air throughout New Mexico and produces a state of bliss for chileheads.

According to one old Spanish saying, "*A la primera cocinera se le va un chile entero*" ("To the best lady cook goes the whole chile").

The Later Invasion of Old World Foods

Unlike livestock, imported grains such as wheat were not immediately successful in New Mexico. Corn was still raised on small plots by Hispanics and Native Americans, but wheat and other crops did not flourish until the arrival of the railroads. In fact, agriculture was so primitive in the region that one critic, Antonio Barreiro, wrote in 1832: "Agriculture is utterly neglected, for the inhabitants of this country do not sow any amount, as they might do to great profit without any doubt. They sow barely what they consider necessary for their maintenance for part of the year, and the rest of the year they are exposed to a thousand miseries."

The situation improved shortly after the U.S. Army raised the U.S. flag over the Palace of the Governors in Santa Fe in 1846, and New Mexico was opened to further settlement by American pioneers. The introduction of modern tools and techniques and new crops such as apples, peas, melons, and others helped the farmers greatly. By 1900, more than 5 million acres were under cultivation in New Mexico. Gradually, wheat surpassed corn in the state. In 1987, corn production was 7.6 million bushels, and wheat was 10.8 million bushels. However, wheat tortillas have not supplanted corn tortillas.

Cattle had been introduced by Oñate but did not assume a significant role in New Mexico until after the Civil War. Soon after the great cattle drives to the New Mexico gold mines in 1890, there were 1.34 million head of cattle in the state. Remarkably, the figures almost a hundred years later (1988) are almost identical— 1.32 million head.

After the Homestead Act of 1862 and the arrival of the railroad between 1879 and 1882, settlers from the eastern United States flooded into the state. The railroad also led to the first railroad restaurants, the Harvey House chain. New Mexico boasted sixteen of these establishments, including five that were the grandest of the system: Montezuma and Castañeda in Las Vegas,

6-3 The Agave, Source of Food—and Tequila

La Fonda in Santa Fe, Alvarado in Albuquerque, and El Navajo in Gallup. Harvey hired 18- to 30-year-old young women as hostesses, and they were quite an attraction on the Western frontier, where-women were scarce. Humorist Will Rogers once said, "Fred Harvey kept the West in food and wives."

The Harvey Houses attempted to bring "civilized" food to the frontier, and early menus reveal dishes such as chicken croquettes, baron of beef, turkey stuffed with oysters, vermicelli with cheese à la Italian, and the ever-delectable calf's brains scrambled with ranch eggs. Mexican food was considered too native for travelers and rarely appeared on hotel and restaurant menus.

The railroads brought the settlers, and these pioneers brought new food crops. At first, vegetables such as tomatoes, asparagus, cabbage, carrots, lettuce, onions, and peas were produced in home gardens on a small scale, but after extensive irrigation facilities were constructed shortly after the turn of the twentieth century, commercial vegetable production began.

In addition to these vegetables, several other notable crops appeared, namely fruits and nuts. Although the nuts were relatively new, fruit growing was actually a rejuvenation of a very old enterprise—winemaking.

THE COLUMBUS EXCHANGE

Here is a basic list of Old World and New World foodstuffs. Some foods, such as coconuts, mushrooms, venison, fish, shellfish, crustaceans, ducks, rabbits, horseradish, and various beans and berries, are native to both worlds.

Old World Foods

Apples, bananas, barley, basil, beef, beer, beets, black pepper, cabbage, capers, celery, cheese, cherries, chicken, cilantro, cinnamon, citrus fruits, cucumber, cumin, eggplant, garlic, ginger, grapes, lamb, lettuce, melons, mint, mustard seed, nutmeg, olives, onions, parsley, peaches, peas, pistachios, plums, pork, rice, soybeans, spinach, turnips, wheat, wine

New World Foods

Allspice, amaranth, avocados, bay leaf, Brazil nuts, butternuts, cactus, cashews, cassava, *cherimoyas*, chile peppers, chocolate, corn, culantro, guava, hickory nuts, lima beans, papayas, passion fruits, peanuts, pecans, pineapples, pinto beans, potatoes, pulque, pumpkins, quinoa, squash, strawberries, sweet potatoes, tamarillos, tomatillos, tomatoes, turkey, vanilla, walnuts

The European grapes that had been established in southern New Mexico in the seventeenth century did well, and, by the 1800s, wine was being produced from the Mexican border to Bernalillo, the heart of the wine production area. By the middle of the nineteenth century, New Mexico was producing more wine than California and, in 1880, produced just fewer than 1 million gallons.

But a series of natural, economic, and political disasters ruined the wine industry.

First, the flood of 1897 was followed by a severe drought. Soon after these discouraging developments, grape growers discovered that cotton was far more profitable. Finally, Prohibition completely wiped out what was left of the wine industry, and New Mexico grape growing fell from 3,150 acres to a mere 8 acres.

But during the 1970s and 1980s, the wine industry in New Mexico made a dramatic recovery. Spurred by foreign investment from the French, Italians, Germans, and Swiss, new vineyards were planted all over the state, and the total acreage is now nearly 5,000. New Mexico has sixteen wineries in production and numerous wine festivals and has finally rediscovered part of its heritage.

A similar situation occurred with apples. Although they have been grown in New Mexico since the early 1600s, extensive cultivation did not really begin until after the Americans arrived. Today, apples are grown in the Mimbres and Ruidoso valleys in the southern part of the state and between Santa Fe and Taos in the north.

One of the most famous apple growers in New Mexico is Fred Dixon, who moved to the state in the early 1940s. He took over a former dude ranch in northern New Mexico and transformed it into very productive orchards, which featured his own patented varieties, Champagne and Standard Winesap. The only problem with apples is that when an early spring frost hits the apple blossoms, the crop is ruined. For example, in 1988, the apple crop was 10 million pounds; a year later, it was only half that figure.

Other tree crops that have prospered in the state are pecans and pistachios. The largest nut industry in New Mexico is pecan growing, as evidenced by the huge pecan forests (actually groves) that stretch north and south of Las Cruces. The trees were introduced from Texas and northern Mexico and first planted at the Fabian Garcia Agricultural Science Center in Mesilla in 1915 and 1916. The original planting was just four acres, and many of those trees are still producing.

The first recorded commercial pecan production in the state was in 1920, when a mere 626 pounds were harvested. Pecans did not enjoy much popularity in New Mexico until the 1960s, when the orchards totaled 6,000 acres. It takes a lot of room to grow pecans, and that's why there are nearly 21,000 acres with about 1.1 million trees in New Mexico, an average of about fifty-two trees per acre. By contrast, Texas has well over 70 million pecan trees, but most of them are wild. A saying that "Texans will buy anything with pecans in it" bodes well for the New Mexico crop. In 1986, 27 million pounds of pecans were produced in New Mexico, about 10 percent of the total U.S. production.

Also in the shell game of nut growing in New Mexico are pistachios. They thrive in the Tularosa Basin because the climate and altitude are similar to those of the noted pistachio-growing regions of Iran and Turkey. Pistachio trees are smaller than pecan trees, growing only to about thirty feet, so about 120 trees can be planted per acre. They are hardy, tolerant of drought and alkaline soils, and can live to be hundreds of years old.

The primary pistachio grower in New Mexico is Eagle Ranch Pistachio Groves in Alamogordo, which markets the tasty nuts under the brand name Heart of the Desert. Eagle Ranch is owned by Marianne and George Schweers, who started their groves in 1974 with 200 two-year-old trees. They now have more than 3,000 trees and can harvest as much as 1,800 pounds an acre.

Alamogordian pistachios are marketed in small designer burlap bags and sold by mail order and in gift shops. They are touted as health nuts because they are cholesterol-free, high in fiber, and low in saturated fats. They are a snack food, are used in pâtés and sausages, are the greenish ingredient in pistachio ice cream, and can be substituted for other nuts in cooking. In fact, they make an excellent pesto if piñon nuts cannot be found.

The appearance of the newer food crops, together with experimentation by talented chefs, has led to the development of what is called New Southwest cuisine. Some of the tenets of this style of cooking are the use of fresh, locally produced crops, the elimination of fattening or high-cholesterol ingredients, the regular appearance of more exotic chiles (rather than just the usual New Mexican varieties), and a dedication to the beautiful presentation of the meal. Another tenet is the use of game and indigenous crops, which, of course, returns us to pre-Columbian times. In fact, there is quite a bit of the oldest Southwest in New Southwest cuisine.

"Southwestern cuisine today is frozen in time," says Mark Miller of Santa Fe's Coyote Cafe. "It neither looks to the past nor progresses into the future. In New Mexico, for instance, most people think the 'traditional' foods can be traced back only a few generations to the Spanish, when in reality the food tradition extends all the way back to the ancient Anasazi culture."

   Although disconcerting to some, the innovations of the New Southwest chefs are fully in keeping with historical tradition—the interaction of various cultures with different ideas of what constitutes Southwestern cookery. In New Mexico, the traditional cuisine based on corn, beans, squash, and chiles will probably be cooked for centuries to come with little or no change. But that doesn't mean all New Mexico cooking will remain static.

   Traditional New Mexican cuisine today enjoys a rich heritage that has evolved from Native American, Mexican, and European sources. Despite its uniqueness, only recently has it achieved the fame it justly deserves—perhaps due to tourism and a resurgent interest in ethnic cuisines. In addition to its traditional elements, the cuisine of the state will continue to evolve as long as innovative chefs create new combinations of the foods being produced around them.

6-4 A Little New Mexico Food Humor

Recipes

CLASSIC NEW MEXICO RED CHILE SAUCE

This basic sauce can be used in any recipe calling for a red sauce, either traditional Mexican or New Southwestern versions of beans, tacos, tamales, and enchiladas.

10 to 12 dried whole red New Mexican chiles
1 large onion, chopped
3 cloves garlic, chopped
3 cups water

Place the chiles on a baking pan and bake in a 250° oven for 10 to 15 minutes or until the chiles smell like they are toasted. Take care not to let them burn. Remove the stems and seeds and crumble into a saucepan.

Add the remaining ingredients, bring to a boil, reduce the heat, and simmer for 20 to 30 minutes.

Puree the mixture in a blender until smooth and strain if necessary. If the sauce is too thin, return it to the stove and simmer until it has been reduced to the desired consistency.

Variations: Spices such as cumin, coriander, and Mexican oregano may be added to taste. Some versions of this sauce call for the onion and garlic to be sauteed in lard— or vegetable oil these days—before adding the chiles and water.

YIELD: 2 TO 2½ CUPS
HEAT SCALE: MEDIUM

HUEVOS RANCHEROS

These ranch-style eggs are ubiquitous throughout the Southwest and appear in many variations. This is the one served in New Mexico.

>   2 **cups red chile sauce (see recipe, p. 150)**
>   2 **medium tomatoes, chopped**
>   4 **corn tortillas**
>   **Oil for frying**
>   8 **eggs**
>   ½ **cup grated cheddar cheese**

Heat the chile sauce and tomatoes in a large saucepan.

Fry each tortilla in the hot oil in another pan for a few seconds until soft; then drain.

Crack the eggs into the sauce and poach them.

To serve, place a tortilla on each place and slip the eggs and sauce on top. Garnish with shredded cheese and serve.

SERVES: **4**
HEAT SCALE: MEDIUM

6-5 Chile Sign Outside of Hatch

BISCOCHITOS

These traditional cookies, based on earlier Mexican recipes, were created by the descendants of the earliest Spanish settlers of New Mexico. Now they are staples gracing holiday tables, usually served following midnight church services and the lighting of hundreds of luminarias or *farolitos*.

½ **pound lard**
1 **cup sugar**
1 **teaspoon anise seeds**
1 **egg**
2 **tablespoons brandy or sherry**
3 **cups flour**
1½ **teaspoons baking powder**
½ **teaspoon salt**
1½ **teaspoons ground cinnamon**
2 **tablespoons sugar**

Whip the lard using a mixer at high speed to create a very light, airy texture, much like whipped cream. (This is the secret to feather-light cookies.)

Add the sugar very slowly and continue beating until well mixed; add the anise seeds, egg, and brandy. Continue to beat until fluffy and somewhat frothy. Add the flour, baking powder, and salt all at once and stir on the lowest speed until they are well mixed and a smooth dough results.

Chill the dough in the freezer until firm. Allow at least 2 hours in the freezer for the tenderest cookies.

To roll, place a ball of dough about 3 or 4 inches in diameter on a lightly floured marble or wood surface. Roll out, using a very light stroke with a rolling pin. The dough should resemble pie pastry more than cookie dough.

Using a sharp knife or cookie cutter, cut the dough into the desired shape—a *fleur-de-lis* is usually preferred. Dust the shapes with a cinnamon-sugar mix and bake at 350° until just done, 8 to 10 minutes. Traditionally, they are served white—never browned or even golden.

YIELD: **18 LARGE COOKIES**

—JANE BUTEL

GREAT NEW MEXICAN RESTAURANTS ✓

These restaurants serving New Mexican food have come to our attention through visits or recommendations from knowledgeable chileheads. The following list is by no means exclusive.

CARLSBAD

Cortez, 506 S. Canal (505-885-4747)

CLOVIS

Guadalajara Restaurant, 916 W. First Street (505-769-9965)
Juanitos Restaurant, 1608 Mabry Drive (505-762-7822)
El Monterrey, 118 Mitchell (505-763-4031)

ESPAÑOLA

Ranch O Casados, 411 N. Riverside (505-753-2837)

FARMINGTON

The Paddock, 315 N. Auburn Avenue (505-327-3566)
Skyliner Gallery, Navajo and Municipal Road (505-327-0436)

continued

GALLUP

Pedro's Mexican Restaurant, 107 Burke
Street (505-863-9755)

GRANTS

Jaramillo's Mexi-Catessen, 213 N. 3rd
(505-287-9308)

HOBBS

La Fiesta, 604 E. Broadway
(505-397-1235)
El Matador, 4428 Lovington Highway
(505-392-2321)

LAS VEGAS

Estella's Cafe, 148 Bridge Street
(505-454-0048)
Plaza Hotel, 230 Old Town Plaza
(505-425-3591)

PORTALES

La Hacienda, 909 N. Avenue K
(505-359-0280)

RATON

El Matador, 445 S. Second Street
(505-445-9575)

continued

ROSWELL

Los Ranchos, 911 E. Second Street
(505-622-9545)
El Toro Bravo, 102 S. Main Street
(505-622-9280)

RUIDOSO

Casa Blanca, 501 Mechem Drive
(505-257-2495)

SILVER CITY

Jalisco Cafe, 103 S. Bullard
(505-388-2060)

TAOS

Andy's "La Fiesta" Restaurant, Ranchos
de Taos (505-758-9733)
Casa de Valdez, S. Santa Fe at Estes
Road (505-758-8777)
Chile Connection, Ski Valley Road
(505-776-8787)
Roberto's, Kit Carson Road
(505-758-2434)

STACKED RED CHILE ENCHILADAS

Here is our second "red" enchilada recipe, the classic enchilada dish served at the early 1960s Albuquerque restaurant, Videz, owned by Pete Benavidez. The restaurant was torn down to make way for Interstate 40, but the recipe lives on.

6–8 **dried red New Mexican chiles, stems and seeds removed**
   1 **clove garlic**
   1 **teaspoon ground Mexican oregano**
      Salt to taste
  ½ **pound pork, cubed from a roast, chops, or bones with meat**
   1 **to 1½ pounds very lean ground beef**
      Salt and pepper to taste
 12 **corn tortillas**
      Vegetable oil for frying
   2 **cups grated cheddar or Monterey jack cheese**
   1 **medium onion, chopped**

Cover the chiles with very hot water and soak for 20 to 30 minutes or until limp and partially rehydrated. Put the chiles in a blender (they should loosely fill ¾ of the container; if more, make two small batches). Fill the container nearly to the top with water. Add the clove of garlic and sprinkle with oregano. Add a little salt at this stage, if you wish. Blend 2 to 3 minutes on high or until a homogeneous or orangish-red mixture is obtained.

Pour the mixture into a saucepan and add the pork. Cook, covered over very low heat or uncovered at a slight bubble, for 2 to 3 hours. If cooked uncovered, periodically add water to original level to maintain proper consistency (which we can only describe as medium soupy).

Remove the pork pieces and save for another meal such as *carne adovada*. Refrigerate the chile sauce to cool. Remove any fat that congeals on top.

Season the beef with a little salt and pepper and sauté until the meat is no longer pink.

Combine the sauce and beef and simmer, covered, for an additional 30 to 45 minutes.

Fry three tortillas per person in a couple inches of oil until they are slightly harder than taco shells. As they are removed from the oil with tongs, submerge each in the red chile pot. Remove, place on a plate, and top with cheese and onion.

Continue the process until the tortillas are stacked three high on each plate.

Ladle the red chiles, including a small amount of the meat, over the tortilla stack until the chile is puddled up as deep as it will stand around the base of the stack. Cover the enchilada lightly with grated cheese and bake at 250° for 20 minutes.

SERVES: **4**

HEAT SCALE: **MEDIUM**

—PETE BENAVIDEZ, DICK BEESON, AND NANCY GERLACH

CALABACITAS

This recipe combines two other Native-American crops, squash and corn, with chiles. One of the most popular dishes in New Mexico, it is so colorful and tasty that it goes well with a variety of foods.

- **3 zucchini squash, cubed**
- **½ cup onion, chopped**
- **4 tablespoons butter or margarine**
- **½ cup chopped green New Mexican chiles, roasted, peeled, stems removed**
- **2 cups whole kernel corn**
- **1 cup milk**
- **½ cup grated Monterey jack cheese**

Sauté the squash and onion in the butter until the squash is tender.

Add the chiles, corn, and milk. Simmer the mixture for 15 to 20 minutes to blend the flavors. Add the cheese and heat until the cheese is melted.

SERVES: **4 TO 6**
HEAT SCALE: **MEDIUM**

—NANCY GERLACH

CHAPTER

7

LAS CRUCES

Las Cruces, New Mexico's second largest city, is undergoing a transition from a farming community to a metropolitan area, which is reflected in its standing as one of the top ten fastest growing regions of the country. Although there are still chile, onion, and cotton fields in the city limits, residents fear the loss of their rural identity.

History and Sightseeing

Early Spanish settlements in the area did not begin in Las Cruces itself. The little town of Doña Ana, north of Las Cruces, was first settled in 1839. Ten years later, the first buildings were erected in Las Cruces, and Mesilla, south of Las Cruces, was founded shortly afterward because of some unusual circumstances.

In 1846, the United States declared war on Mexico and claimed New Mexico as its own. When U.S. troops moved into the Mesilla Valley in 1848, half the population of Doña Ana and Las Cruces founded Mesilla, which was still in Mexico because it was then south of the Rio Grande. Mesilla remained in Mexico and Las Cruces in the Territory of New Mexico until 1854, when Mexico sold 30,000 square miles of land to the United States during the Gadsden Purchase. On July 4, 1854, the purchase was celebrated in the Plaza at Mesilla, but many of the residents missed it because they had moved farther south to remain Mexican citizens.

Mesilla flourished despite the departure of many of its citizens and soon became a booming town of 5,000—larger than Las Cruces or El Paso. In fact, for a while, Mesilla was the largest city west of San Antonio. Part of its success was because Mesilla was chosen as a major station along the 2,800-mile Butterfield Stage Route from St. Louis to San Francisco.

In 1861, Mesilla was briefly the capital of the Confederate Territory of Arizona and headquarters for Lt. Col. John Robert Baylor, Rebel military governor of the Southwest. But the town was retaken by Union forces from California thirteen months later. In 1863, nature played a cruel trick on Mesilla as the Rio Grande shifted course and turned the town into an island.

During the 1870s, Mesilla was occasionally the scene of violence. In 1871 rival Democratic and Republican factions started a bloody riot on the Plaza that left nine dead and fifty wounded, and, in 1880, it was the site of the first trial of Billy the Kid. He was found guilty of murder, sentenced to hang, but escaped and later participated in the Lincoln County War.

When, in 1881, the Santa Fe Railroad selected Las Cruces rather than Mesilla for its route, Mesilla declined in importance as a territorial city. Las Cruces soon became the commercial center of the Mesilla Valley, a fertile agricultural region. Farmers grew pecans, onions, alfalfa, vegetables, and of course, the famous New Mexico chile peppers.

The Las Cruces area offers some interesting historical sights. The Old Armijo House, on Lohman Avenue (505-524-2833), is more than 120 years old and has been restored and stocked with original furnishings. The Amador Hotel, another famous site, is one of the earliest buildings in town. It was built in 1850 at Amador and Water streets by Don Martín Amador and has been a hotel, post office, jail, and courthouse. As a hotel, the Amador hosted such luminaries as Pat Garrett, Billy the Kid, and Mexico's President Benito Juárez. It now houses the Doña Ana County offices, and special rooms upstairs have been restored with period furniture and artifacts.

The Branigan Cultural Center, in the Downtown Mall (505-524-1422), houses artifacts from nearby Fort Selden and produces shows by local artists and craftspersons. The center also presents lectures, concerts, and performing arts. The facility has a gallery, museum, and auditorium. An interesting sight downtown at Water and Lohman avenues is El Molino, a grinding wheel from an 1853

7-1 Historic La Posta in Mesilla

flour mill that commemorates the work and hardships of the early settlers.

New Mexico State University, south of University Avenue, houses several museums and galleries worth visiting. The University Museum in Kent Hall (505-646-3739) has displays of artifacts from prehistoric and historic Native American cultures of the region, plus traveling shows and art exhibits. The University Art Gallery in Williams Hall (505-646-2545) offers monthly exhibits of historical and contemporary art, plus a permanent collection of prints, photographs, and folk art. Visitors interested in the latest advancements in science and technology will be fascinated by the Southwest Residential Experiment Station, which has eight working solar photovoltaic prototypes on display. Guided tours can be arranged by calling the visitor center (505-646-1049).

Mesilla, also called La Mesilla and Old Mesilla, is a charming village that retains much of the feel of Spanish colonial days. A major tourism center, similar to Albuquerque's Old Town, Mesilla (located southwest of Las Cruces on Avenida de Mesilla) has restaurants, shops, galleries, and a museum. The Plaza, site of celebrations and riots, has been well-preserved and serves as the center of town. The San Albino Mission, with its twin towers, adjoins the Plaza. It was founded in 1851 by Fray Ramón Ortiz. The Gadsden Museum on Barker Road (505-526-6293) displays artifacts and relics relating to Mesilla's turbulent history.

For more information on the Las Cruces and Mesilla areas, contact the Las Cruces Convention and Visitors Bureau, 311 North Downtown Mall, Las Cruces, NM 88001 (505-524-8521).

Redesigning Chile Peppers

The founding of the New Mexico College of Agriculture and Mechanical Arts in 1888 ushered in a new era for the Las Cruces area. The college, which later became New Mexico State University with the world's largest campus (6,250 acres), not only assisted in bringing Las Cruces into the modern age by educating the youth of New Mexico, its researchers also assisted local growers with the latest techniques in horticultural science.

The most immediate problem was chile peppers. There was no control at all over what seeds were planted, so farmers could never predict how large the pods would be—or how hot. The demand for chiles was increasing as the state's population grew, so it was time for modern horticulture to take over.

In 1907, Fabian Garcia, a horticulturist at the Agricultural Experiment Station at the College of Agriculture and Mechanical Arts, began his first experiments in breeding more standardized chile varieties. In 1908, he published "Chile Culture," the first chile bulletin from the Agricultural Experiment Station. In 1913, Garcia became director of the station and expanded his breeding program.

Finally in 1917, after ten years of experiments with various strains of *pasilla* chiles, Garcia released New Mexico No. 9, the first attempt to grow chiles with a dependable pod size and heat level. The No. 9 variety became the chile standard in New Mexico until 1950, when Roy Harper, another horticulturist, released New Mexico No. 6, a variety that matured earlier, produced higher yields, and was wilt-resistant and less pungent than No. 9.

The New Mexico No. 6 variety was by far the biggest breakthrough in chile breeding. According to the late Dr. Roy Nakayama, who succeeded Harper as director of the agricultural station, "The No. 6 variety changed the image of chile from a ball of fire that sent consumers rushing to the water jug to that of a multipurpose vegetable with a pleasing flavor. Commercial production and marketing, especially of green chiles and sauces, have been growing steadily since people around the world have discovered the delicious taste of chile without the overpowering pungency."

In 1957, the New Mexico No. 6 variety was modified, made less pungent, and renamed New Mexico No. 6–4. The No. 6–4 variety became the chile industry standard in New Mexico, and more than thirty years later, it was still the most popular commercially grown chile in the state. Other chile varieties, such as Big Jim and New Mexico R-Naky, became popular, but only with home gardeners.

Today, Dr. Paul Bosland, who took over the chile breeding program from Nakayama, is developing new varieties that are resistant to chile wilt, a fungal disease that can devastate fields. He has also created varieties to produce brown, orange, and yellow *ristras* for the home decorating market. The breeding and development of new chile varieties—in addition to research into wild species, postharvest packaging, and genetics—are on-going major projects at New Mexico State.

Visitors to the region are often eager to visit the chile fields and watch harvesting in progress. Such excursions are possible,

Not Everyone Liked Chiles at First

Susan Magoffin, the teen-age bride of American trader and agent Samuel Magoffin, wrote in her diary in 1846 about her first taste of New Mexican green chile stew: "Oh how my heart sickened to say nothing of my stomach . . . [from] a mixture of meat, chilly verde & onions boiled together completing course No. 1. . . . There were a few mouthfuls taken, for I could not eat a dish so strong, and unaccustomed to my palate."

Susan did become accustomed to spicy food, however, and even wrote a "cookery book" so that her friends in the states (New Mexico was a territory, of course) could experience New Mexican cuisine.

but don't be disappointed to find, for the most part, the only thing happening is chiles growing—except, of course, during the Whole Enchilada Fiesta in Las Cruces or the Hatch Chile Festival.

The best way to tour the chile fields is to drive north from Las Cruces on Highway 185 (the back way) to Hatch, and then proceed farther north on Highway 187 through the chile-growing towns of Salem, Garfield, Derry, and Arrey. Signs point the way to chile farms on the side roads. During the winter, of course, you will see only fallow fields (except for some onions or lettuce), but during the summer months there are thousands of acres planted in chiles and cotton. During chile harvesting (late July to September for green, October to December for red), you will see teams of pickers roaming through the fields carrying buckets full of green chiles or jalapeños, which are then dumped into large, wooden-sided carts. Photography is permitted from a distance, but do not trespass, interfere with the pickers, or take any chiles. The pungent pods are available by the bushel from roadside stands.

The Department of Agronomy and Horticulture at NMSU will occasionally conduct tours of their greenhouses, laboratories, and acres of exotic chile plants by appointment only (505-646-3405)—and usually only for people who have some professional connection to botany, horticulture, or food manufacturing.

Both south and north of Las Cruces are extensive pecan groves. No trespassing is allowed, but there is one retail shop, Stahmann's Country Store, south of Mesilla (see below).

Markets, Bakeries, Retail Shops, and Wineries

During the chile season, the pods are available everywhere. Roadside stands are common around the Plaza in Mesilla and along the route through Hatch. Chiles are also plentiful in supermarkets throughout the area.

ADELINA'S PASTA SHOP

2790 Highway 28 South, Mesilla (505-527-1970). *Open Monday–Friday, 2 p.m.–6 p.m.; Saturday, noon–5 p.m.* VISA, MC; NO LIQUOR.

There is a passion for pastas in New Mexico, especially pepper pastas. Adelina Willem makes them in her adjacent pasta factory and sells them in the shop. Her full line of dried pastas, like rotini and linguine, comes in black pepper, red chile, green chile, and jalapeño flavors. She also sells green chile pesto, basil pesto, green chile alfredo, and roasted pepper sauce. Mail order is available.

CHILE GOURMET   ✓

2340 S. Highway 28, Mesilla (505-525-2266). *Open daily,*
10 a.m.–6 p.m. NO CREDIT CARDS; NO LIQUOR.

When you see Stuart Hutson's llamas, you know you're there. This retail outlet for Rancho Mesilla chile farm sells farm-fresh produce in season (chiles, garlic, pecans) and fresh frozen green chile yearlong. It also carries Peruvian and Mexican imports, such as rugs and pottery. The store has a mail-order catalog and will ship frozen chiles anywhere in the United States.

DOMAINE CHEURLIN WINERY
                                                                 ✓

Warm Springs Blvd. and Highway 195, Truth or Consequences (505-744-5418). *Open daily, 7:30 a.m.–3:30 p.m.; tours Monday–Friday, Saturday–Sunday, 7 a.m.–3:30 p.m., and by appointment.*

The vineyards were established in 1980 and now produce the grapes for perhaps the finest Champagne in the Southwest.

7-2 The Peerless Pods of Southern New Mexico

They also make a Chardonnay and sell it and their Champagne by the bottle and by the case. Tours and wine tasting are conducted yearlong. Call for directions.

GOING NUTS IN MESILLA

Highway 28 South, at Bouty Road intersection (505-525-9555). *Open Monday–Saturday, 10 a.m.–5 p.m.; Sunday, 1 p.m.–4 p.m.* MAJOR CREDIT CARDS; NO LIQUOR.

This store is the retail outlet for the Salopek Orchards, so the house specialty is pecans. But when they say "Going Nuts," they mean it, as they also offer pistachios, peanuts, almonds, walnuts, Brazil nuts, filberts, and piñons. And since they're in the middle of chile country, they also sell chile-flavored pecans and pistachios, and pecan chile brittle.

HATCH CHILE EXPRESS

622 Franklin, Hatch (505-267-3226). *Open Monday–Saturday, (usually) 9 a.m.–5 p.m. (January–July); daily, August–December.* VISA, MC; NO LIQUOR.

Owners Jo and Jimmy Lytle are one of the major chile growers in the region, so it makes sense that their shop carries thirty-four varieties of chiles, including piquin, serrano, cayenne, árbol, and even fresh (in season) and dried Habanero. They also sell chile *ristras* and chile food items, such as jams, jellies, preserves, dip mixes, and candies. The chile pepper non-food items include cookie cutters, fishing lures (we're not making this up), salt and pepper shakers, ceramic bells, hummingbird feeders (we're still not making this up), and, for hard-core chileheads, the chile pepper–emblazoned bikini panties (we promise). Don't miss a stop here.

J&P GROCERY

201 East Union, Mesilla Park (505-526-9664). *Open Monday–Saturday, 7:30 a.m.–7 p.m.* NO CREDIT CARDS; NO LIQUOR.

Established in 1965, J&P is a combination grocery, restaurant, and carry-out. It's the place to go for red chile beef jerky, *carne adovada,* burritos, and sandwiches. Locals love J&P's organically grown turkeys.

STAHMANN'S COUNTRY STORE

Highway 28, south of Mesilla in the middle of a vast pecan grove (505-525-3470). *Open Monday–Friday, 9 a.m.– 5:30 p.m.; Saturday and Sunday, 11 a.m.–4 p.m.* MAJOR CREDIT CARDS; NO LIQUOR.

Stahmann's sells the Del Cerro brand of pecans grown in its orchard, plus twenty-five different candies—most of which, naturally, feature pecans. As might be expected, there are chile-flavored pecans and pecan brittle. The store also carries gift items.

THREE ANGELS BAKERY

½ mile west of Hillsboro on NM 152 (505-895-5695). *Open Sunday–Thursday, 7 a.m.–5 p.m.* MAJOR CREDIT CARDS; NO LIQUOR.

It is nothing short of incredible that a bakery this good is located so far from a major city. But the Maccarone family makes it work as they pump out blue corn chile bread, zante currant bread, oat-pecan bread, and freshly ground blue corn and pinto bean flour. It's worth a trip to this former ghost town and present artists' colony just for the bread.

Restaurants

LOS ARCOS

1400 North Date Street, Truth or Consequences (505-894-6200). *Open Sunday–Thursday, 5 p.m.–10:30 p.m.; Friday and Saturday, 5 p.m.–11 p.m.* MAJOR CREDIT CARDS; LIQUOR LICENSE.

This is neither a New Mexican nor a Southwestern restaurant, but it's worth a stop because it is simply the best steak house in New Mexico. The reason is simple: The beef is personally selected by owners Robert Middleton and Earl Whittemore and aged by them in their own coolers. The result is a very thick, meltingly tender, flavorfully char-broiled, extremely satisfying steak. Yes, they'll put green chiles on it if you ask. Seafood is also served.

BIG JOHN'S BARBECUE

810 S. Valley Road, Las Cruces (505-523-9347). *Open daily, 11 a.m.–8:30 p.m.* VISA, MC; BEER AND WINE.

People drive all the way from El Paso for Big John's barbecue, which includes Texas-style brisket, ribs, sausage, and chicken, plus excellent fried catfish and side dishes of coleslaw and fried okra.

CHOPE'S BAR AND CAFE

Highway 28 in La Mesa, 16 miles south of Las Cruces (505-233-9976). *Open daily for lunch, noon–1:30 p.m.; dinner, 6 p.m.–8:30 p.m.* NO CREDIT CARDS; LIQUOR LICENSE.

In business for more than fifty years, Chope's is legendary in southern New Mexico. This small joint is the watering hole for politicians, university professors, and chileheads who appreciate the hot chile that is grown nearby. Everything is excellent, but try especially the *chiles rellenos* and the enchiladas.

7-3 The Indoor Patio at Peppers in Mesilla

My Brother's Place

334 S. Main, Las Cruces (505-523-7681). *Open Monday–Thursday, 11 a.m.–9 p.m.; Friday and Saturday, 11 a.m.–10 p.m.* MAJOR CREDIT CARDS; LIQUOR LICENSE.

Recommended by *Ford Times* magazine, My Brother's Place has chile-oriented specialties, as might be expected. The three most popular dishes are their green enchiladas, beef fajitas, and barbecue platter.

Nellie's Cafe

1226 West Hadley, Las Cruces (505-524-9982). *Open daily, 8 a.m.–8 p.m.; closed Sunday.* NO CREDIT CARDS; NO LIQUOR.

In business for more than twenty years and with a reputation for serving the hottest chile in Las Cruces, Nellie's is popular with the locals because of its authentic New Mexican cuisine. Try Sopaipilla Compuesta, their *gorditas*, or Chile Relleno Meat Bañados, which is a burrito smothered in chile sauce.

Owl Bar

Highway 380 in San Antonio, 9 miles south of Socorro (505-835-9946). *Open Monday–Thursday, 8 a.m.–9:30 p.m.; Friday and Saturday, 8 a.m.–10 p.m.; closed Sunday. Steakhouse open Friday and Saturday, 5 p.m.– 9:30 p.m.* VISA, MC; LIQUOR LICENSE.

This legendary bar, open since 1945, is a compulsory stop on the trip from Albuquerque to Las Cruces or El Paso. In the parking lot, a BMW will be parked between a Harley and a pickup—a sure sign of the diversity of the clientele. Sure, you can order a variety of New Mexican foods, but the house specialty is a green chile cheeseburger, so have one with green chile cheese fries and a Dos Equis. Heaven. Co-author Wilan once ate two green chile cheeseburgers in rapid succession and then ordered a third, to the embarrassment of co-author DeWitt—who told the waitress it was for him. The all-time record seems to have been set by the former head of the FBI in Albuquerque, who once ate six green chile cheeseburgers, a bowl of beans and chile, an order of fries, and a piece of chocolate cake—all at one sitting. You might run into anyone at the Owl—from Sen. Pete Dominici, to beauty pageant hopefuls, to the local basketball team, to bird-watchers from nearby Bosque del Apache Wildlife Refuge, to tourists from the People's Republic of China, Germany, or Israel.

PEPPERS

On the Plaza in Mesilla (505-523-4999). *Open Monday– Saturday, 11 a.m.–10 p.m.; Sunday, noon–9 p.m.* MAJOR CREDIT CARDS; LIQUOR LICENSE.

This restaurant, in an old adobe on the National Register of Historic Sites, is atypical of the area because New Mexican specialties take a back seat to innovative hot and spicy dishes using poblano and chipotle chiles. Its unique entrees include Chile Molido Spit-Roasted Chicken, Shark Fajitas (occasionally), Mexican Wontons, Spicy Baby Back Ribs, and Banana Enchiladas for dessert. There is a small retail store in the front of the restaurant. The indoor patio is intimate and warm.

LA POSTA

Just off the Plaza in Mesilla (505-524-3524). *Open Sunday– Thursday, 11 a.m.–9 p.m.; Friday and Saturday, 11 a.m.– 9:30 p.m.* MAJOR CREDIT CARDS; BEER AND WINE.

Without question, the most famous restaurant in the area is La Posta (the mail station). Originally built as a stage station along the Butterfield Overland Mail Route, this building is more than 175 years old and has been a restaurant since 1939. In fact, it is one of two waystations on the entire stage route still serving visitors—the rest were burned to the ground by Apaches. Several dining rooms in the sprawling complex feature authentic New Mexican foods (try the Tostada Compuesta) amid plants, tropical birds, and stagecoach artifacts. Because it serves so many tourists, its chile specialties tend to be milder than usual, so chileheads should request their sauces extra-spicy.

LA RISTRA

939 East Main, Las Cruces (505-523-0991). *Open Sunday– Thursday, 11 a.m.–8 p.m.; Friday and Saturday, 11 a.m.– 9 p.m.* VISA, MC; BEER AND WINE.

In addition to the usual enchiladas and *chiles rellenos*, Las Ristra offers two delicious specialties: homemade *gorditas* (which they call Mexican hamburgers) and Tacos Rancheros, which are soft tacos filled with *machaca* that they make from shredded brisket. Reservations are recommended Thursday to Sunday.

ROBERTO'S

908 East Amador, Las Cruces (505-523-1851). *Open Monday–Saturday, 7 a.m.–8 p.m.* NO CREDIT CARDS; NO LIQUOR.

Roberto's has been selling tortillas since 1968 and opened as a full-fledged restaurant in 1987. It serves the usual New Mexican dishes and specializes in tamales, burritos, and *gorditas*, which they make by stuffing fresh corn dough with either beans or a combination of beef, lettuce, and tomato, which is then fried.

THE SPANISH KITCHEN

129 East Madrid, Las Cruces (505-526-4275). *Open daily, 7 a.m.–8:45 p.m.* NO CREDIT CARDS; NO LIQUOR.

New Mexican food is the specialty here, with owner Manuel Monfivaiz serving the combo dish, red chili con carne enchiladas. Of course, his chili con carne stands alone quite well without being made into enchiladas. Also, try the Spanish rice.

Recipes

SOPA SECA WITH GARBANZOS

This dish, translated as dry soup, is actually a variant of Spanish rice, which was brought to Mexico by early Spanish settlers and eventually made its way northward. More modern versions substitute coiled vermicelli, broken into small, rice-sized pieces.

½ **cup green New Mexican chiles, chopped**
1 **onion, chopped**
2 **cloves garlic, minced**

3 **tablespoons bacon fat**
1 **cup long grain rice**
2 **cups chicken broth**
1 **cup finely chopped tomatoes**
1 **cup canned garbanzo beans, drained**
   Salt and pepper to taste

Sauté the first three ingredients in the bacon fat until the onion is soft. Add the rice and cook over low heat until the rice is browned. Add the broth and tomatoes and bring to a boil.

Transfer the mixture to an oven-proof 1 quart or larger casserole dish and bake covered at 350° for about 45 minutes. Remove the cover during the last 10 minutes for a crispier rice. Add the garbanzos and seasoning and stir during the last 5 minutes of cooking.

SERVES: **4**
HEAT SCALE: **MILD**

GREEN CHILE STEW

This is the beef stew or macaroni and cheese of New Mexico—a basic dish with as many variations as there are cooks. Add a warmed flour tortilla and you have a complete meal.

7-4 La Ristra Restaurant in Las Cruces

2 **pounds lean pork, cubed**
2 **tablespoons vegetable oil**
1 **large onion, chopped**
2 **cloves garlic, minced**
6 **to 8 green New Mexican chiles, roasted, peeled,
   stems and seeds removed, chopped**
1 **large potato, peeled and diced (optional)**
2 **tomatoes, peeled and chopped**
3 **cups water**

Brown the pork in the oil. Add the onion and garlic and sauté for a couple of minutes.

Combine all the ingredients in a kettle or crockpot and simmer for 1½ to 2 hours or until the meat is very tender.

SERVES: **6**
HEAT SCALE: MEDIUM

—NANCY GERLACH

CHILAQUILES

This extremely simple breakfast dish takes only a few minutes to prepare. It is rarely found in restaurants.

1 **dozen corn tortillas**
  Vegetable oil for frying
2 **cups salsa, bottled or homemade**
2 **cups Monterey jack cheese**

Cut the tortillas in quarters and fry them in the oil until slightly crisp.

Place a layer of 16 wedges on the bottom of a 1 quart casserole dish. Add ⅓ of the salsa and sprinkle ⅓ of the cheese on top. Repeat this process twice more.

Bake for 20 minutes at 350°.

SERVES: **4**
HEAT SCALE: **MILD TO MEDIUM (DEPENDING ON THE SALSA)**

WINTER SQUASH AND APPLE CHOWDER WITH CHILE-DUSTED CROUTONS

This hearty soup combines several fall crops from northern New Mexico, namely squash, apples, and red and green chiles. Add a salad, crusty bread, and a nice New Mexican wine for a memorable meal.

Winter Squash and Apple Chowder

- 1 **medium onion, diced**
- 2 **tablespoons butter or margarine**
- 1½ **pounds hubbard or butternut squash, peeled, seeded, and cut into 1-inch cubes**
- 3 **tart green apples, peeled, cored, and chopped**
- ¼ **cup chopped green New Mexican chiles, roasted, peeled, and stems and seeds removed**
- 4 **cups chicken stock or broth**
- 1 **teaspoon grated lemon peel**
- 2 **cups diced cooked chicken**
  Freshly ground black pepper
- 2 **tablespoons applejack or Calvados**
  Salt to taste
- 1–2 **teaspoons cider vinegar (optional)**

Sauté the onion in the butter until soft. Add the squash and apples and sauté for another 3 minutes.

Add the chiles and stock and bring to a boil. Reduce heat, cover partially, and simmer about 30 to 45 minutes until the squash and apples are very tender.

Add the lemon peel, chicken, black pepper, applejack, and salt and simmer for an additional 15 minutes. Add vinegar if the soup is too sweet.

Top with croutons and serve.

SERVES: **4 TO 6**
HEAT SCALE: **MEDIUM**

Chile-Dusted Croutons

3 **slices of white bread, crusts trimmed, cut in cubes**
1 **clove garlic, sliced**
3 **tablespoons butter**
2 **teaspoons ground red New Mexican chiles**
½ **teaspoon ground cumin**

Spread the bread cubes on a baking sheet and let them dry out at room temperature for 3 hours.

Sauté the garlic in the butter for a couple of minutes, then remove the garlic and discard. Add the chiles and cumin and quickly toss the bread until all the cubes are coated with the mixture.

Bake the croutons on a cookie sheet at 350° for 10 minutes or until they are golden brown.

—NANCY GERLACH

7-5 Look for Llamas at the Chile Gourmet in Mesilla

ROASTING, PEELING, AND PROCESSING PEPPER PODS

Travelers to New Mexico during late summer and early fall see forty-pound sacks of green chiles in supermarkets and roadside stands and are often tempted to buy a whole sack. But then what do you do with them?

New Mexican chiles are usually blistered and peeled before being used in recipes. Blistering or roasting the chiles requires heating the fresh pods to the point that the tough transparent skin separates from the meat of the chile so it can be removed.

To roast and peel chiles, first cut a small slit in the chile close to the stem end so that the steam can escape and the pod won't explode. The chiles can be placed on a baking sheet and put directly under the broiler or on a screen on the top of the stove. They can also be plunged into hot cooking oil to loosen the skins.

Our favorite method, which involves meditation with a six-pack of Santa Fe Pale Ale, is to place the pods on a charcoal grill about five to six inches from the coals. Blisters will soon indicate that the skin is separating, but be sure the chiles are blistered all over or they will not peel properly. Although the chiles may burn slightly, take care that they do not blacken or they will be nearly impossible to peel.

Immediately wrap the chiles in damp paper towels and place them in a plastic bag to steam for ten to fifteen minutes. The best way to avoid chile burns is to wear rubber gloves

continued

during the peeling process. Remove the skin, stem, and seeds of each pod and chop coarsely. Place the chopped chile in plastic ice cube trays and freeze solid. Pop the cubes out and place them in Ziploc freezer bags for easy access to whatever amount of chile is needed in a recipe. The taste of New Mexico will keep in your freezer for at least a year. (Some mail-order firms sell fresh green chiles in season; see Mail-Order Sources, Appendix 1.)

MESILLA PECAN TARTS

Here's a simple but delicious dessert that captures the flavor of New Mexico's largest nut crop.

  3 **ounces cream cheese, softened**
½ **cup butter, softened**
  1 **cup sifted flour**
  1 **egg, slightly beaten**
¾ **cup brown sugar**
  1 **teaspoon vanilla**
  1 **tablespoon butter, softened**
¾ **cup chopped pecans**

Blend the cream cheese and ½ cup butter until smooth. Add the flour and blend well. Chill the dough in the refrigerator for at least 2 hours. Shape the dough into 2 dozen 1-inch balls and press into 1¾-inch muffin or tart pans.

Blend the remaining ingredients until they are thoroughly mixed. Fill each section of the tart pan with a portion of the mixture. Bake for 20 minutes at 375° and cool on wire racks before removing the tarts from the pans.

YIELD: **24 TARTS**

CHAPTER

8

ALBUQUERQUE

A metropolis of half a million people in the center of a vast state with a small rural population, Albuquerque has often been forgotten by tourists and criticized by other New Mexico cities for its size and supposed emphasis on sprawling growth, freeways, and commerce rather than history or the arts. But the real Albuquerque is a city that cares about all aspects of its historical, cultural, and natural environments.

Early History

The "Duke City" was named in honor of Don Francisco Fernandez de la Cueva Enriquez, eighth Duke of Alburquerque (the extra "r" was later dropped) and Viceroy of New Spain. The name Albuquerque is said to be a corruption of *albus quercus* (Latin for white oak). The Dukedom of Alburquerque still exists, and visits by the current Spanish duke are always the height of the social season in this city.

Albuquerque was founded in 1706 by families from nearby Bernalillo on the site of today's Old Town Plaza. One of the first buildings was San Felipe de Neri Church (rebuilt in 1793), an interesting blend of Spanish colonial, Gothic, and Pueblo Revival architectural styles. It is open to the public for visits and prayers. Albuquerque soon became a major trade center along the Camino Real de Tierra Adentro (Royal Road of the Interior), the main road from Mexico City to El Paso del Norte to Santa Fe, also called the Chihuahua Trail.

In her 1947 book, *Albuquerque*, Erna Fergusson discussed the long tradition of New Mexican cooking, which stretched back to the early days of the settlement of the town. "The larder was limited. Beef, mutton, pork and fowl were varied by game and dried buffalo meat from the plains. Vegetables grew but were used in sauces and gravies rather than alone. Fruit was eaten fresh in its short season, and dried on wide trays for storing. Corn was used in every way, from soup to desserts, and the lowly brown bean appeared at every meal. Chile grew in every man's garden and was the only condiment. A limited diet, but good cooks invented

THE TWO STATE "VEGETABLES"

In 1965, the New Mexico Legislature was locked in a bitter struggle, with the pinto bean growers on one side and the chile pepper producers on the other. Each group was lobbying fiercely for its crop to be named the official state vegetable. New Mexico politics being what they are, there was only one real solution: name them both as state co-vegetables.

The only problem, as agronomists and horticulturists point out, is that neither beans nor chiles are vegetables. Beans are legumes like the peanut (which is not a nut), and chiles are fruits.

The politicians didn't care. If it's eaten like a vegetable, a vegetable it must be, they reasoned. Well, beans are beans, but chiles are a bit more complicated. Botanically, they're berries. Horticulturally, they're fruits. When used in their green form, the produce industry calls them vegetables. When dried in their red form, they're a spice. No wonder the politicians got confused.

many a savory combination and the modern epicure rates New Mexican cookery—when properly done—with the best."

During the Indian wars and Civil War, Albuquerque became a principal supply center for the forts being built throughout the Southwest, and warehousing became an important business. In the early to mid-1800s, the area around Albuquerque was the largest sheep-growing district in the state, which meant mutton was a large part of the diet. Subsistence farming was common on small parcels of land in the north and south valleys, and extra fruit and vegetables were peddled to nearby pueblos. During a cattle boom after the Civil War, particularly during the 1880s, beef replaced mutton as the most common meat served in Albuquerque.

The railroad arrived in Albuquerque in 1881, transforming it into the trade center for the entire state. Another settlement two miles east of the Old Town Plaza was dubbed New Town and now serves as the downtown area. The principal industries at the turn of the century were wool, livestock, alfalfa, and lumber.

The hot spot in town soon became the Alvarado Hotel. This magnificent structure was built at a cost of $200,000 and opened in 1902. It was considered the "finest railroad hotel on Earth" and was hotel magnate Fred Harvey's prime lodging creation. Located along the railroad tracks facing First Street, the Alvarado featured eighty-eight guest rooms, a gigantic dining room, Spanish-tiled roofs, many patios with cascading fountains, and beautiful Harvey Girls, the hostesses who served "all you could eat" for $1.

Many celebrities stayed at the Alvarado: Rudolph Valentino, Albert Einstein, Charles Lindbergh, Joan Crawford, Katherine Hepburn, and Jack Benny, to name just a few. U.S. presidents selecting the Alvarado included William H. Taft (who reputedly got stuck in the bathtub), Herbert Hoover, Woodrow Wilson, Franklin D. Roosevelt, and Theodore Roosevelt.

The Alvarado fell on hard times when serious competition— for example, the first Hilton—opened. Eventually, the hotel was abandoned, despite efforts to preserve it. One of Albuquerque's architectural masterpieces—as well as a significant part of the city's food history—was demolished in 1970.

Food and Sightseeing

The food scene in Albuquerque is incredibly varied. In addition to an extraordinary number of restaurants serving New Mexican dishes, most of the other world cuisines are well represented—especially those famous for serving hot and spicy dishes. There are many Chinese restaurants serving Sichuan and Hunan dishes, four Thai restaurants, two Cajun places, three East Indian establishments, and several hot and spicy barbecue joints. Unfortunately, its only Caribbean restaurant closed recently.

Food collectors will love the markets and shops in Albuquerque, which have chiles galore, plus other Mexican and Southwestern ingredients. Four shops are devoted just to chile peppers, and most of the specialty food stores carry Southwestern foods as well as cookbooks.

In addition to eating, there's lots to do and see in Albuquerque. The Albuquerque Museum (2000 Mountain Road NW in Old Town, 505-243-7255) has assembled the largest collection of Spanish colonial artifacts in the United States and uses it as a centerpiece for a permanent exhibit entitled Four Centuries: A History of Albuquerque. The New Mexico Museum of Natural History (1801 Mountain Road NW, 505-841-8837), is a two-minute walk from Old Town and traces the region's 4.6-billion-year geology, paleontology, botany, and zoology. The Maxwell Museum of Anthropology (off University two blocks north of Central, 505-277-4404) has great displays of Indian artifacts and explains the human habitation of the area.

The Sandia Mountains rise 5,000 feet above Albuquerque and are preserved as part of the Cibola National Forest and the Sandia Wilderness Area, so within fifteen miles of downtown are golden eagles, black bears, and mountain sheep. It's fun to take the Sandia Peak Tramway (505-298-8515), the world's longest tram, up to the top of the mountain, where you'll find a ski area, wildlife, great views, and a bar and restaurant.

The Rio Grande Nature Center (2901 Candelaria NW) has interesting exhibits and walking tours of the *bosque*, the twenty-mile cottonwood forest that lines both sides of the Rio Grande. The Rio Grande Zoological Park (903 10th Street SW) is one of the finest zoos in the country and offers such interesting exhibits as Cat Walk with its cheetah run, Jungle Habitat with exotic birds, and Ape Country. The recently opened Petroglyph National Monument (west of Coors Road on Unser Boulevard) protects the artistic rock carvings that are thousands of years old.

Besides the malls, two shopping areas are popular gathering spots. Old Town (Central and Rio Grande) has twenty-five galleries

8-1 The Monte Vista Fire Station
Restaurant (*Credit:* Chel Beeson)

and about fifty shops offering everything from chile peppers to turquoise jewelry. The University–Nob Hill area, in the 2000–4000 blocks of East Central, offers fashion shops, bookstores, record shops, cafes, restaurants, and other delights.

For more information on Albuquerque, contact the Albuquerque Convention and Visitors Bureau, P.O. Box 26866, Albuquerque, N.M. 87125 (1-800-284-2282 or 1-505-243-3696).

Markets

CARAVAN EAST GROWER'S MARKET

Caravan East parking lot, 7605 Central NE (no phone). *Open daily, 6 a.m.–noon (summer through November).* NO CREDIT CARDS; NO LIQUOR EXCEPT AN OCCASIONAL BEER IN A COOLER.

Local growers meet at the market to share the fruits (and vegetables) of their gardens. As you might expect, a number of varieties of chiles, as well as other native crops like piñons, squash, corn, and beans are available.

La Familia

134 Isleta SW (505-873-0490). *Open Monday–Saturday,
8 a.m.–7 p.m.; Sunday, 9 a.m.–6 p.m.* NO CREDIT CARDS; NO
LIQUOR.

Calling themselves "the chile store and more," La Familia is
famous for its *carne adovada* and homemade *chicharrónes.*
The market also specializes in food items imported from Mexico, such as salsas, candies, and sodas. During chile season,
La Familia keeps five roasters constantly working to prepare
hundreds of forty-pound sacks of green a day. Owner George
Benavidez, when asked to estimate how much green chile he
sells annually, said, "One million pounds."

Flea Market

New Mexico State Fairgrounds, Central and Louisiana (no
phone). *Open Saturday and Sunday, 7 a.m.–4 p.m., except
during the State Fair in September.* NO CREDIT CARDS; NO
LIQUOR.

This huge operation is entirely outdoors and most items sold
are the usual used hammers and worn-out eight-track tape
machines. However, fresh produce and chiles in season, plus
the items "imported" from Mexico in the back of pickups, are
available. Sporadically, a wide variety of food items is available, but the total sensory experience of the flea market
(where decades ago a broke co-author DeWitt used to peddle
loofah sponges) is a real trip and well worth the time.

The Grocery Emporium

1403 Girard NE (505-265-6771). *Open Monday–Saturday,
8 a.m.–7 p.m.; Sunday, 9 a.m.–5 p.m.* VISA, MC; NO LIQUOR.

This store, crammed full of domestic and international foods,
is a confusing maze of sights and smells. Although there is
seemingly no organization to the shelves here, owner David

8-2 Robb Richmond of Robb's Ribbs with Smoked
Specialties (*Credit:* Chel Beeson)

Bromberg can find anything you need—like tamarind juice, Madras curry powder, or his own justly famous green chile turkey sausage, winner of a people's choice award at the 1992 National Fiery Foods Show. New Mexican foods are scattered among offerings from the Middle East and Southeast Asia.

J. MICHAEL'S

2400 Rio Grande NW (505-764-9090). *Open daily, 7 a.m.–8 p.m. (winter); 7 a.m.– 9 p.m. (summer).* VISA, MC; LIQUOR SALES.

The nine different varieties of cheesecake offered here are foodie heaven. J. Michael's also has New Mexican products, unusual deli foods (jalapeño cheese bread), breakfast burritos, 200 varieties of wine, a huge imported beer selection, and—of course—super fresh meats, produce, and pastas.

LOUIE'S PRODUCE

622 Coors SW (505-831-5940). *Open daily, 9 a.m.–5 p.m.* NO CREDIT CARDS; NO LIQUOR.

Outside, the sign says "Louie's Chile," and inside are some of the 2 tons of red chile pods they sell annually. In addition to New Mexican varieties, Louie's has canned Mexican chiles, árbol in season, *chile pasado*, plus beans, New Mexico fruit, and corn husks. Ever watchful of the customer's health, it has a complete line of *remedios* (medicinal herbs). Louie's will ship dry chiles and chile products—call for details.

TA LIN SUPERMARKET

230 Louisiana Blvd. SE (505-268-0206). *Open Monday– Saturday, 9 a.m.–7:30 p.m.; Sunday, 8 a.m.–6 p.m.* NO CREDIT CARDS; NO LIQUOR.

This Asian-oriented market also has an astounding collection of Latin American foodstuffs, including the unusual, hard-to-find specialty items like guava paste, mango pickles, taro, and seven kinds of bananas. Their collection of worldwide hot sauces is hard to believe.

TULLY'S MEAT MARKET

1425-A San Mateo NE (505-255-5370). *Open Monday– Friday, 9 a.m.–6 p.m.; Saturday, 9 a.m.–5:30 p.m.* NO CREDIT CARDS; NO LIQUOR.

Think you're going to escape hot and spicy food by going to an Italian market? No way. Try their *putanesca* sandwich or *pannino*, which combines sausage, cheese, and green chile all baked together. Tully's also carries great meats, cheeses, pastas, sausages, and exotic olives.

Retail Shops

BUENO FOODS FACTORY STORE

2001 Fourth Street SW (505-243-2722). *Open Monday–
Friday, 9 a.m.–4 p.m.* NO CREDIT CARDS; NO LIQUOR.

Bueno is the largest food processor in New Mexico and the
only one to offer authentic New Mexican frozen entrees. The
store is dwarfed by the huge processing plant, but you can
find red chile powders and pods, dried *chile pasado,* blue corn
meal, packaged spices and herbs, and frozen green chile
entrees.

CARMEN'S OF NEW MEXICO USA

401 Mountain Road NW (505-842-5119). *Open Monday–
Friday, 9 a.m.–5 p.m.; some Saturdays—call first.* VISA, MC;
NO LIQUOR.

This small shop and mail-order operation carries only New
Mexico specialty food products such as *sopaipilla* mix, blue
corn meal, and dozens of chile varieties. Additionally, Carmen's markets its own line of complete New Mexican dinners,
including a salsa mix, a recipe book, and the necessary ingredients for the dinner. Call about mail orders.

CHILE HILL EMPORIUM

Highway 44 just west of Bernalillo, adjacent to Coronado
State Monument (505-867-3294). *Open Monday–Saturday,
9:30 a.m.–6 p.m.; Sunday, noon–6 p.m.* VISA, MC; NO
LIQUOR.

This charming shop is an ode to New Mexico food products,
with not only red chiles and *ristras* but also *posole,* salsas,
blue corn masa, and homebaked oven bread from the nearby
pueblos. Non-food items include books, maps, T-shirts, and
cards. Fresh green chiles are available in season.

CHILE PATCH USA

*204-B San Felipe NW (505-242-4454). Open daily, 9 a.m.–
7 p.m. (winter); 9 a.m.–9 p.m. (summer).* MAJOR CREDIT
CARDS; NO LIQUOR.

Everything in this Old Town shop relates to the chile. Owner
Martina Kirk has her own line of chile-emblazoned clothing,
and her store carries every imaginable food and non-food item
concerning chile peppers. Tastings and samplings run continuously on salsas, hot sauces, candies, nuts, chips, and more.
Call for mail-order information.

THE BEST CHILI DEBATE GOES ON AND ON

Regardless of geographical location, every cook
in the Southwest has his or her own perfect
recipe for chili. In 1969, *Life* magazine ran an
article on Texas chili con carne that prompted
Arch Napier of Albuquerque to fire off a letter
of protest.

"Sirs," he wrote, "you are giving this exciting food a bad name by linking it to the crude
stuff served in Texas. Texas chili is a test of
endurance, primarily useful for terrorizing
tourists and fracturing oil wells. Last year, the
Texans had a kind of chili cooking contest—
conducted like a shoot-out—and it was publi-
cized on the front page along with crimes and
disasters. When New Mexico chili cuisine is discussed in our newspapers, it is usually carried
on the Art and Music pages."

FREMONT'S

556 Coronado Center Mall (505-883-6040). *Open Monday–Friday, 9:30 a.m.–9 p.m.; Saturday, 9:30 a.m.–6:30 p.m.; Sunday, 9:30 a.m.–5:30 p.m.* MAJOR CREDIT CARDS; NO LIQUOR.

Thousands of food items from all over the world are crammed into this shop in Coronado Center. Besides local specialties, Fremont's carries caviar from Russia, biscuits from England, balsamic vinegar from Italy, and hundreds of Asian items.

THE HERB STORE

107 Carlisle SE (505-255-8878). *Open Monday–Saturday, 10 a.m.–6 p.m.; Sunday, noon–5 p.m.* VISA, MC; NO LIQUOR.

Here's the place for herbheads, with over 350 varieties available, plus thirty Chinese herbs. For culinary use, more than 100 spices and a number of excellent teas are sold here.

THE PEPPER EMPORIUM

328 San Felipe NW in Old Town (505-242-7538). *Open daily, 9 a.m.–5 p.m. (winter); 10 a.m.–6 p.m. (summer).* 104 Winrock Center Mall (505-881-9225). *Open Monday–Friday, 10 a.m.–6 p.m.; Saturday, noon–5 p.m.* 201 3rd NW in the Hyatt Regency (505-766-9119). *Open daily, 9 a.m.–5 p.m.* MAJOR CREDIT CARDS; NO LIQUOR.

In addition to their own New Mexico–style brand of foods, Jan and Dirk Schneider sell every imaginable chile pepper food item, including pods, powders, jams, jellies, candies, salsas, sauces, and on and on. Popular non-food items include T-shirts, books, posters, dishware, and mugs. Call about mail orders.

POTPOURRI

121 Romero NW in Old Town (505-243-4087). *Open Monday–Saturday, 10 a.m.–8 p.m.; Sunday, 10 a.m.–6 p.m.* MAJOR CREDIT CARDS; NO LIQUOR.

Potpourri has perhaps the widest selection of hot and spicy products in Albuquerque. Owner Abraham Santillanes scours the food shows and magazines to find interesting spicy products like pineapple salsas and salsa-filled chocolate truffles. Expect tastings on the weekends. In addition to foods, he carries hundreds of cooking utensils and a great selection of Southwestern cookbooks.

READ ON

10200 Corrales Road NW (505-898-0000). *Open Monday– Thursday, 9 a.m.–8 p.m.; Friday, 9 a.m.–9 p.m.; Saturday, 9 a.m.–6 p.m.; Sunday, 9 a.m.–5 p.m.* VISA, MC; NO LIQUOR.

This bookstore is listed as a food source because it has the largest collection of Southwestern and Mexican cookbooks in Albuquerque.

Bakeries and Wineries

ANDERSON VALLEY VINEYARDS

4920 Rio Grande NW (505-344-7266). *Open Tuesday– Sunday, noon–5:30 p.m. for wine tastings and tours.* VISA, MC; WINE SALES BY GLASS OR BOTTLE.

Central New Mexico's most notable winery, Anderson Valley specializes in Chardonnay and Cabernet Sauvignon Reserve. Anderson has a wine room available for special events, plus a gift shop.

GOLDEN CROWN PANADERÍA

1103 Mountain Road NW (505-243-2424). *Open Monday– Saturday, 6 a.m.–3 p.m., or closes when sold out.* VISA, MC; NO LIQUOR.

Bread sculptor Pat "Hot Buns" Morales has created a bull for an investment firm, a B-52 bomber for a party, a castle for the Duke of Albuquerque, and a three-breasted French woman (mythological, of course) for a gift, so you can trust his chile pepper-shaped bread that he ships by UPS. Call him for mail-order information. When visiting, try the green chile bread (you may have to call for it in advance) or any other Mexican bakery item (*bolillos*, yum).

GRUET WINERY

3758 Hawkins NE (505-344-4453). *Open Monday–Friday, 10 a.m.–5 p.m.; by appointment on weekends.* VISA, MC; WINE SALES.

This winery, located in an industrial park, makes good sparkling wines despite its pedestrian location. It specializes in brut and blanc de noirs, made by Methode Champenoise. Gruet has a tasting room, and you can buy wine by the bottle or case.

ISLETA PUEBLO BREAD SALES

Various locations (505-869-3111). NO CREDIT CARDS.

Bread baked in traditional *hornos* in Isleta Pueblo, south of Albuquerque off I-25, is available for sale at the following locations in the pueblo: beside the church after 9 a.m.; at Lino's Cigarettes, Highway 47 at the 147 interchange; and at Smoke 'n Save, Old Highway 85 and Coors Road.

MEL'S BAKERY AND CHILE

1926 Isleta SW (505-877-0305). *Open Monday–Friday, 7:30 a.m.–6 p.m.; Saturday, 8 a.m.–4 p.m.* NO CREDIT CARDS; NO LIQUOR.

Only in New Mexico would you find a combination bakery and chile market. Mel offers freshly made whole wheat and corn tortillas daily, plus some pastries such as *empanadas* and *biscochitos*. He also sells red chile pods, ground piquin, frozen green chiles, and *chile pasado*.

LA MEXICANA TORTILLA COMPANY

1523 4th Street SW (505-243-0391). *Open Monday–Saturday, 7:30 a.m.–5:30 p.m.* NO CREDIT CARDS; NO LIQUOR.

For sixty years, La Mexicana has been cranking out corn and flour tortillas, plus blue corn tortillas and freshly made tamales. Its bakery produces Mexican items such as *bolillos* and tortilla chips. A small Mexican market area carries canned foods and salsas.

Restaurants

CASA VIEJA

4541 Corrales Road, Corrales (505-898-7489). *Open Tuesday–Sunday, 6 p.m.–10 p.m.* MAJOR CREDIT CARDS; LIQUOR LICENSE.

Casa Vieja offers romantic dining at its best here in the oldest house in Corrales, built in 1706. Owner Rob Kellner and owner/chef Jean-Pierre Gozard do a top-notch job with continental cuisine like veal saltimbocca, have a marvelous wine list, but have not been able to shake the all-encompassing cult of the chile. In the back of the restaurant, with limited seating, is the Gourmet Pizzaria. Its specialty? Red Chile Cheese Pizza, of course.

CHICHARRONERIA OROZCO

722 Isleta SW (no phone yet). *Open daily, 9 a.m.–8 p.m.* NO CREDIT CARDS; NO LIQUOR LICENSE.

We have no idea if this fascinating place will make it, but we wish them luck. Few restaurateurs would dare to open such a specialty place devoted to three different *chicharrones*, plus *carnitas* and fried *colas de pavo* (turkey tails). However, they do serve lamb ribs, pork ribs, and pig's feet—there they go again.

LOS CUATES

4901 Lomas NE (505-255-5079). *Open daily, 11 a.m.–9 p.m.* VISA, MC; LIQUOR LICENSE.

Named "the twins" for Frank Barela's own twins, this highly regarded New Mexican restaurant is appreciated because of its complimentary salsa and excellent *carne adovada* and *chiles rellenos*.

DURAN CENTRAL PHARMACY

1815 Central NW, near Old Town (505-247-4141). *Open Monday–Friday, 9 a.m.–6:30 p.m.; Saturday, 9 a.m.–2 p.m.* NO CREDIT CARDS; NO LIQUOR.

Now we have chiles combined with drugs and colognes! This forty-eight-seat restaurant adjacent to the pharmacy is famed for its red chile sauce, which tops great enchiladas and burritos. Locals and politicos gravitate here.

E. J.'S COFFEE, TEA, AND RESTAURANT

2201 Silver SE (505-268-2233). *Open Monday–Thursday, 7 a.m.–11 p.m.; Friday, 7 a.m.–midnight; Saturday, 8 a.m.–midnight; Sunday, 8 a.m.–6 p.m.* VISA, MC; NO LIQUOR.

Some of best places to eat breakfast in Albuquerque are near the University of New Mexico campus, as is E.J.'s. Early delights include huevos rancheros, *quesadillas*, and breakfast burritos. Desserts are a specialty, like eight different cheesecakes (baklava and Fuzzy Navel) and hazelnut tortes. If you come just for the great coffee, be prepared to discuss the imagery of Navajo darkness in the works of Tony Hillerman.

FRED'S BREAD AND BAGEL

3009 Central Avenue NE (505-266-7323). *Open daily, 7 a.m.–11 p.m.* NO CREDIT CARDS; NO LIQUOR.

Another great breakfast place near UNM, Fred's is rapidly gaining fame for its green chile bagels and green chile cheese bread. This combination bakery/coffeehouse also chases down and cooks free-range turkeys, which they roast and carve. for sandwiches. Fred doesn't exist; owner Aaron Hendon freely admits he just wanted a name that rhymed with *bread*.

THE FRONTIER RESTAURANT

2400 Central SE (505-266-0550). *Open 24 hours a day, 7 days a week.* VISA, MC; NO LIQUOR.

Here it is, the people zoo of Albuquerque—and it's open all night! You're likely to meet everyone from a TV news anchorperson, to a professor of semiotics, to a self-proclaimed medicine man. Breakfast—quick and spicy and served cafeteria-style—is available all day and all night; their Western Hash Browns with Cheddar Cheese and Green Chile with Ranchero Sauce are recommended.

GARCIA'S

1726 Central SW (505-842-0273). *Open Monday–Thursday, 6:30 a.m.–3 p.m.; Friday and Saturday, 6:30 a.m.–midnight.* 1113 4th Street NW (505-247-9149). *Open Sunday–Thursday, 6:30 a.m.–10 p.m.; Friday and Saturday, 6:30 a.m.–midnight.* NO CREDIT CARDS; NO LIQUOR.

The original 4th Street location of these family restaurants is the kitsch capital of the Southwest, with the most ridiculous decorations imaginable, including a mechanical monkey on a tightrope. We love it, and we love their *carne adovada*, green chile stew, homemade flour tortillas, and *biscochitos*, the official New Mexico state cookie.

GRANDMA'S K & I DINER

2500 Broadway SE (505-243-1881). *Open Monday–Friday, 6 a.m.–3 p.m.* NO CREDIT CARDS ("BUT WE TAKE HOT CHECKS AND COLD CASH"); NO LIQUOR.

This charmingly madcap diner is the home of the Travis Mexican Special, Grandma Warner's own burrito smothered in red and green chiles that will serve an entire family of four for the price of a single meal. Some customers have been so intimidated they have ordered a "one-eighth Travis." Grandma serves about 15 gallons of green chile and 400 pounds of french fries a day, which is a testament to her popularity.

M & J'S SANITARY TORTILLA FACTORY

403 2nd Street SW (505-242-4890). *Open Monday–Friday, 9:30 a.m.–4 p.m.* NO CREDIT CARDS; NO LIQUOR.

The Factory's salsa is a killer, so don't miss it—and it's free. House specials are *carne adovada* chicken, *chiles rellenos*,

8-3 Dave Bromberg Outside His Grocery Emporium
(*Credit:* Chel Beeson)

and stuffed *sopaipillas*. This is a hangout for local politicos,
so you might have to eat next to a lawyer. Oh, well.

EL MODELO MEXICAN FOODS

1715 2nd Street SW (505-242-1843). *Open daily, 8 a.m.–
6:45 p.m.* MAJOR CREDIT CARDS; NO LIQUOR.

It's carry-out only at this landmark of New Mexican foods,
open since 1929 in the same location. El Modelo specializes
in preparing very large quantities and will be glad to cater
your next chile cookoff. Try the tamales, the *carnitas*, and the
stuffed *sopaipillas*.

MONROE'S RESTAURANT

1520 Lomas NW (505-242-1111) and 6051 Osuna NE
(505-881-4224). *Open daily, 9 a.m.–9 p.m.* MAJOR CREDIT
CARDS; BEER AND WINE.

These two restaurants use over 100,000 pounds of green chiles annually, and they're all chopped by hand. Their signature items are green chile cheeseburgers, taco fingers, blue corn enchiladas, and a simple bowl of green chiles. They are good about accommodating their menu to customers' desires, so go ahead and order that Blue Corn Carne Adovada Enchilada.

MONTE VISTA FIRE STATION RESTAURANT

3201 Central NE (505-255-2424). *Open Monday–Friday, 11 a.m.–2:30 p.m.; Monday–Saturday, 5 p.m.–10:30 p.m. Bar open daily until 2 a.m.* MAJOR CREDIT CARDS; LIQUOR LICENSE.

First, the venue: This three-story former firehouse was designed by famed architect John Gaw Meem in the Pueblo Revival style. It was built in 1936 as a WPA project and gorgeously restored and renovated as a restaurant in 1985. The main dining area is the former bay for fire trucks. Second, the food: Lovingly created by executive chef Rosa Rajkovic, the innovative cuisine here almost defies description. The menu is so vast and changes so often you never know what's coming—from Mushroom Ravioli to every imaginable incarnation of duck. Rosa doesn't slight the chiles, either. Highly recommended.

EL NORTEÑO

7306 Zuni SE (505-256-1431). *Open Sunday–Thursday, 10 a.m.–9 p.m.; Friday and Saturday, 9 a.m. 10 p.m.* VISA, MC; BEER AND WINE.

It's a family affair at this wonderful northern Mexican restaurant. The entire Nuñez family pitches in to serve the greatest soft tacos this side of Guadalajara. You can mix and match about fifteen fillings, including *carne al carbón*, *barbacoa*, *lengua*, *cabrito*, and *carne asada*. Top them with pico de gallo or their famous El Norteño Guaca-Chile Salsa.

OLD TIME BARBECUE

4300 Coors Blvd. SW (505-877-8383). *Open Tuesday–Saturday, 11 a.m.–8 p.m.; closed Sunday and Monday ("gone fishin'"—and he means it).* NO CREDIT CARDS; NO LIQUOR.

Henry Clopton is the acknowledged master of barbecue in Albuquerque, combining Alabama techniques with New Mexico spiciness. His techniques yield the tenderest ribs and brisket imaginable, and his sausage has amazing texture, taste, and tang. Occasionally, Henry will have something special, something that's not on the menu, like barbecued breast of lamb. Be sure to ask—and if you love barbecue, don't miss Henry's Old-Time Barbecue. And try the soups—Henry loves to make 'em.

EL PALENQUE

3248 Isleta SW (505-877-8871). *Open daily, 9 a.m.–9 p.m.* NO CREDIT CARDS; BEER AND WINE.

El Palenque's food is not New Mexican but Mexican—from the north and fiery hot. In fact, the Holguins swear their green chile sauce (made with jalapeños) is *levanta muertos* (enough to raise the dead). Try the *barbacoa* and be brave—try the *buche* (lips). The Tacos al Pastor are good, too, and are served with three sauces.

EL PATIO

142 Harvard SE (505-268-4245). *Open Monday–Saturday, 11 a.m.– 9:30 p.m.; Sunday, 2 p.m.–8 p.m.* VISA, MC; BEER AND WINE.

The patio is nice in the summer at this small, quaint New Mexican place near the university. David and Gloria Sandoval have fashioned a great, understated restaurant with modest prices. Chef Tom Baca refuses to compromise on the heat of his chile and often fends off complaints about it being too hot by shrugging and saying, "There're other restaurants around." Try the Green Chile Chicken Enchiladas, the Blue

Corn Red Enchiladas, or the Chiles Rellenos. El Patio is, in our opinion, the best New Mexican restaurant in Albuquerque.

PETE'S CAFE

105 N. 1st Street, Belen (505-864-4811). *Open Monday–Thursday, 11 a.m.–8 p.m.; Friday and Saturday, 11 a.m.–8:30 p.m.* VISA, MC; BEER AND WINE.

This is the place for chiles in Belen, south of Albuquerque. Pete's is renowned for its red and green sauces, as well as its other New Mexican specialties. The *sopaipillas* and *natillas* are particularly good. Their sauces can also be purchased for takeout.

THE MEANING OF "MEXICAN"

Albuquerque has nearly 100 Mexican restaurants listed in the Yellow Pages, and all but three serve *New Mexican* rather than Mexican meals. The locals make that distinction to avoid being accused of serving the American Mexican food found in, say, Baltimore.

It's interesting to note that national restaurant chains specializing in Mexican food have not fared well in Albuquerque. Both Chi Chi's and Garcia's of Scottsdale failed in the city because their versions of Mexican were too bland for local palates. The only chain that has flourished is Taco Bell, but its success is the result of fast, cheap food rather than great Mexican cuisine.

And the two or three restaurants that do serve Mexican food in Albuquerque? Ah, they're called *Mexico* Mexican, to distinguish them from, say, Maryland Mexican. El Palenque and El Norteño serve authentic northern Mexican specialties.

THE QUARTERS

905 Yale SE (505-843-7505). *Open Monday–Saturday,*
11 a.m.–3 p.m. and 5 p.m.–9 p.m. MAJOR CREDIT CARDS;
LIQUOR LICENSE.

Since co-author DeWitt has eaten lunch here about 1,000 times (once a week for twenty years will do it!), it has been adequately tested. The Quarters is famed for its barbecue, but the size and quality of the numerous sandwiches, combined with a policy of liberal pouring at the bar, are what keep people pouring in. This is probably the best all-around lunch place in the city.

RESTAURANT ANDRÉ

1100 San Mateo NE (505-268-5354). *Open Monday–Satur-*
day, 11:30 a.m.–2:30 p.m. and 5:30 p.m.–9 p.m.; Sunday,
10 a.m.–2 p.m. and 5 p.m.–9 p.m. MAJOR CREDIT CARDS;
LIQUOR LICENSE.

Chef André loves to hunt and fish, so expect to see plenty of game and fish on the menu, in addition to his New Southwest items, like a mixed grill. Experimentation is key here, and innovations crop up constantly. Try the Tuna Scallopine with Red Hot and Sour Cabbage or the Calamari with Three Dipping Sauces. The desserts are always great, and the Sunday brunch is outstanding.

RIO GRANDE CANTINA

1100 Rio Grande Blvd. NW (505-242-1777). *Open daily,*
11:30 a.m.–2 a.m. MAJOR CREDIT CARDS; LIQUOR LICENSE.

Brothers Kenny and Arthur Walker are the only restaurateurs in New Mexico who grow their own chiles for their restaurant. Three acres produce enough chiles for one year, Arthur tells us. We love to sit out on the patio under the Russian olive tree, munching on chips and their great pico de gallo salsa (winner of people's choice for best fresh salsa at the National Fiery Foods Show). Try any New Mexican specialty here, or the Little Ricky Burger if you want an interesting burger. Their Sopa de Lima is so good we stole the recipe for you.

ROBB'S RIBBS

2412 San Mateo Place NE (505-884-7422). *Open Tuesday– Friday, 11 a.m.–2 p.m. and 4:30 p.m.–8 p.m.; Saturday, 11 a.m.–8 p.m.* NO CREDIT CARDS; NO LIQUOR EXCEPT MAYBE IN SOME OF THE SAUCES.

Barbecue master Robb Richmond is also the manufacturer of the consistent people's choice barbecue sauce winner in the National Fiery Foods Show. He also makes a fiery Habanero BBQ sauce. At Robb's unassuming strip-center restaurant, try his ribs, his brisket, and his side dishes, such as Green Chile Cheese Corn Puddin', and his Bread Puddin' with Whiskey Sauce. His barbecue sauce is available in jars.

8-4 The Legendary Henry Clopton, BBQ Guru of New Mexico (*Credit:* Chel Beeson)

SADIE'S

6132 4th NW (505-345-5339). *Open Monday–Friday,*
11 a.m.–10 p.m.; Saturday, noon–10 p.m.; Sunday, noon–
9 p.m. VISA, MC; LIQUOR LICENSE.

Originally atop a bowling alley, Sadie's has its own place now,
and it's a good one. This family-owned and family-run restaurant makes a full selection of powerful and tasty New Mexican
favorites like enchiladas. Nothing new here, but it's all great.

Recipes

NEW MEXICO CARNE ADOVADA

This simple but tasty dish evolved from the need to preserve meat
without refrigeration, since chiles act as an antioxidant and prevent the meat from spoiling. It is a common restaurant entree in
New Mexico.

> 1½ **cups crushed dried red New Mexican chiles, seeds**
>   **included**
> 4 **cloves garlic, minced**
> 3 **teaspoons dried oregano**
> 3 **cups water**
> 2 **pounds pork, cut in strips or cubed**
>
> Combine the chiles, garlic, oregano, and water and mix well
> to make a caribe sauce.
>   Place the pork in a glass pan and cover with the sauce.
> Marinate overnight in the refrigerator.
>   Bake in a 300° oven for a couple of hours or until the
> pork is very tender and starts to fall apart.
>
> SERVES: 6
> HEAT SCALE: HOT
> SERVING SUGGESTIONS: Fill a flour tortilla with *carne ado-*
> *vada* to make a burrito, use as a stuffing for *sopaipillas,* or
> use as filling for enchiladas. If quartered potatoes are add-
> ed during the last hour of baking, the dish becomes a stew.

Grilled Marinated Chicken Breasts with Roasted Poblano-Piñon Salsa

Rosa Rajkovic, executive chef at the Monte Vista Fire Station, prepared this recipe at the 1992 National Fiery Foods Show. The foodies who tasted it were delighted with the intriguing blend of fresh, spicy flavors.

8 chicken breasts, boned and skinned

Fresh Herb Marinade

- 1 cup canola oil
- ¼ cup champagne wine vinegar
- 3 tablespoons fresh lemon juice
- 2 tablespoons Dijon mustard
- 2 tablespoons chopped fresh parsley
- 1 tablespoon chopped fresh basil
- 1 tablespoon chopped fresh marjoram
- 1 tablespoon chopped fresh chives
- 1 tablespoon chopped fresh tarragon
- 1 tablespoon chopped fresh oregano
- ¼ teaspoon salt
- ⅛ teaspoon freshly ground black pepper

Combine all ingredients and mix well. Marinate the chicken breasts for at least 4 hours, preferably longer. Grill the breasts over an aromatic wood such as mesquite or pecan and serve them topped with the salsa.

Roasted Poblano-Piñon Salsa

- 6 poblano chiles, roasted, peeled, seeds and stems removed, chopped
- 1 eggplant, peeled, sliced lengthwise, salted and blotted, then baked and chopped
- 4 tomatoes, peeled, cored, seeded, and chopped
- ½ cup roasted piñon nuts

¼ **cup virgin olive oil**
2 **tablespoons balsamic vinegar**
3 **tablespoons fresh lime juice**
3 **scallions, chopped**
3 **tablespoons cilantro, chopped**
2 **cloves garlic, chopped**
  Salt to taste

Combine all ingredients and allow to sit at room temperature for at least 1 hour to blend the flavors.

SERVES: **8**
HEAT SCALE: MILD

HONEY-DRENCHED SMOKED TURKEY BREAST WITH RAINBOW CHILE-MANGO SALSA

This is one of our favorite summer dishes. The turkey breast should be smoked with either hickory or pecan wood. Do not use mesquite because the flavor is too intense for smoking.

Turkey

1 **cup honey**
½ **cup soy sauce**
1 **turkey breast**

Combine the honey and soy sauce to make a basting sauce. Drench the breast with a thin coating of sauce.

Place the breast on a cookie sheet in the smoker and smoke with indirect smoke for 4 to 5 hours, depending on the size of the breast and the heat of the smoke. Continue basting as the breast smokes. The skin on the breast will turn dark brown, almost black, and should be removed before carving.

Rainbow Salsa

2 **red jalapeño chiles, chopped fine**
2 **green serrano chiles, chopped fine**

2 **yellow wax hot chiles, chopped fine**
1 **red onion, diced**
2 **tomatoes, cored and diced**
1 **mango, peeled and pitted**
2 **tablespoons cooking oil**
1 **tablespoon vinegar**
Fresh cilantro leaves for garnish

Combine the first five ingredients in a bowl. Puree the mango with the oil and vinegar in a blender, then add it to the other ingredients. Mix well.

To serve, spoon some of the salsa on top of a slice of smoked turkey breast and garnish with cilantro leaves.

SERVES: **12 OR MORE**
HEAT SCALE: **MEDIUM**

CANTINA SOPA DE LIMA

The motto of the Rio Grande Cantina, a popular watering hole and lunch spot near Old Town, is *"Salud Amor y Pesetas y Tiempo Para Disfrutarlas,"* which translates loosely as "To Health, Love and Money and the Time to Enjoy Them." This spirited soup is one of the Cantina's enjoyable signature items.

1 **green New Mexican chile, roasted, peeled, seeds and stem removed, chopped**
⅓ **cup chopped onions**
2 **teaspoons vegetable oil**
4 **cups chicken broth**
1 **cup shredded chicken**
Salt to taste
1 **tomato, chopped**
1 **freshly squeezed lime**
4 **large lime slices for garnish**
16 **tortilla chips for garnish**

Sauté the chile and onion in the oil until the onion is soft but not browned. Add the chicken broth, chicken, and salt; cover and simmer 20 minutes. Add the tomato and simmer

8-5 They Do Things Differently at the K & I Diner (*Credit:* Chel Beeson)

5 minutes longer. Stir in the lime juice, taste, and add more if needed. Serve in bowls garnished with 1 lime slice and 4 tortilla chips.

SERVES: **4**
HEAT SCALE: **MILD**

NATILLAS

This pudding is a wonderful end to a traditional New Mexican meal. The consistency should be that of a soft custard, and it can be served either warm or cold.

¾ **cup sugar**
2 **tablespoons flour**
½ **teaspoon salt**
2 **eggs, separated**
2 **cups milk**
½ **teaspoon vanilla**
  Ground cinnamon

Combine the sugar, flour, and salt. Beat together the egg yolks and 2 tablespoons of the milk. Add to the sugar mixture and beat until well combined.

Bring the remaining milk to just below boiling, or scald the milk. Add the egg yolk and sugar mixture, stirring constantly. Reduce the heat and simmer for 10 minutes, being sure to stir constantly until it has the consistency of a thick custard sauce.

Remove from the heat, allow to cool, and stir in the vanilla.

Beat the egg whites until stiff.

Fold the custard mixture into the beaten egg whites. Sprinkle with the ground cinnamon and let sit for 30 minutes.

Refrigerate or serve warm.

SERVES: **4 TO 6**

—NANCY GERLACH

CHAPTER

---◆◆---

9

SANTA FE AND NORTHERN NEW MEXICO

S anta Fe lays claim to having the oldest house in America, which is only the tip of the iceberg of other declarations of ancient status. Its lengthy history has led to many claims of antiquity for buildings, such as the oldest mission church in the United States. Santa Fe itself is often referred to as the oldest continually occupied city in the United States, the oldest seat of government in the United States, and sometimes simply the oldest city.

Sorry folks, it's just not that old; 400 years is simply a tick of a clock when compared to, say, the 6,000 years that have elapsed since the city of Sumer was established on the site of Babylon. Juan de Oñate established the first Spanish settlement in this region in 1598, and Santa Fe was made the capital of the frontier of New Mexico in 1610, forty-five years after St. Augustine, Florida, was settled. But such facts do not qualify either city for the title of the oldest.

Since Santa Fe rests upon the ruins of an ancient pueblo, the title of Oldest City in the United States must go to an Indian settlement rather than a Spanish town. In reality, Santa Fe is the second-oldest city *founded by Europeans* in this country. No one knows for certain which Indian ruin is the most ancient, but the consensus seems to be that Acoma Pueblo is the oldest continually occupied settlement in the Southwest, dating to about A.D. 1000, or 600 years before Santa Fe.

A Food Mecca for Centuries

The Spaniards who first settled Santa Fe brought with them the necessary livestock to grow herds of cattle, sheep, and horses, and the seeds to plant the crops they needed. Since Santa Fe was the terminus of the 1,500-mile Camino Real from Mexico City, it became a trading center and both the beginning and end for the caravans of wagons that traveled along the Royal Road. The wagons unloaded in the Plaza in Santa Fe, and vigorous trading was done in foodstuffs.

Another town that became a trading mecca was Taos. During the early 1700s, the village became one of the most important trade centers in New Spain by holding what became known as the Taos Trade Fairs. And during the early 1800s, Taos was headquarters for many of the famous mountain men who trapped beaver and other fur-bearing animals in the surrounding mountains. The town became one of the most important markets for beaver pelts in North America, and where there's trading, there's food.

Interestingly enough, most of the food was of New World origin—namely, corn, beans, and squash. Wheat adapted well to the high valleys of Taos and Peñasco, but not to the lower elevations. Barley was used primarily for feeding livestock. Historian Marc Simmons commented about the early Spanish agriculture: "Other field crops included the *frijol* bean, horsebean, peas, squashes and pumpkins, melons, chile, tobacco, and cotton. Only a limited variety of garden vegetables seem to have been cultivated in the later Colonial period. Onions and garlic were regarded as staples in the diet, but other things, such as cucumbers, lettuce, beets, and the small husk-tomato, are mentioned in the documents only rarely. The potato was practically unknown."

The establishment of the Santa Fe Trail from Missouri in the 1820s and contact with Americans led to even more trading (which was prohibited by Spain, necessitating smuggling). Soon, Santa Fe was the terminus of *two* major trade routes. After it fell to the Americans in 1846, Santa Fe really opened up.

By then, champagne and oysters were available, and flour for making bread sold for $2.50 per *fanega* (144 pounds). About this time, Lt. James Abert was traveling extensively throughout New Mexico. Later, in his book, *Through the Country of the Comanche Indians*, he described the market at Santa Fe: "The markets have . . . great quantities of 'Chile Colorado' and 'verde,' 'cebollas' or onions, 'sandias' or watermellons, 'huevos' or eggs, 'uvas' or grapes, and 'piñones,' nuts of the pine tree."

Prices were relatively high. Corn was $2 a bushel; beef and mutton, 8 to 10 cents a pound; sugar and coffee, 25 cents a pound; and tea was very expensive at $1.25 a pound. About this time, W. W. H. Davis traveled to Santa Fe and sampled the native cuisine. In *El Gringo*, he described his encounter: "The meal was a true Mexican dinner, and a fair sample of the style of living among the better class of people. The advance guard in the course of the dishes was boiled mutton and beans, the meat being young and tender, and well flavored. These were followed by a *sui generis* soup, different from any thing of the kind it had been my fortune to meet with before. It was filled with floating balls about the size of a musket bullet, which appeared to be a compound of flour and meat. Next came mutton stewed in *chile* (red peppers), the dressing of which was about the color of blood, and almost as hot as so much molten lead."

After mentioning the *albóndigas* soup and the mutton, Davis described the standard beans, tortillas, and *atole*, and then commented on chile: "Besides those already enumerated, there are other dishes, some of which have come down from the ancient inhabitants of the country. The *chile* they use in various ways— green, or *verde*, and in its dried state, the former being made into a sort of salad, and is esteemed to be a great luxury."

Santa Fe survived the Civil War without a scratch and did well under U.S. control. Hotels and restaurants flourished with the coming of the railroad in the early 1880s, but they had to put up with unprecedented lawlessness. As historian Warren Beck noted: "During the period following the Civil War and lasting approximately until the turn of the century, New Mexico experienced a wave of rampant lawlessness unparalleled in the history of the United States. It was an era when stealing, killing, and lynching were so common as to be hardly worthy of mention in the press. . . . Other parts of the nation had experienced a breakdown in law and order, but in few areas had it lasted or been as complete as it was in the territory of New Mexico."

Reasons for the wave of lawlessness included New Mexico's reputation for being a land of great treasures; its remoteness, which tended to attract criminals on the run; and the federal government in Washington, which regarded the territory as an outpost in a wilderness and virtually ignored the needs of its citizens.

During the years immediately following the Civil War, Santa Fe witnessed a dazzling diversity of crime: the death of a judge in a gunfight, the theft of government funds, the mass murder of nine innocent travelers, and a colossal diamond hoax.

During the years following World War I, Santa Fe began to emerge from obscurity as the city—and the rest of the state—was discovered by artists such as Peter Hurd and Georgia O'Keeffe; authors such as Willa Cather and D. H. Lawrence; as well as prominent sculptors, poets, photographers, and musicians. The high concentration of artists in the city, combined with Santa Fe's tradition as an Indian trading center, produced one of the top art sales markets in the world. More than 150 art galleries, concentrated principally around the Plaza and along Canyon Road, now feature local as well as international artists, and special events such as Indian Market in mid-August ensure that the ancient artistic traditions are kept alive.

Historic Sightseeing

Within walking distance of the Plaza, there's a lot of history to see. Don't miss the Loretto Chapel at 219 Old Santa Fe Trail and its supposedly miraculous staircase. Santa Fe's most famous church is St. Francis Cathedral, at San Francisco Street and Cathedral Place. Construction was begun by Santa Fe's first archbishop, Frenchman Jean-Baptiste Lamy in 1869, who is buried beneath the altar. Santuario de Guadalupe, located at Guadalupe and Agua Fria streets, features displays of Spanish colonial art and religious artifacts, including a large painting of Our Lady of Guadalupe, patron saint of Mexico.

One of the oldest mission churches in the United States, San Miguel Chapel, at Old Santa Fe Trail and De Vargas Street, was totally rebuilt (including new foundations and walls) after it was burned to the ground during the Pueblo Revolt. So to say this building is the oldest church is a fallacy akin to claiming one has Abe Lincoln's original axe, except for three new handles and four new heads.

Behind San Miguel Chapel is a privately owned gift shop that proclaims itself the oldest house in the United States. This claim is totally unsubstantiated because the structure was built in 1740

9-1 The Inn of the Anasazi, Just off the Plaza

on the site of an Indian pueblo dating back to 1250. As indicated above, such claims are arbitrary, and people making them should visit Acoma Pueblo.

Called the Roundhouse by locals, the State Capitol (Paseo de Peralta and Old Santa Fe Trail) was built in 1966 in the shape of the Zia symbol, the New Mexico state insignia. Built in 1610, the Palace of the Governors on the Plaza was originally part of the royal *presidio* of Don Pedro de Peralta, the first colonial governor of New Mexico. It served as the residence and offices of succeeding Spanish, Mexican, and U.S. governors.

Located just off the Plaza at Palace Avenue and Lincoln Street, the Museum of Fine Arts houses a permanent collection of more than 8,000 works of regional art. Other great collections are housed at the Laboratory of Anthropology and the Museum of Indian Arts and Culture, located in the Camino Lejo museum complex (south of town off Old Santa Fe Trail), which also includes the Museum of International Folk Art and the Wheelwright Museum. The Museum of International Folk Art has collected more than 120,000 objects from 100 countries.

For more information about Santa Fe, contact the Santa Fe Convention and Visitors Bureau, P.O. Box 909, Santa Fe, NM 87504 (505-984-6760).

The Restaurant Scene

People used to joke that Santa Fe was the only city in the United States with more art galleries than gas stations. Well, there are now more restaurants than galleries! The tradition of great restaurants in Santa Fe was born forty-five years ago when Rosalea Murphy opened The Pink Adobe. As Rosalea recalls, when "the Pink" first opened, Santa Fe was not the tourist mecca it is today, but rather a "lazy, sleepy town." She served 25-cent Pink Dobeburgers, imported chicken enchiladas from Mexico, and eventually became the first chef in Santa Fe to serve seafood. Rosalea never bothered to obtain a liquor license until 1972, when she realized visitors expected fine restaurants to serve mixed drinks.

Today the restaurant is located in a 300-year-old former barracks for Spanish soldiers, Barrio de Analco, one of the oldest parts of Santa Fe. Despite its name, the Pink Adobe is no longer pink but a shade of sandstone. Santa Fe's Historical Design Review Board has refused to allow the restaurant to be painted its original color because, according to the board, pink is not an earth tone. During a hearing on the issue, Rosalea presented several samples of pink rocks collected in the desert and mountains around Santa Fe, but the board still refused permission for her to paint the Pink Adobe pink.

The Dragon Room bar of the Pink was named one of the nineteen best bars in the world by *Newsweek International* in 1986, perhaps because the Pink is *the* hangout for visiting celebrities. Such notables as John Erlichman, Robert Redford, Cher, and Vincent Price often frequented the Pink. In 1981, Paul Newman wandered into the Pink but, according to Rosalea, "No one recognized him, and I think he was upset because we didn't make a fuss over him. One thing you get here is privacy and, besides, we didn't really know him." Such indifference to celebrities is one aspect of an attitude called Santa Fe blasé. The owner of a gallery close to the Pink Adobe once sold a work of art to *Star Trek* actor Leonard Nimoy and, after examining the name and address on the check, remarked: "Nimoy, huh? I knew some Nimoys back in Cleveland."

An Alternative Guide to the City Different

Santa Fe too tame for you? Well, Pancho Epstein's *Santa Fe Olé!* is subtitled *A Guide to the Real Santa Fe*, but actually is a droll, fantasy-induced tour guide to the City Different. Included in his listings are the following imaginary foodie haunts:

Anasazi Brewery.   Established in A.D. 1275, it is the oldest continuously operating brewery in the world. According to Pancho, "These created-in-Santa Fe beers contain the highest alcoholic content of any brew in the world and produce an hallucinogenic effect."

Dyed Blue Corn Meal Manufacturing Company.   Developed by the same people who brought you the atomic bomb, Los Alamos National Laboratories, this blue corn meal "has the exact formula of color, texture, and taste to deceive out-of-state visitors, and the blue corn tortilla has its normal moldy look that so appeals to travelers."

Anglo Herb Store and Food Market. "The owners sell only the highest quality artificially produced and preserved health products manufactured in America. The pharmacy's catchy motto is, 'If you've got a symptom, we've got a drug.'"

continued

Armida's Vegetarian Bountiful Barbecue.
"This is the only vegetarian restaurant in the world that barbecues all its food. From all-vegetable fajitas to flan, everything has that wonderful mesquite flavor at Armida's. This is one of the real 'in' places for Santa Fe's holistic new-age crowd."

For more of Pancho Epstein, contact Southern Rockies Publishing Company, 2074 Calle Contento, Ste. 1002, Santa Fe, NM 87505.

Rosalea has become a celebrity herself because of the Pink Adobe. She has appeared on the PBS series "Great Chefs of the West," and her cookbook, *The Pink Adobe Cookbook,* has received excellent reviews. In it, Rosalea reveals all her culinary secrets—including the recipe for Steak Dunigan—but is not worried about losing any restaurant business to people cooking her recipes at home.

There are more fine restaurants per capita in Santa Fe than probably anywhere else in the United States. As is true of New Mexico in general, people living in and visiting the "City Different" love their food spicy hot. In fact, a study done by *Chile Pepper* magazine a few years ago determined that Santa Fe is the fiery food capital of the country, based on the number of Mexican restaurants compared to the population. (Incidentally, Las Cruces was second, Austin third, San Antonio fifth, El Paso sixth, Albuquerque tenth, and Tucson twelfth; of all the cities in this book, only Phoenix didn't place in the top fifteen.)

Despite the heat of Santa Fe food, visitors should note that there is a wide variety of cuisines available to sample because Santa Fe attracts great culinary artists as well as great visual artists. Since Santa Fe restaurants usually are crowded, especially during the summer, calling in advance for hours and reservations is suggested.

Within a few of blocks of the Plaza in Santa Fe, foodies can indulge every gastronomic whim imaginable. Want to buy the hottest salsa known to man? Like some to-die-for blue corn enchiladas with killer red chiles? Care to taste some New Mexican wines? Need a *ristra* for your front porch? How about some cast bronze chile pulls for your kitchen cabinets? It's all here in Santa Fe, but be forewarned: Before trying the restaurants, you should learn about some of the dining rituals first.

How to Order Enchiladas in Santa Fe

Picture this: You're sitting in a typical New Mexican restaurant in Santa Fe, there are red *ristras* on the wall, the smell of roasting chiles is in the air, and the traditional melody of "I Shot the Sheriff" by Bob Marley is blasting from the speakers. You have that eerie sensation of *veja du*—the feeling that you've never been here before in your entire life!

Your waitress is dressed in granola-girl style—complete with sandals and beaded headband—and professes to be, actually, a native crafts and crystal artist who is just waitressing until her artwork is picked up by enough galleries. She has a bad case of Santa Fe blasé, and unless you have your own show on network TV or paint endless variations on chubby Navajo women examining their big toes, you're nobody, Buster. In fact, she figures you for a gringo tourist from the East who's going to (naturally) *attempt* to order the enchiladas. Trouble is, she's right. It's time to play the Santa Fe Enchilada-Ordering Ordeal.

"I'd like the enchiladas, please," you state confidently, not realizing you're about to be given the third degree with the same intensity the Commies used on Frank Sinatra in *The Manchurian Candidate*.

"Red or green?" she snaps. She's not asking about your living room decor, but rather the type of chile sauce you want. To avoid seeming like a gringo tourist from Back East, you counter with a question of your own.

"Which is hotter?"

"Green," she grunts.

"I'll take it," you reply—and foolishly relax.

"Blue or regular?" she asks fiendishly. She's not inquiring about your mood, but rather your preference for either blue or yellow (regular) corn tortillas. Since you frequent trendy New Southwest restaurants Back East, you reply,

"Blue."

"Stacked or rolled?" is her next baffling question. She's asking whether you want your tortillas stacked, with the filling in between, or individually rolled with the filling inside. You haven't a clue as to which one is tastier, but you remember Sophia Loren's Mexican blouse when she was ordering enchiladas at the cafe in *Pancho Villa Rides Again* and you answer,

"Stacked."

Then she grills you about the filling: "Beef or chicken?" At last, you think, the questions are getting easier.

"Beef!" you shout proudly, remembering how cute Cybill Shepherd looked when she was gobbling hamburgers on the National Beef Council TV spots, even though she said in a later interview that she avoided eating red meat. But then the waitress—whose name tag you now notice reads "Spirit Child"—asks a mystical question:

"Ground or shredded?"

Since you have a bona fide degree from a big shot college, you're smart enough to figure it out on your own that any old meat grinding machine can turn out ground beef, but it takes an authentic, certified New Mexican chef to hand-shred the stewed *machacha* beef for tacos or enchiladas. You answer:

"Shredded, what else?" with just a hint of sly mockery tinged with studied boredom in your voice. Despite your bravado, you're ill-prepared for the next question from waitress Spirit Child, which is tricky indeed.

"Egg?" she asks with fake innocence.

Panic sets in. If you answer yes, does that mean the chef will mix a couple of scrambled eggs with your shredded beef? If you answer no, are you violating some sacred Santa Fe enchilada-eating ritual? Never fear, the answer is easier than you think. The eggs are fried and should only be accepted with breakfast enchiladas—and, of course, to accompany Easter, Cinco de Mayo, or Mother's Day brunches. So your answer is a simple:

"No."

"Oven, microwave, or radiant heat process?" she asks, but you're not fooled a bit by this technical jargon. And besides, it's not your job to cook the damned enchiladas.

"Chef's choice," you reply loftily.

"*¿Cerveza?*" Her sudden shift to a foreign language momentarily confuses you. Then your steel-trap, instant-recall, database program-like mind accesses a language file, and your favorite four-letter word appears translated upon the screens of your retinas: BEER.

You dissolve into a pitiful abyss of depression as you realize you have absolutely no idea whatsoever what beer is *de rigueur* in Santa Fe. But your Back-East instincts hold true, and you bail yourself out by demanding:

"Have the maitre d' send the beer steward with a list."

Defeated, the waitress slinks off to fling your order at the chef. The beer steward appears from nowhere and reads from a scroll: "To accompany your green-blue-stacked-shredded beef-no egg-chef's choice enchiladas," he pronounces, "may I suggest a presumptuous but titillating Tusker imported from Kenya, a more full-bodied Xingu, the Black Beer from the Amazon, or maybe a Mamba?"

"On tap?" you demand haughtily.

"Uh, sorry, Señor, but only in bottles," apologizes the embarrassed steward.

"It's okay this time," you sneer. "Bring me a Santa Fe Pale Ale—and don't let it happen again."

Congratulations. You have passed the Santa Fe Enchilada-Ordering Ordeal. Now you will be allowed to buy T-shirts emblazoned with cartoon coyotes wearing neckerchiefs.

A Living Museum

EL RANCHO DE LAS GOLONDRINAS

Off I-25 at exit 271, 15 miles south of Santa Fe (505-471-2261). *Open Wednesday–Sunday, 10 a.m.–4 p.m.*
(June, July, and August). Call for tour times, festival dates, and other information.

El Rancho de las Golondrinas (Ranch of the Swallows) was the last stopping place along the Camino Real between Mexico City and Santa Fe. Imagine a small colonial village restored to the way it was during the seventeenth and eighteenth centuries—with a chapel, shepherd's kitchen, *torreon* (defensive tower), weaving rooms, and village store. Then

9-2 Mark Miller Instructs at the Santa Fe Chile and Wine Fiesta

imagine this village as a living museum, complete with volunteers dressed in authentic costumes who demonstrate weaving, spinning, threshing, farming, and blacksmithing.

The museum features special Spring, Summer, and Harvest Festivals during the first weekends of June, August, and October, when Spanish folk dances with traditional music are performed. Open houses are held the first Sundays in July, August, and September, when visitors may take self-guided tours. The museum is closed from November through March.

Cooking Schools

SANTA FE COMMUNITY COLLEGE

P.O. Box 8741, Santa Fe, NM 87504 (505-438-1363). NO CREDIT CARDS; NO LIQUOR.

On Saturdays during the summer, chef and culinary arts director Bill Weiland teaches visitors how to prepare the corn and chile cuisine of northern New Mexico. The fees are reasonable, and potential cooks can write for a free catalog of summer cooking classes.

SANTA FE SCHOOL OF COOKING

116 West San Francisco (upper level) (505-983-4511). *Open daily, 9:30 a.m.–5:30 p.m. (winter); 9:30 a.m.–6 p.m. (summer).* VISA, MC; BEER AND WINE.

This combination cooking school and retail shop offers classes on traditional New Mexican food preparation conducted by guest chefs. The school also conducts culinary tours of northern New Mexico. Reservations for classes and tours are necessary. New Mexican specialty foods are featured in the retail shop.

Winery and Breweries

LA CHIRIPADA WINERY

Highway 76, off Highway 68 between Santa Fe and Taos, in Dixon (505-579-3337). *Open Monday–Saturday, 10 a.m.– 5 p.m.* VISA, MC; WINE SALES.

The "Lucky Break" winery produces about 3,000 cases a year of its Primavera White and Rio Embudo Red wines, which it sells by the case. A good time to visit the tasting room is during the Artist's Studio Tour, the first weekend in November. The winery is located in beautiful mountain country.

PRESTON BREWERY

Highway 68 in Embudo, between Santa Fe and Taos (505-852-4707). *Open Tuesday–Sunday, noon–8 p.m. (April to first weekend in November).* VISA, MC; BEER AND WINE.

A fascinating place that's an easy stop on the road between Santa Fe and Taos, this brew-pub-restaurant-smokehouse-gallery-craft store is justly famous for its green chile beer, which, according to owner/brewmaster Preston Cox, "has a green chile taste and a little afterburn." The brewery, overlooking the rushing Rio Grande, is located in a former railroad depot that's listed on the National Register of Historic Sites. The restaurant serves smoked and grilled meats, plus northern New Mexican specialties served inside or outside on the patio near the river. Brewery tours are permitted, but call ahead. Call about mail order for their smoked meats. They can also help schedule whitewater rafting trips during the spring.

Santa Fe Brewing

Flying M Ranch, Box 83, Galisteo (505-988-2340). Call for directions. *Open Monday–Friday, 9 a.m.–5 p.m.; Saturday, noon–4 p.m. (summer). Saturday tours available.* NO CREDIT CARDS; BEER AVAILABLE.

This brewery produces seven beers: wheat beer, pale ale, brown ale, Old Pojoaque Porter, fiesta ale, raspberry ale, and their never-to-be-forgotten Chicken Killer Barley Wine. It's best to call for their rather complicated schedules of tours, tastings, and lunches. The beers have won several awards, including Best of Show at the New Mexico State Fair and a bronze medal at the Great American Beer Festival in Denver.

Markets and Retail Shops

Note: Many of the gift shops around the Plaza carry food items, but it's not possible to list all of them. Our recommendations are limited to those establishments devoted to local food products.

Chile, Etc.

3472 Cerrillos Road (505-471-3749). *Open Monday–Saturday, 10 a.m.– 5 p.m.* VISA, MC; NO LIQUOR.

Looking for chile dishes and other New Mexican foods in every conceivable form? Here it is, including frozen green chiles, *ristras*, wreaths, salsas, and dozens of other products. It also carries Mexican chiles, Ecuadorian clothing, chile pottery and jewelry, and a wide selection of international hot sauces. Write for a mail-order catalog to P.O. Box 16274, Santa Fe, NM 87506.

THE CHILE SHOP

109 E. Water Street (505-983-6080). *Open Monday–
Saturday, 9:30 a.m.–5 p.m. (winter); Monday–Saturday,
9:30 a.m.–5:30 p.m. and Sunday, noon–4 p.m. (summer).*
VISA, MC; NO LIQUOR.

Founded in 1985, this was the first shop in the country devoted entirely to products made from the peerless pods. It's a
small shop, to be sure, but it's crammed with the very best
chile pepper food and non-food items, with an emphasis on
unique salsas and cookware. There is also a good selection of
books and cloth goods emblazoned with chiles. Call about
mail order.

COYOTE CAFE GENERAL STORE

132 W. Water Street (505-982-2454). *Open daily, 11 a.m.–
7 p.m. (winter); daily, 11 a.m.–9 p.m. (summer).* MAJOR
CREDIT CARDS; NO LIQUOR.

With a collection of 120 or more hot sauces and salsas, the
owners of this shop are making a statement about its stand
on hot and spicy—they love it! A bakery and deli offer cheeses,
breads, and fresh salsas. In addition to a complete line of
dried chile pods and powders, the Coyote has a huge collection
of Southwestern and chile pepper cookbooks, plus gift baskets, clothing, and unique pottery. Call about mail order.

THE FRUIT BASKET

Highway 68, between Santa Fe and Taos, in Velarde
(505-852-2310). *Open daily, 9 a.m.–4 p.m.* MAJOR CREDIT
CARDS; NO LIQUOR.

This roadside market has been serving travelers since the
early 1940s when the Velarde family established it to sell locally grown fruits and produce. During the chile season, the
Fruit Basket sells land races of chiles grown only in northern
New Mexico—and if you ask nicely they'll give you a tour of
their orchards and chile fields, but call the day before. *Ristras*
are available yearlong; garlic ropes, in October; and apples
and other fruits, in season.

JACKALOPE

2820 Cerrillos Road (505-471-8539). *Open (winter) Monday–
Saturday, 8:30 a.m.–5:30 p.m., and Sunday, 9:30 a.m.–
5 p.m.; (summer) Monday–Saturday, 8:30 a.m.–7 p.m., and
Sunday 9:30 a.m.–6 p.m.* MAJOR CREDIT CARDS; NO LIQUOR.

What a zoo—literally, because this unique place has its own
zoo-quality prairie dog village as well as an aviary. Ostensi-
bly, Jackalope is a two-and-one-half-acre pottery and folk art
store, with items from all over the world. Additionally, it sells
Santa Fe– and New Mexico–made food products such as cookies, jellies, salsas, and chiles. Try the frito pie in the small
cafe and enjoy the entertainment on the patio in the summer.
This is a fun place to visit for a "jackalopian experience," says
owner Darby McQuade. Its name refers to the legendary jackalope, part jack rabbit and part antelope, which occasionally
is spotted hopping across Cerrillos Road.

MONET'S KITCHEN

124 M Bent Street, Taos (505-758-8003). *Open daily,
10 a.m.–6 p.m.* MAJOR CREDIT CARDS; NO LIQUOR.

In addition to a strong collection of cookbooks, kitchenware,
and gadgets, Monet's offers a fine selection of hot and spicy
foods, much of it produced in New Mexico. It is one of the few
places where you can find locally harvested mushrooms.

SALMAN RANCH STORE

Highway 518, north of Las Vegas, in La Cueva (505-
387-2900). *Open daily, 9 a.m.–5 p.m. (August to October);
Monday–Saturday, 10 a.m.–4 p.m. (rest of the year).*
VISA, MC; NO LIQUOR.

If you like raspberries, a visit to Salman is worth a trip to
the country. There're twenty acres of them here in the late
summer and fall on a ranch so scenic it's on the National
Register of Historic Sites. The Salman family makes their
own raspberry jams (20,000 jars in 1991) and vinegars, which
they sell with other New Mexican food products. If you'd like
to picnic, feel free to use the tables inside the livestock cor-

rals. The Salmans ship their jams and vinegars; call for mail order information.

SANTA FE AREA FARMERS' MARKET

Sanbusco Market parking lot, Guadalupe and Montezuma (505-471-4711). *Open Tuesday and Saturday, 7 a.m.– 11:30 a.m. (summer and fall).* NO CREDIT CARDS; NO LIQUOR.

Growers and food manufacturers come out in full force during the summer and fall. Virtually every northern New Mexico product is available for sale, which is a boon for tourists and locals alike. Although visitors are unlikely to take home 15 pounds of purple cabbage, they will enjoy the salsas, jams, jellies, and chiles.

SANTA FE SCHOOL OF COOKING.

See Cooking Schools section.

TAOS COOKERY

113 Bent Street, Taos (505-758-5435). *Open daily, 10 a.m.–5 p.m. (winter); daily, 10 a.m.–6 p.m. (summer).* MAJOR CREDIT CARDS; NO LIQUOR.

Shoppers will find an extensive collection of Southwestern foods here, including salsas, chile pastas, cookies, jams, and candy. General cooking supplies are available, as well as Steve Kilborn's exquisite pottery with chile motifs.

WILD OATS COMMUNITY MARKET

1090 S. St. Francis (505-983-5333) and 1708 Llano (505-473-4943). *Open daily, 8 a.m.–11 p.m.* VISA, MC; NO LIQUOR.

These environmentally conscious, full-service natural grocery stores have taken Santa Fe by storm—and for good reason. Their meats and produce are totally natural or organic and contain no preservatives or hormones. The markets have perhaps the finest collection of New Mexico–produced foods from local cottage industries, including a great selection of fresh and bottled salsas. A bakery and deli on the premises has great food items, so Wild Oats is the place to go if you're planning a vacation picnic. Tasting fairs and entertainment are usually held on weekends.

Santa Fe Restaurants

There are so many good restaurants in Santa Fe and northern New Mexico that space constraints make it impossible to list all of them. In addition to the ones we recommend, we suggest visitors pick up a copy of *New Mexico ñ la Carte*, which publishes complete menus and is available on local newsstands.

BLUE CORN CAFE

133 Water Street (505-984-1800). *Open daily, 11 a.m.– 11 p.m.* MAJOR CREDIT CARDS; LIQUOR LICENSE.

You have to love a restaurant that proclaims: "Not responsible for chile that's too hot" on its menu. This new eatery, with its painted floor and Santa Fe Modern decor, is quickly catching on with locals and tourists alike. Try the Galisteo Burrito, stuffed with beef, green chile, and Indian potatoes, or the Achiote-Grilled Chicken with Refried Black Beans. Other specialties include Blue Corn Posole and Grilled Corn and Chipotle Soup.

9-3 The Refurbished Train Station, Tomasita's

LA CASA SENA

125 E. Palace, in Sena Plaza (505-988-9232). *Open daily, 11:30 a.m.–3 p.m. and 5:30 p.m.–10 p.m.; cantina open daily, 5 p.m.–11 p.m.* MAJOR CREDIT CARDS; LIQUOR LICENSE.

La Casa Sena was built by Major José Sena in the late 1860s in the classic adobe style and is now on the National Register of Historic Sites. While it was Sena's residence, the hacienda hosted such notable guests as L. Bradford Prince, territorial governor from 1889 to 1893, and Col. Kit Carson of Taos. Its historic architecture, combined with extensive collections of Southwest, Indian, and Taos art, gives the restaurant an elegant yet warm ambience. La Casa Sena uses as many as seventeen varieties of chiles in its recipes—which is probably why it is a major sponsor of the Santa Fe Chile and Wine Fiesta, held each year in late September. The *Santa Fe New Mexican* described La Casa Sena as showing "luminescent signs of star quality" and, to Chef de Cuisine David Jones, that means a dedication to native heritage, local produce, and constant innovation. Interesting dishes from a recent menu included Filete Bistec, a mesquite-grilled filet of beef with a Hatch green chile and tree oyster mushroom sauce; and Corona del Cordero, a rack of fresh prime Rocky Mountain lamb marinated in red chile pesto, served with jalapeño jelly and red chile-piñon cream sauce.

THE COYOTE CAFE

132 W. Water Street (505-983-1615). *Open daily, 6 p.m.–9:30 p.m.; Saturday and Sunday, 11:30 a.m.–2 p.m.* MAJOR CREDIT CARDS; LIQUOR LICENSE.

The Coyote Cafe provides a truly unique dining experience because anthropologist-turned-executive-chef Mark Miller offers a different menu each day as he re-creates Southwestern and Latin American dishes that pre-date the arrival of the Europeans. It is difficult to suggest any particular menu item because the choices change so much, but the following are some samples from past menus: Barbecued Duck Crepas, layered corn crepes with roast duck, barbecue sauce, and corn chile relish; Red Chile Quail, fresh Texas bobwhite quail marinated in dried chiles and wild mushrooms; and Grilled Prime Ribeye, a pecan-grilled ribeye steak with roasted garlic and orange-chipotle butter. Incidentally, Mark has taken the Santa Fe restaurant scene by storm. Since relocating from Berkeley in late 1986, he has managed to make the Coyote the top-grossing single-establishment restaurant in the city. The Rooftop Cantina, open daily, 11:30 a.m.–9:30 p.m. (May to October) serves *tortas*, duck *quesadillas*, and Ensenada-style tacos.

E.K. MAS

319 S. Guadalupe (505-989-7121). *Open daily, 11:30 a.m.– 2 p.m. and 5:30 p.m.–9:30 p.m.* MAJOR CREDIT CARDS; BEER AND WINE.

The name is a pun on the Spanish phrase *y que mas*? ("and what more?"). Nothing more is the obvious answer at this modest restaurant with its innovative cuisine and international menu. While sipping one of fourteen wines offered by the glass, choose from delicacies like Wild Mushroom Strudel, Satay with Thai Peanut Sauce, Grilled Mahi-Mahi with Red Chile Cream, or Roast Duckling with Warm Apple Chutney. It's nice to dine on the patio during the summer.

INN OF THE ANASAZI

113 Washington Avenue (505-988-3030). *Open daily, 7 a.m.– 10:30 a.m., 11:30 a.m.–2:30 p.m., and 5:30 p.m.–10:00 p.m. (winter); dinner extended until 11 p.m. in the summer.* MAJOR CREDIT CARDS; LIQUOR LICENSE.

This elegant inn and restaurant, decorated in ancient Indian motifs, is reputedly the most expensive hotel in Santa Fe. Well, we can't speak for the rooms, but the food is worth it, with such offerings as Venison Chile with Aged Cheddar Quesadilla, Navajo Flatbread with Fire-Roasted Sweet Peppers, or Vegetable Empanadas with Yellow Mole. Guests may dine in the Library, the Wine Cellar (700 bottles on display), or in one of the private dining rooms. Over seventy-five wine selections are available by the glass.

THE OLD MEXICO GRILL

2434 Cerrillos Road (505-473-0338). *Open daily for lunch, 11:30 a.m.–3 p.m.; daily for dinner, 5 p.m.–9 p.m. (winter) and 5 p.m.–9:30 p.m. (summer).* MAJOR CREDIT CARDS; LIQUOR LICENSE.

This grill specializes in dishes from Old rather than New Mexico, such as Mole Poblano, Paella Mexicana, Tacos al Pastór, and Carne Asada à la Tampiqueña. Many specialties are grilled over mesquite wood or prepared on a French rotisserie. The *New York Times* noted: "The dishes are filled with flavor, light and vibrant." Everything is freshly prepared, and the restaurant can handle vegetarian requests.

PEPPERS RESTAURANT AND CANTINA

2239 Old Pecos Trail (505-984-2272). *Open Monday–Saturday, 11 a.m.–9:30 p.m. (winter); Monday–Saturday, 11 a.m.–10 p.m. (summer).* MAJOR CREDIT CARDS; LIQUOR LICENSE.

You'll find a nice ambience here, especially on the patio while watching the sun set over mesa and mountain and listening to mariachi music. The food isn't fancy, just the great, hearty dishes of the north. Try the Pecos Trail Plate, a New-Mex combo, with one of Peppers' margaritas; then progress to Margarita Pie for dessert.

THE PINK ADOBE

406 Old Santa Fe Trail (505-983-7712). *Open daily, 11:30 a.m.–2 p.m. and 5:30 p.m.–9:30 p.m.* MAJOR CREDIT CARDS; LIQUOR LICENSE.

The popular dinner menu, which rarely changes except for specials, offers an eclectic selection of complementary cuisines: French, Creole, Spanish, and, of course, New Mexican. The Enchilada Pink Adobe is a classic regional dish featuring blue corn tortillas, jack cheese, red chile meat sauce, pinto beans, and a guacamole salad. The Pink Adobe excels in combining the essence of this regional cuisine with unexpected ingredients. Its most popular dish is Steak Dunigan, a New York–cut sirloin smothered in mushrooms and green chile sauce. Other creative variations on New Mexican cuisine include Green Chile Risotto and Rolled Stuffed Breast of Veal New Mexican.

THE PLAZA CAFE

54 Lincoln Avenue (505-982-1664). *Open daily, 7 a.m.– 10 p.m.* VISA, MC; BEER AND WINE.

According to historian Orlando Romero, the Plaza is the oldest, continually operating restaurant in Santa Fe. Established in 1928 and conveniently located on the Plaza, it has a very casual atmosphere. The Razatos family serves an eclectic mix of American, New Mexican, and Greek specialties, including roast beef soft tacos, blue corn enchiladas, *moussaka*, and *gyros* sandwiches. Try the homemade fruit pies for dessert.

RANCHO ENCANTADO

Highway 22, north of Santa Fe, in Tesuque (505-982-3537). *Open daily, 7:30 a.m.–10 a.m., 11:30 a.m.–2 p.m., and 6 p.m.–9:30 p.m.* MAJOR CREDIT CARDS; LIQUOR LICENSE.

The food is as delightful as the environs at the "enchanted ranch" outside of Santa Fe. Chef Karen Woods recommends the Roasted Pepper Stuffed with New Mexico Goat Cheese for an appetizer, the Loin of Pork with Ancho Chile-Cherry Sauce and Apple-Pecan Fritters for an entree, and either the Fried Green Chile Ice Cream or the Red Chile Honey Piñon Tart for dessert. Whatever your desire (and there's a lot more, such as Grilled Honey-Glazed Rack of Lamb), it's wise to make reservations.

SANTACAFE

231 Washington Avenue (505-984-1788). *Open Monday–Thursday, 11:30 a.m.–2 p.m. and 6 p.m.–10 p.m.; Friday and Saturday, 5:30 p.m.–10:30 p.m.* VISA, MC; LIQUOR LICENSE.

The Southwest meets Asia at Santacafe, one of Santa Fe's toniest spots. Come to think of it, the Santacafe cookbook, *East Meets Southwest*, is available for sale at the restaurant. The menu changes seasonally, but some recent menu choices included Smoked Pheasant Spring Rolls with Four-Chile Dipping Sauce, Grilled Filet Mignon with Mole Verde Sauce, and

Oriental Duck Breast with Sweet and Sour Sauce. Recommended desserts are the Santa Cafe Brownie All-the-Way or the Three-Layer Chocolate Mousse Cake.

SANTA FE DELI

1501 Paseo de Peralta, in the Hotel Santa Fe (505-982-1200 ex. 6014). *Open daily, 7 a.m.–10 p.m.* MAJOR CREDIT CARDS; LIQUOR LICENSE.

One of the few delis with a happy hour and live entertainment, Santa Fe is a great cool-down spot after all that chile. It serves a good selection of fresh sandwiches, salads, and soups, plus assorted cakes for dessert.

TECOLOTE

1203 Cerrillos Road (505-988-1362). *Open Tuesday–Sunday, 7 a.m.–2 p.m.* MAJOR CREDIT CARDS; BEER AND WINE.

The "Owl" is *the* place for breakfast in Santa Fe. This eighty-two-seat restaurant has a comfortable, diner-like atmosphere. Try the Atole-Piñon Pancakes, a breakfast burrito in the morning, or a traditional northern New Mexican enchilada plate with *posole* in the afternoon. The Pork Chops Verde are smothered in green chiles and cheese and are highly recommended. "Good meals at reasonable prices" is the motto here. Works for us.

LA TERTULIA

416 Agua Fria (505-988-2769). *Open Tuesday–Sunday, 11:30 a.m.–2 p.m. and 5 p.m.–9:30 p.m.* MAJOR CREDIT CARDS; LIQUOR LICENSE.

"The Party" or "Gathering Place" is the turnaround name of this former convent that was part of the Guadalupe Mission Church complex. Beautifully restored now, it serves traditional northern New Mexican specialties, and, surprisingly, Spanish Paella with Chorizo, which is highly recommended. Great food served in a warm, relaxed atmosphere.

Rancho de Chimayó

When Florence Jaramillo first opened Rancho de Chimayó in 1965, everyone told her she was crazy to attempt to operate a fine restaurant twenty miles from Santa Fe and off the established tourist track. But Florence had a hunch that the combination of traditional Hispanic New Mexican cuisine, beautiful Chimayó Valley, and the sprawling Jaramillo hacienda which had belonged to her husband's grandparents, would make her restaurant unique.

She was right, but the struggle took over five years of hard work. In addition to limited financing, none of her food suppliers would deliver out of town, so Florence was forced to drive into Santa Fe to buy everything necessary for preparing and serving fine food. On one trip back to the rancho, she recalls, she was stopped for speeding by a state police officer who asked the usual question, "What's the hurry?" Florence got out of the car, opened the trunk, and showed the officer 300 pounds of fresh meat that would spoil if she didn't speed back to Chimayó. She got off with a warning, and the pork for the *carne adovada* made it safely into the kitchen.

In the early days, visitors from other parts of the country would ask, "Is it safe to drink the water?" and "Should we pay in pesos?" Florence would then patiently explain that New Mexico became a state in 1912 and readily accepts dollars. The most frequently asked question still is "Why is this chile so hot?" The

continued

answer to that one is easy. Rancho de Chimayó uses locally grown Chimayó chiles, which are more fiery than most New Mexico chiles, as indicated by their smaller pods. Hatch Valley chiles from the southern part of the state serve as a backup because local growers alone cannot meet the demand of the restaurant, which uses an astounding two to three *tons* of green chiles a year and about 1,000 pounds of red chiles, which weigh considerably less than the green because they are dried.

During the summer, Rancho de Chimayó opens its multiterraced patio, increasing the number of tables to 200 to accommodate the flood of diners. The restaurant serves an incredible *1,000* meals a day during its peak summer business, which usually revolves around a holiday such as Father's Day or the Fourth of July. Such a large volume requires a staff of 130, recruited mostly from Chimayó and nearby towns. Florence believes working at Rancho de Chimayó has helped educate the young people of the area to the cosmopolitan ways of the outside world. In fact, many of her employees paid their college expenses with salaries and tips earned at the restaurant.

TINY'S LOUNGE

1015 Pen Road Shopping Center, southeast corner of St. Francis and Cerrillos Road (505-983-9817). *Open Monday–Saturday, 10 a.m.–2 a.m.* MAJOR CREDIT CARDS; LIQUOR LICENSE.

Not the usual tourist hangout, this lounge is strictly for locals and politicos, and the food is unspoiled by any concessions to outsiders. All of the New Mexican specialties are great; try the *flautas* and the fajitas. For dessert, the traditional *capirotada* can't be topped.

TOMASITA'S

500 S. Guadalupe Street (505-983-5721). *Open Monday– Saturday, 11 a.m.–10 p.m.* VISA, MC; LIQUOR LICENSE.

Lodged in a former train station, this New Mexican restaurant serves margaritas by the liter and hot red chile sauce by the gallon. Specialties are the *chiles rellenos* and the *carne adovada* (served on Friday) but the blue corn, red chile cheese enchiladas—the key comparison dish for New Mexican restaurants—are nothing short of superb. In our opinion, Tomasita's is the best New Mexican restaurant in Santa Fe.

Taos and Elsewhere Restaurants

APPLETREE RESTAURANT

123 Bent Street, Taos (505-758-1900). *Open Monday– Saturday, 11:30 a.m.–3 p.m.; daily, 5:30 p.m.–9 p.m.; Sunday, 10 a.m.–3 p.m. (brunch).* MAJOR CREDIT CARDS; BEER AND WINE.

From its Shrimp Quesadillas to the Chimayo Chicken to the Sun-Dried Tomato Pesto Pasta, the Appletree proves it is an eclectic, international restaurant. The menu changes seasonally, vegetarian entrees are available, and breads and pastries are sold at the bakery on the premises.

BENT STREET DELI AND CAFE

120 Bent Street, Taos (505-758-5787). *Open daily, 8 a.m.– 8 or 9 p.m.* VISA, MC; BEER AND WINE.

Have a bowl of green chile served with jalapeño corn muffins. Or how about The Taos—turkey, bacon, green chiles, and guacamole wrapped in a flour tortilla? For dinner, try the Margarita Shrimp—shrimp marinated in a margarita and then stir-fried with mandarin oranges and scallions. This deli is innovative and fun.

CAFE ABIQUIU

Highway 84 at the Abiquiu Inn, Abiquiu (505-685-4378). *Open (winter) daily, 5 p.m.–9 p.m.; Saturday and Sunday, 8 a.m.–2 p.m.; (summer) daily, 8 a.m.–2 p.m. and 3 p.m.– 9 p.m.* MAJOR CREDIT CARDS; NO LIQUOR LICENSE.

If you're heading north from Santa Fe to the scenic beauty of Georgia O'Keeffe country in the winter, be sure to call ahead for reservations. This interesting cafe combines Middle Eastern and Southwestern specialties, and the combination works. The kabobs are good, as are the red or green chile prime rib burritos, a house specialty. The hamburgers and salads are also recommended.

THE CHILE CONNECTION

Ski Valley Road, Taos (505-776-8787). *Open daily, 4 p.m.– 10 p.m. (winter); daily, 5:30 p.m.–10 p.m. (summer).* VISA, MC; LIQUOR LICENSE.

This great hangout, at mile marker No. 1 on the road from Taos to Ski Valley, not only has wonderful dishes devoted to chiles, but also the finest liquor selection in the state, including twenty single malt scotches and a Cognac collection so fine that a glass sells for $700! For food, in addition to the northern New Mexican red chile specialties, try the buffalo dishes, including buffalo fajitas or a mesquite-grilled buffalo steak.

DOC MARTIN'S

125 Paseo del Pueblo N., Taos (505-758-1977). *Open daily, 7 a.m.–2:30 p.m. and 5:30 p.m.–9:30 p.m.* MAJOR CREDIT CARDS; LIQUOR LICENSE.

Located in the historic Taos Inn, Doc Martin's has a great tradition of serving innovative food. Executive Chef Karen Lubliner oversees the creation of wonders such as Citrus-Ancho Glazed Snapper, Pork Tenderloin with Achiote Orange

Sauce and Garlic, and Breast of Chicken Sauteed with Anchos and Pasillas Sauced with Garlic Cream. It serves a *quesadilla* of the day (try the peppered salmon) and great desserts, too.

RANCHO DE CHIMAYÓ

Highway 520 in Chimayó (505-984-2100). Call for directions. *Open Tuesday–Sunday, 11:30 a.m.–9 p.m. (winter); daily, 11:30 a.m.–10 p.m. (May–September).*

There is nothing nouveau on the menu at Rancho de Chimayó, just the classic cuisine of northern New Mexico. The favorites are Carne Adovada, pork marinated in red chiles and served with *posole*; and Fajitas al Estilo Chimayó, beef marinated in chiles and wine, then grilled, sliced, and served with a spicy pico de gallo salsa. According to Florence Jaramillo, more and more of her customers are requesting vegetarian entrees, so she has removed the traditional lard from all her recipes and replaced it with high-quality vegetable oil. During the summer, dining outdoors on the huge patio is a delightful experience.

Recipes

POSOLE WITH CHILE CARIBE

This is the classic version of *posole* as prepared in northern New Mexico. Serving the chile caribe as a side dish instead of mixing it with the *posole* allows guests to adjust the heat to their own taste.

Posole

- **2 dried red New Mexican chiles, stems and seeds removed**
- **8 ounces frozen *posole* corn or dry *posole* corn, soaked in water overnight**

1 teaspoon garlic powder

1 medium onion, chopped

6 cups water

1 pound pork loin, cut in ½-inch cubes

Combine all the ingredients except the pork and boil at medium heat for about 3 hours or until the *posole* is tender, adding more water if necessary.

Add the pork and continue cooking for 30 minutes, or until the pork is tender but not falling apart. The result should resemble a soup more than a stew.

Chile Caribe

6 dried red New Mexican chiles, stems and seeds removed

2 quarts water

1 teaspoon garlic powder

Boil the chile pods in the water for 15 minutes. Remove the pods, combine with the garlic powder, and puree in a blender. Transfer to a serving bowl and allow to cool.

Note: For really hot chile caribe, add dried red chile piquins, cayenne chiles, or árbol chiles to the Anaheims.

Serve the *posole* in soup bowls accompanied by warm flour tortillas. Three additional bowls of garnishes should be provided: chile caribe, freshly minced cilantro, and freshly chopped onion. Each guest can then adjust the pungency of the *posole* according to individual taste.

SERVES: 4

HEAT SCALE: MEDIUM, BUT VARIES ACCORDING TO THE AMOUNT OF CHILE CARIBE ADDED.

Blue Corn Tamales with Spiced Goat Cheese

Tamales are very versatile and are no longer made with just traditional ingredients. For example, this recipe uses goat cheese, which is made everywhere in the Southwest.

Masa

1 package dried corn husks
  Water
2 cups blue corn masa
1 teaspoon salt
2 cups chicken broth
⅓ cup shortening

Filling

6 serrano chiles, stems removed, chopped
4 ounces goat cheese (or substitute feta cheese)
¼ cup onion, finely chopped
⅓ cup heavy cream
¼ cup fresh cilantro, chopped
¼ cup piñon nuts

Soak the corn husks in hot water for 15 to 30 minutes, or until they are soft and pliable.

Mix together the masa and salt. Slowly add the broth until the mixture holds together.

Whip or beat the shortening until fluffy. Add the masa to the shortening. Drop a teaspoonful of the dough into a glass

9-4 Enjoy the Sunset at Peppers

of cold water; if it floats, it is ready. If it sinks, continue to beat and test the mixture until it floats.

Combine all the filling ingredients.

To assemble, overlap a couple of the corn husks so they measure about 5 by 8 inches. Put 2 tablespoons of the masa in the center of the husk; pat or spread the dough thinly and evenly into a 2 by 3 rectangle.

Put about 2 teaspoons of filling down the center of the masa and fold the husk around the masa and filling; firmly tie each end of the tamale, being careful not to squeeze it.

Place a rack in the bottom of a steamer or large pot over a couple of inches of boiling water. Put the tamales on the rack and cover with additional husks or a towel to absorb the moisture. Bring the water to a boil and steam for 2½ hours or until done.

YIELD: **12 TO 18 TAMALES**
HEAT SCALE: **MILD**

—NANCY GERLACH

GRILLED MARINATED PORK TENDERLOIN WITH ROASTED CORN AND POBLANO CHILE RELISH

Pork Tenderloin

- 2 jalapeño chiles, stems and seeds removed, and chopped
- ½ cup sherry vinegar
- 1 cup olive oil
- 1 teaspoon garlic, chopped
- 1 teaspoon shallots, chopped
- 1 teaspoon cumin
- 1 teaspoon salt
- 4 8-ounce pork tenderloins, fat removed
  Roasted Corn and Poblano Chile Relish

9-5 A Confirmed Chilehead's Heaven

Combine the first seven ingredients in a bowl. Add the pork and marinate for 3 hours at room temperature.

Remove the pork from the marinade and grill or broil until just done. Slice the pork into medallions and fan out the pork medallions on individual serving plates.

Carefully spoon out the Roasted Corn and Poblano Chile Relish on the medallions so they are half covered.

Roasted Corn and Poblano Chile Relish

    1 **teaspoon vegetable oil**
    1 **red bell pepper**
    2 **poblano chiles, stems and seeds removed**
    2 **ears of corn, roasted and kernels cut off the cobs**
    3 **tablespoons shallots, finely chopped**
    3 **tablespoons garlic, finely chopped**
    1 **bunch cilantro, chopped**
1½ **cups olive oil**
  ½ **cup sherry vinegar**
      Salt and pepper to taste

Lightly brush the vegetable oil on the bell pepper and the *poblanos* and roast them over a gas flame until the skin is blackened. Peel off the skins, remove the seeds, and dice the chiles.

Combine the chiles with the rest of the ingredients, mix well, and allow to sit for at least 2 hours to blend the flavors.

SERVES: **4**
HEAT SCALE: MEDIUM

—COURTESY OF LA CASA SENA IN SANTA FE

PIÑON FLAN WITH CARAMEL SAUCE

Flan is a traditional Mexican custard dessert that has been adopted all over the Southwest. This version is flavored with another favorite Southwestern taste, that of piñon nuts.

- **2 cups sugar**
- **⅔ cup water**
- **3½ cups whole milk**
- **1 vanilla bean**
- **6 eggs**
- **1 teaspoon each ground cinnamon, nutmeg, ginger**
- **1 tablespoon dark rum (optional)**
- **1 cup whole shelled piñon nuts**

Put 1 cup sugar and the water in a heavy saucepan; stir over low heat until the sugar is dissolved. Increase the heat and boil until the mix is a light brown. Reduce the heat and simmer until the syrup is an amber color, swirling the pan occasionally to push any crystals back into the syrup. Allow to cool slightly and pour evenly into six warmed custard cups, coating the cups with the caramel sauce.

Scald the milk and vanilla bean. Remove from heat and allow to cool. Remove the vanilla bean.

Beat the eggs, spices, and rum until foamy. Whisk in the remaining 1 cup sugar and the piñons. Gradually add the milk, stirring until the sugar is dissolved.

Pour the mixture into the custard cups. Place the cups in a pan with enough hot water to come half-way up the sides of the cups.

Bake in a 350° oven for 60 to 70 minutes or until a thin knife inserted halfway between the center and the edge of the custard comes out clean.

To serve, run a thin knife around the outside of the cup and invert the custard onto a dish. The piñons should be on top. Let the custard sit at room temperature for 10 minutes to set before serving.

SERVES: **6**

PART
FOUR

ARIZONA

The spread was excellent in variety and style.... The sight of the little roasted porkers, chickens, and other fixings caused our bosom to swell and our heart to beat with emotion.

—NEWSPAPERMAN JOHN MARION,
DESCRIBING ONE OF THE FIRST THANKSGIVING
DAY DINNERS AT GOVERNOR A. P. K. SAFFORD'S
RESIDENCE IN PRESCOTT IN 1869

CHAPTER

10

DESERT DINING

Today, Arizona is a vibrant state with millions of residents, in addition to the many tourists who revel in the luxury of its resorts. But such growth was slow in coming. Arizona remained sparsely settled (as compared to New Mexico and Texas) until the arrival of cattlemen and miners during the mid-1800s. There was no Camino Real connecting the region with Mexico City and the rest of the interior, so settlement and trade from the south was slow in developing.

The first trickle of Spanish pioneers faced many hardships in what is now southern Arizona: the heat, lack of water, hostile Apaches, and a scarcity of what they considered to be proper food. But they didn't let a lack of larder bother them—they brought their own.

Domesticating the Desert

The Spanish had already settled New Mexico for a century before they undertook the taming of the Sonoran desert near what is now Tucson. It wasn't until 1700 that Padre Eusebio Francisco Kino, a Jesuit priest, founded San Xavier del Bac Mission, said to be the finest example of mission architecture in the United States. Kino spent the last twenty-four years of his life on a missionary tour of Sonora and Arizona, which covered 75,000 miles and resulted in the founding of seventy-three *vistas* (local churches) and twenty-

243

nine missions. In addition to converting the Native Americans to Christianity, Kino—and the Spanish settlers who followed after his death in 1711—introduced cattle, sheep, goats, horses, mules, and chickens into Arizona. The Spanish planted wheat, barley, grapes, onions, garlic, cabbage, lettuce, carrots, peaches, apricots, pomegranates, figs, pears, peaches, quinces, and mulberries.

Chile peppers were probably introduced about this time as well, though any records about them appear to be lost. We do know that in 1776, as the colonies were fighting for their independence from England, Fray Pedro Font was describing the agriculture and food of the Spanish settlers of the desert in his diary: "They plant with a stick and grow maize, beans, squash, and chiles. With their fingers, they eat tortillas and beans, chiles, and tomatoes. They begin their day hours before breakfast, stopping about 10 a.m. for maize cereal, sweet with honey or hot with red pepper. The main meal is in the early afternoon, usually tortillas, beans, and salsa. On special occasions, bits of meat in cornmeal are steamed in husks."

Font's description of tamales is still accurate today, and despite the introduction of European foods into Arizona, the Spanish padres were quite aware of the native plants growing around them. In 1794, the improbably named missionary, Ignatz Pfeffercorn, described his encounter with the wild chile, the chiltepin: "After the first mouthful, the tears started to come. I could not say a word and believed I had hell-fire in my mouth. However, one does become accustomed to it after frequent bold victories, so that with time the dish becomes tolerable and finally very agreeable."

In the late eighteenth and early nineteenth centuries, there was very little development of Arizona crops and food because of cultural and political turmoil. First, the Spanish battled the Yumas and the Apaches. Then, during the Mexican wars of independence from Spain (1811 to 1822), the northern settlements such as Arizona were neglected, and thousands of lives were lost as the Indians destroyed ranchos, haciendas, and mining camps. In 1824, Mexico became a republic and established the Territory of Nuevo Mexico, which included the present states of New Mexico and Arizona, with Santa Fe as the capital. The territory had about 4,500 inhabitants, and New Mexico had about 20,000 non-Indians. Arizona, however, had been almost totally abandoned, leaving only two tiny settlements, Tucson and Tubac, each protected by a small garrison of Mexican soldiers.

Arizona Food Events

Southwest Salsa Challenge, Hayden Square, Tempe, mid-April (602-266-8427).

Tucson Culinary Festival, El Conquistador Resort, Tucson, late August (602-742-7000).

La Fiesta de Viños, Bisbee, mid-September (602-432-3332).

Scottsdale Culinary Festival, Scottsdale Mall, third or fourth week in April (602-994-2787).

Tucson Meet Yourself, El Presidio Park, downtown Tucson, early October (602-621-3392).

La Fiesta de los Chiles, Tucson Botanical Gardens, late October (602-326-9225).

The 1846–48 war between Mexico and the United States was soon concluded to America's advantage, with virtually no fighting in the Territory of Nuevo Mexico; by the early 1850s, American pioneers began trickling into Arizona, attracted by the high prices paid by military posts for hay, corn, and beef. But the pioneers' attraction soon turned to aversion because settlers and soldiers alike complained of the heat and dryness. One soldier's journal of the time reported: "Everything dries. There is no juice left in any living thing. Bacon is eaten with a spoon and chickens hatched come out of the shell cooked."

Food on the Frontier

Nevertheless, the arid conditions of the Arizona deserts were actually a boon for some foods. The ancient Indian method of preserving meat—drying it in the sun—was reborn as jerky for the Americans and *carne seca* for the Mexicans. In 1844, Josiah Gregg, in his book *Commerce of the Prairies*, described how the pioneers in their caravans treated meat—mostly buffalo: "They find no difficulty in curing their meats even in mid-summer, by slicing it thin and spreading or suspending it in the sun; or if in haste, it is slightly barbecued. This is done without salt, and yet it rarely putrifies. The flesh [can be] 'jerked' or slightly barbecued, by placing it upon a scaffold over a fire. The same method is resorted to by Mexicans when the weather is too damp or cloudy for the meat to dry in the open air."

The meats used to make jerky were, in addition to buffalo, venison, beef, and even pork. The Americans apparently did not season the jerky, except for sprinkling it with a little salt. However, the Mexican version, *carne seca*, was seasoned with vinegar, black pepper, and some salt before drying and then was rubbed with garlic and sprinkled with chile powder after it had dried completely in the sun. In some cases, the *carne seca* was lightly smoked over mesquite wood before air-drying. The key to proper drying was to slice the meat along the grain as thinly as possible. When dry, the meat could be stored indefinitely.

Another staple of the settlers was sourdough, a bread that made its own yeast. The starter was simply flour mixed with warm water that was allowed to sit in the open. Yeasts occurring naturally in the air would settle on the starter, multiply furiously, and cause the starter to ferment. This process usually took between three and five days; the starter was usually kept in a wooden keg or a porcelain crock, but never in a metal container. Early cookbooks suggested wrapping a blanket around the starter in cold weather, or even taking it to bed with the cook in the event of a hard freeze! The starter would last only about two weeks before it had to be renewed.

When the cook was ready to make bread, it was a simple matter to mix the starter with more flour and water and make a dough. After retaining a cup or two of the dough for more starter, the remaining dough was allowed to proof or rise, then pushed down for a second proofing. After the dough had risen the second time, it was baked.

One of the most basic and necessary cooking tools of the frontier, the Dutch oven, was a precursor of the crockpot. The spider Dutch oven was a heavy, cast-iron pot with three legs and a thick lid. It served as a combination kettle, frying pan, and oven that could be hung above a fire or set in the coals, and sometimes coals were placed on the lid. Sourdough biscuits were commonly baked in this manner, and the method was known to Mexicans as *entre dos fuegos* (between two fires). Meats were commonly cooked with vegetables in a Dutch oven to make a pot roast. A ranch cook about the turn of the century described the food of the frontier:

10-1 Citrus Ranks High Among Arizona Crops

"Frijole beans, potatoes, and hot biscuits were served at every meal. Lick [syrup] took the place of butter. Dried fruit cooked with plenty of sugar was the usual dessert. Huge Dutch ovens were used for outside cooking."

In 1860, a census of sorts was taken in Arizona, and the population of the territory was determined to be 6,482—and that only included settlers, soldiers and "tame" Native Americans. By contrast, the population of New Mexico was about 70,000. The price of imported food was outrageous: flour was $55 a barrel; sugar, coffee, tea, and bacon were 75 cents a pound; butter was $2 a pound; and eggs were $2 a dozen—a fortune back then.

But the high price of food did not prevent the opening of restaurants. In 1864, the Juniper House, a combination hotel and restaurant, opened in Prescott, the territorial capital. On the menu was fried venison and chili for breakfast, roast venison and chili for dinner, and simply chili for supper. On a sadder note, that same year Kit Carson destroyed the Navajo peach orchards during the relocation of the tribe to New Mexico. In doing so, he wiped out the peaches that had been imported by the Spanish nearly two centuries earlier.

During the Indian wars, around 1873, one of Gen. George Crook's most trusted Indian scouts, Wales Arnold, ordered breakfast: "I want a can of peaches, six biscuits, a dozen eggs scrambled with green chiles, and a quart of hot coffee." The meal probably cost $4, a fortune for breakfast in those days. But prices were bound to get better as more settlers arrived in Arizona Territory, and modern transportation and agriculture techniques found their way into Arizona.

In 1879, Miss Nellie Cashman opened Delmonico's Restaurant on Church Plaza in Tucson. The restaurant had a Mexican cook, and meals were priced at four bits—50 cents. The food prices in the grocery stores that year were fluctuating; tea had doubled to $1.50 a pound while the price of sugar dropped to 50 cents a pound.

Finding firewood to cook the food was always a problem on the frontier, so the ingenious pioneers resorted to using hay boxes to save fuel. They would take a metal box or a trunk, make certain it was airtight, and pack it three-quarters full of finely cut, fresh hay. Then they made depressions in the hay large enough to hold a Dutch oven or other cook pot. The food was brought to the boiling point on the stove or over the fire; then the pot was transferred to the hay box. Pillows were placed over the pots for insulation, the top closed, and the meal continued to cook. The method took twice as long as stove cooking, but it saved fuel and many cooks swore that the food tasted better.

Beginning in 1870, the Salt River irrigation project produced 35,000 irrigated acres near Phoenix, leading to extensive citrus production. By 1885, Territorial Governor Frank A. Tritle commented that "orange trees loaded down with excellent fruit in the gardens of Phoenix show that climate and soil are well adapted to their culture." The first commercial orange groves were planted in 1891 at Ingleside, northeast of Phoenix, and grapefruit growing began in 1894. Severe freezes as low as twelve degrees nearly wiped out citrus in 1913, but the industry rebounded. Indeed, the Arizona 1983 citrus crop was valued at $53 million, but citrus orchards are continually threatened by development.

In 1912, dates were introduced into the Salt River Valley, and, in 1920, the first pecan orchards were planted. The pecan acreage grew to 4,000 in 1932, but later declined to 500 acres because of the inferior adaptability of older varieties. The Western Schley, introduced from New Mexico, was well adapted, and acreage zoomed to its current 22,000.

By 1920, Arizona's population had increased to 334,162—an increase of more than 5,000 percent in a mere sixty years. Much of that increase was the result of a change in immigration patterns. As the population of northern Mexico—particularly Sonora—increased, it was natural that immigrants would move even farther north and cross the border into Arizona. And, of course, they brought their own cuisine with them.

Sonoran-Style Food

Unlike the food in New Mexico and Texas, Mexican cooking was not well established in Arizona until much later. Whatever Mexican cuisine had been established there was wiped out in the early 1800s and did not reappear until the immigration from Mexico began later in the century. In fact, as late as 1880, the Mexican-American population of Arizona was fewer than 10,000 people. Thus, Arizona versions of *norteño* cookery were developed at least two centuries after New Mexicans were growing and eating their own heavily spiced versions.

Generally speaking, Arizona cuisine is not as fiery as that of New Mexico or Texas; the most widely used chiles are mild New Mexican types, and many Sonoran recipes do not include chiles. Mexican *poblanos* and dried *anchos* are surprisingly uncommon except in heavily Hispanic neighborhoods. These general rules are often contradicted when the fiery chiltepin enters the picture. This progenitor of the modern chile pepper grows wild in Sonora and southern Arizona on perennial bushes, as in Texas. The red, berry-like pods are harvested and dried and then crushed and sprinkled over soups, stews, and salsas.

However, as is true for the entire country, jalapeños and the hotter New Mexican varieties are steadily invading Arizona. Growers are increasing the size of their fields, and more of the fiery fruits are being imported from New Mexico. Jalapeños, chipotles, and serranos are also being imported from Mexico; so, as with the rest of the country, Arizona is starting to heat up.

Perhaps the most basic Sonoran-style dish is *machaca*, which evolved from *carne seca*. These days, the words are used interchangeably in Arizona, but they are actually two different things. In frontier times, dried beef was rehydrated, then allowed to stew with chiles and tomatoes until it fell apart. These days, since it is no longer necessary to dry meat, *machaca* is simply meat stewed, again with chiles and tomatoes, until it can be shredded (the Spanish verb *machacar* means to pound). The shredded meat is then used to stuff *burros*, as burritos are called in Arizona.

Another basic Sonoran-style dish is *chiles rellenos*, like this recipe from the *Bazar Cook Book*, published in 1909 by the Ladies'

Aid Society of Tucson's First Congregational Church: "Take green chile peppers, roast on top of the stove, roll in cloth to steam until cold, then peel (after being steamed in this way, the skins are easily removed). Cut off tops. Scoop out carefully to remove the seeds and veins and fill with mixture made of grated Mexican cheese, chopped olives, chopped onion. Dip in egg and cracker meal and fry in hot lard as you would oysters. Serve hot."

In Arizona, *huevos rancheros* are surprisingly served Texas-style, with fried eggs served over wheat or corn tortillas and then smothered in a mild *ranchero* sauce, which often contains tomatoes. There are at least three different Sonoran-style enchiladas served in the state. One version, prepared around Douglas where most of the New Mexican chiles are grown, is similar to New Mexican enchiladas in that it uses a chile sauce rather than a gravy. Another is more like the Tex-Mex enchiladas, and a third has been moved virtually intact from Sonora.

In the westernmost part of the Southwest, wheat tortillas are more popular than corn, primarily because farmers in Sonora and Arizona grow more wheat than corn. These tortillas are usually quite large—as much as sixteen inches across—and are stuffed with meat, beans, and cheese; called burros, they are more popular than enchiladas.

Perhaps the most famous Arizona specialty dish is the *chimichanga*, a dish whose name is translatable only as thingamajig. It is a burrito (usually stuffed with beans or ground meat, chiles,

10-2 The Margarita Is a Favorite Drink in Arizona

10-3 The Barrel Cactus, Source of Water in the Desert

and cheese), which is deep-fat fried and served with guacamole and a pico de gallo salsa.

Anne Lindsay Greer, an expert on Southwestern cuisine, observes of Arizona food: "Though 'Sonoran style' is the popular term used to describe this food, fast-food chains have had a devastating effect on the regional idiom, particularly in the western part of the state. 'Authentic' Sonoran style is more likely to be found around Tucson, where the peasant roots of the cuisine are still a source of pride."

In addition to its Sonoran-style establishments, Arizona has seen a steady growth in New Southwest restaurants during the past few years. Restaurants such as Vincent Guerithault on Camelback, the Piñon Grill in Scottsdale, and Janos and Cafe Terra Cotta in Tucson have led the way in combining regional ingredients in often startling new ways.

Followers of Euell Gibbons Take Note

The early settlers of Arizona—like their Native American predecessors—occasionally had to eat every imaginable plant and animal substance. In addition to the native plants mentioned in Part I, here are some other edible oddities.

Acorns. The nuts of oak trees were usually ground into flour, and cakes made from the flour were baked on hot rocks or allowed to dry in the sun.

Creosote bush. The leaves and bark of this pungent bush were used to make medicinal teas and poultices for the relief of arthritis, and the flower buds were also a substitute for capers.

Wild grapes. "The fruit is quite acid and occasionally is used to make vinegar and even wine," wrote Juan Nentvig in 1764.

Diamondback rattlesnakes. The snakes were carefully caught, killed, and skinned, and the meat was cut off, rolled in flour and cracker crumbs, and deep fried.

Bears, squirrels, and more. Bear steaks were fried, and squirrel carcasses were baked. The journals of early explorers and settlers record the consumption of other questionable delicacies, such as skunk, dog, shelf fungus, and sumac berries.

Recipes

SONORAN-STYLE ENCHILADAS, ARIZONA VERSION

For generations, American cooks of Mexican heritage have lived in Arizona and have developed their own interpretations of such classic dishes as enchiladas. Here is our third Southwestern enchilada recipe, as prepared in Phoenix and other parts of southern Arizona. Note its similarity to the Tex-Mex chile gravy.

- 3 tablespoons vegetable oil
- 3 tablespoons flour
- 6 tablespoons red chile powder
- 3 cups water
- ½ teaspoon crushed garlic
- 4 tablespoons vegetable oil
- 6 corn tortillas
- 2 cups cooked ground beef, drained
- ½ cup chopped black olives
- 1 cup grated cheddar cheese
- 1 cup finely chopped onion

Heat 3 tablespoons oil in a skillet and add the flour. Stirring constantly, brown the flour into a roux. Add the chile powder to the water and mix well; add this mixture to the roux. Add the crushed garlic and bring the sauce to a boil. Reduce heat and simmer until thickened, about 15 minutes.

Heat 4 tablespoons oil in a skillet; using tongs, lightly fry each tortilla for about 5 seconds per side to soften them. Do not overcook. Place three tortillas on a plate, spread a row of ground beef over each end, add a little sauce, and roll up. Repeat with the other three tortillas on a second plate. Pour the rest of the sauce over the rolled tortillas on each plate, sprinkle the olives, cheese, and onions over the sauce, and serve immediately. You can keep the plates warm in a 250° oven until the cheese melts slightly.

SERVES: 2
HEAT SCALE: MILD

SCHOLEY BEANS

From the famous Scholey and Stephans Saloon in historic Tomb-stone come the "best darned beans in the state." They were part of the saloon's free lunch.

　1　**quart dried red beans**
　½　**pound salt pork or bacon**
　1　**onion, chopped**
　1　**cup lard (or substitute vegetable oil)**
　5　**red chile pods**
　　Water
　½　**pound round steak**
　1　**cup chopped green New Mexican chiles**
　1　**clove garlic, minced**
　　Salt to taste

Wash and clean the beans; cover with water and soak over-night. In a kettle, combine the beans, salt pork, onion, and lard and cook until the beans are tender. Boil the chile pods

10-4 Sign on a Panadería in South Phoenix

in a little water until they soften. Mash them through a colander and reserve the pulp.

Fry the round steak in its own suet until it is well done and then grind it in a meat grinder. Add the ground meat, chile pulp, green chiles, and garlic to the beans and cook for at least 30 minutes to blend the flavors. Salt before serving.

SERVES: **12**
HEAT SCALE: MEDIUM

ROASTED POBLANO-CORN SALSA WITH MORELS

One of the tenets of New Southwestern cooking is the innovative combination of farm-fresh ingredients. This recipe, made with mostly New World foods, is a good example.

5 ears of corn in husks
5 tablespoons diced morels (or other wild mushrooms)
8 teaspoons olive oil
2 poblano chiles, roasted, peeled, stems and seeds removed, diced
¼ cup sun-dried tomatoes, minced
2 tablespoons cilantro, minced
1 tablespoon chipotles in adobo, minced
2 teaspoons fresh marjoram, minced
1 teaspoon lime juice
Salt to taste

Place the corn on a baking sheet and bake at 400° for 30 minutes, turning often until the corn husks are blackened on all sides. Allow to cool.

Cook the morels in 2 teaspoons of the olive oil until well browned, about 10 minutes.

Shuck the corn and brush with 6 teaspoons of olive oil. Grill or broil the corn until the kernels brown, about 10 minutes. Cut the kernels from the cob and reserve.

10-5 A Little Arizona Food Humor

Combine the corn and morels with the remaining ingredients and mix well. Serve warm on a bed of greens.

SERVES: **4**
HEAT SCALE: **MILD**

Green Chile Pesto on Red Chile Pasta

Several manufacturers produce red chile pastas. If you can't find them, simply add red chile powder to pasta recipes and make your own!

- **5 green New Mexican chiles, roasted, peeled, stems and seeds removed, minced**
- **½ red bell pepper, roasted, peeled, stems and seeds removed, minced**
- **3 cloves garlic, minced**
- **1 cup cilantro (or substitute Italian parsley), minced**
- **½ cup roasted piñon nuts**

1 **teaspoon lime juice**
2 **tablespoons olive oil**
1 **package red chile pasta, cooked al dente in salted water**
1 **cup grated romano cheese**

In a *molcajete* (mortar), crush the first 7 ingredients into a rough pesto.

Toss the pasta with the pesto and sprinkle liberally with cheese.

SERVES: **2 TO 4**
HEAT SCALE: MEDIUM

HELPFUL COOKING HINTS FROM THE FRONTIER

There was no lack of cooking innovation in early Arizona. Here are some helpful hints even for modern kitchens.

- Old bread should be dried thoroughly, ground, and put away to make bread pudding when unexpected guests arrive.
- Dip fish in boiling water for a minute to make them easier to scale.
- A bay leaf will keep weevils out of oatmeal and cornmeal.
- Parsnips, which are peeled, sliced, roasted, and powdered, make an excellent coffee substitute.
- Adding a half-teaspoon of baking soda to the water used to boil beans will eliminate "repeating" and "gas attacks."
- Soak bacon in cold water for a few minutes to reduce curling and shrinking when it is fried.

CHRISTINE'S HOT SAUCE

We confess we've never met Christine. Her recipe was passed on to us by friends in Scottsdale, and it's a good example of an Arizona-style, all-purpose hot sauce that can be used for a chip dip or added to soups and stews.

  2 tablespoons chiltepins
  3 red New Mexican chiles, stems and seeds removed, crushed and rehydrated in ½ cup water
1½ cloves garlic
 ½ onion, minced
 ½ teaspoon cumin
  Pinch of oregano
  Pinch of salt
  2 tablespoons vegetable oil
  2 tablespoons vinegar
  1 8-ounce can tomato sauce

Puree the first 9 ingredients in a blender and place the mixture in a bowl. Add the tomato sauce and mix well.

YIELD: 2 CUPS
HEAT SCALE: HOT

CHAPTER

11

PHOENIX AND SCOTTSDALE

hoenix and its attendant suburbs sprawl across the aptly named Valley of the Sun, which broils in the sun during the fierce summer, yet remains warm and pleasant during the winter. October through May is the time the tourists flock to the numerous resorts that offer golf, tennis, and total relaxation.

Despite the artistic and shopping attractions of Scottsdale, Phoenix remains the dominant city in the area. Besides being the state capital and financial center, it is the home of a major league football team (Cardinals) and a basketball team (Suns). With nearly a million people, Phoenix is America's ninth largest city (some say eighth) according to population, and the largest in land area with nearly 400 square miles.

History and Sightseeing

The ancient Hohokam civilization first settled in the valley and tamed the Salt River for irrigation around 300 B.C. By A.D. 1100, the population of Hohokam settlements approached 100,000, and their culture (along with that of the Anasazi) was the most advanced north of Mexico City in prehistoric times. By 1450, though, the Hohokam civilization had collapsed, and the people had dispersed. Their artifacts remain preserved at the Pueblo Grande

Museum, 4619 E. Washington Street (602-495-0901), including displays of pit houses, irrigation canals, and ball courts.

American settlers began arriving in the area shortly after the Civil War, when the Army built Fort McDowell to provide hay and crops for the fort. Jack Swilling, a former Confederate soldier, was the first to dig out the Hohokam canals and grow irrigated crops. Other farmers soon followed, and a small city was laid out in 1870 and incorporated in 1881. It was named Phoenix by Darrel Duppa, one of the early settlers, who predicted the city would rise from the ashes of the Hohokam civilization like the mythical bird, the phoenix. He was right.

By 1889, Phoenix was large enough to snatch the state capital away from Prescott. After the turn of the century and the construction of Theodore Roosevelt Dam, which provided sufficient water for the city, Phoenix began to boom. It really came into its own after World War II, when its income base changed from farming to manufacturing and tourism.

But evidence of the early Phoenix still remains at Heritage Square, Sixth and Monroe Streets (602-262-5071), where homes built between 1890 and 1930 comprise the last existing block of the original Phoenix town site. Anchored by the Rosson House, which is open for tours, Heritage Square is an interesting diversion in a fast-moving town. So is the Pioneer Arizona Living History Museum, Pioneer Road Exit off I-17 (602-933-0212), with its reconstructed historical buildings of a pioneer town. Blacksmiths, printers, dressmakers, and other craftspeople ply their trades among the exhibits.

One of the finest museums in the world devoted to the native peoples of the Southwest is located in Phoenix. The Heard Museum, 22 E. Monte Vista Road, has extensive and outstanding exhibits on the culture, artifacts, and art of indigenous peoples. Other interesting museums in the Valley of the Sun include Pueblo Grande Museum and Cultural Park, 4619 E. Washington (602-495-0901); Phoenix Art Museum, 1625 N. Central Avenue (602-257-1222) with more than 11,000 works of art; Arizona Museum of Science and Technology, 80 N. 2nd Street (602-256-9388); and Hall of Flame, a collection of antique fire-fighting equipment, 6101 E. Van Buren Street (602-275-3473).

Existing in the desert seems to be the theme of a number of Phoenix attractions. Arcosanti, futuristic architect Paolo Soleri's ecologically designed town, is under construction at Exit 262 off

THE BEST OF THE BEST OF PHOENIX

Nearly 2,000 people cast ballots in the *Arizona Republic*'s 1991 Arizona's Best contest. For food lovers with equally diverse tastes in entertainment, we present the recommendations of the *Republic*'s readers.

Best Museum: Heard Museum, 22 E. Monte Vista Road

Best Place to Buy Desert Plants: Desert Botanical Garden, 1201 N. Galvin Parkway

Best Flea Market: Park and Swap, 3801 E. Washington Street

Best Grocery for Gourmets: Euro Market, 5017 N. Central Avenue

Best Place to Play in the Water: Island of Big Surf, 1500 N. McClintock Drive

Best Southwestern Restaurant: Vincent Guerithault on Camelback, 3930 E. Camelback Road

Best Barbecue (staff recommended): Lovejoy's Kansas City Pit Bar-B-Que, 15414 N. 19th Avenue

I-17 at Cordes Junction (602-632-7135). A foundry, gift shop, bakery, and cafe are in operation. Another architectural masterpiece, Frank Lloyd Wright's Taliesin West, is available for tours (602-860-8810). The Desert Botanical Gardens, 1201 N. Galvin Parkway (602-941-1225), has the country's largest collection of arid-land plants and displays of pre-Columbian food collecting techniques. The world's largest terrarium, Biosphere 2, is in nearby Oracle (602-896-2108). It's either a brilliant scientific endeavor or a boondoggle; perhaps a visit will give a hint which. Daily tours, accommodations, a restaurant, and a gift shop are on the premises. The Desert Center at Pinnacle Peak, 8711 E. Pinnacle Peak Road (602-563-5170), teaches ethnobotany, archaeology, and ancient Indian skills.

Lovers of the outdoors will enjoy the Phoenix Zoo, 5810 E. Van Buren Street, with its special Arizona Exhibit and one of the largest herds of Arabian oryx in the world. Smaller but still interesting is the Roer Bird Farm, 6553 N. 27th Avenue (602-242-2477) and its three acres of exhibits of exotic birds. Also outdoors, and for good reason, is the World's Highest Fountain in aptly named Fountain Hills (602-837-1654). Drive east of Scottsdale and look for the 560-foot plume of water and ponder how much of it evaporates in the Valley's 116-degree summer temperatures.

Other attractions in the valley include Rawhide, 22023 N. Scottsdale Road (602-663-5600), which is a large Western theme park complete with a Wild West museum, twenty retail shops, a saloon, restaurant, and, to assist your digestion, gunfights. The Rockin' R Ranch, 6136 E. Baseline Road in Mesa (602-832-1539) is another Wild West town featuring chuck wagon suppers, gold panning, wagon rides, and entertainment. Castle lovers will enjoy Mystery Castle, 800 E. Mineral Road (602-268-1581), which was built in 1930 by Boyce Gulley for his daughter. It has eighteen rooms and thirteen fireplaces; but, hey, who's counting?

It wouldn't be fair to the Valley not to mention Scottsdale, with its sprawling resorts, shopping malls, art galleries, and numerous restaurants. Old Town, bordered by Brown Avenue, 2nd Street, Indian School Road, and Main Street, is a section of downtown Scottsdale with preserved, frontier-style buildings. From October to May, horse-drawn carriages and open-air trolleys carry visitors to the shops, restaurants, and galleries. Nearby is Fifth Avenue, with its collection of exclusive shops, and Scottsdale Galleria, a mall with its own IMAX theater. Scottsdale rivals Santa Fe as a center for Southwestern art, although the galleries also carry many different styles.

For more information on visiting the region, contact the Phoenix and Valley of the Sun Convention and Visitors Bureau, 400 E. Van Buren Street, Suite 600, Phoenix, AZ 85004 (602-254-6500); or the Scottsdale Chamber of Commerce, 7333 Scottsdale Mall, Scottsdale, AZ 85251 (602-945-8481).

Valley of the Sun Dining

It is no surprise that the style of Mexican food most typical of Arizona originates from Sonora, the neighboring Mexican state.

11-1 The Unusual Los Olivos Restaurant in Scottsdale

Sonora is cattle country, and wheat is one of the primary crops. Flour tortillas, beef, cheese, sour cream, and of course, the ubiquitous chiles and beans are the staples on which the cuisine is built.

After World War II, the widespread use of air conditioning and a flood of young veterans looking for a fresh start and a place to raise families swelled sleepy, dusty little Phoenix to city size. The newcomers learned to eat the hearty, spicy food found in dozens of unpretentious *taquerias* (taco shops) and cafes—tacos, tamales, tostadas, *machaca, quesadillas*, and enough smooth-textured but fiery red sauce to fill the always-dry Salt River.

Woody Johnson, founding father of the Macayo chain, opened what was probably the first "upscale" Mexican restaurant, El Nido, near downtown Phoenix in 1950. The atmosphere may have been fancy but the food was straightforward.

Suddenly, in the early 1970s, things began to change. Along with the complimentary pre-meal basket of chips and familiar squeeze bottle of sauce, shallow bowls of chunky salsa appeared on tables.

A hybrid dish called the *chimichanga* turned up on menus all over town. No one knows what the name means or where it came from. It is basically an enormous burrito with a choice of fillings (such as *machaca*), which is deep-fried and smothered in cheese, sauce, guacamole, and sour cream. The appearance of sour cream has outraged some purists. "As for the person who slopped sour cream on a *chimichanga*, or any Mexican food," said railroader Joe Lancaster, "I use a cowboy phrase, 'Get a rope.'"

The *chimichanga* has always commanded a premium price—based no doubt on its size. An astonishing number of local restaurateurs have taken credit for originating this dish, which rivals fry bread for the Alka Seltzer Award of all time. Claims have also come from Tucson's El Charro, La Frontera in Nogales, and other restaurants all over the state. The consensus seems to be that the *chimi*, as it is fondly known, is the creation of the Garcia family, who also gave birth to the national chain of restaurants of the same name.

Creeping California-ism has brought the taco salad, and fajitas crept up from Texas. Blue corn and green chiles were a welcome infusion from New Mexico. Arizonans also learned in the 1980s that there were other styles of Mexican food besides Sonoran, when restaurants opened offering specialties from Central and Coastal Mexico.

Ask anyone who has lived in Phoenix for any length of time where they head upon returning home after being out of town. Chances are they will tell you Rosita's, La Familia, Don José, or any other of the many Mexican restaurants untouched by time or trend, where they will order a No. 5 plate: taco, tostada, and enchilada awash in that river of sauce.

—ELIN JEFFORDS

Roadside Stands

In the winter months, Bell Road from 32nd Street to Scottsdale Road, and Scottsdale Road, north of Bell almost to Pinnacle Peak, are hotbeds of entrepreneurship. During daylight hours, vendors sell everything from *ristras* and Mexican blankets to cow skulls and fine Tarahumara pottery. Bring cash and feel free to bargain.

Phoenix Markets and Bakeries

ESTRELLA TORTILLA FACTORY

1004 S. Central Avenue (602-253-5947). *Open Monday–Saturday, 7 a.m.–5 p.m.; Sunday, 8 a.m.–noon.* NO CREDIT CARDS; NO LIQUOR.

Since 1945, this tortilla factory and grocery store has been selling corn and flour tortillas, chips, tamales, and basic Mexican ingredients such as beans, salsas and hot sauces, herbs, and more.

EURO MARKET

5017 N. Central Avenue (602-252-3876). *Open Monday–Saturday, 7 a.m.–8 p.m.; Sunday, 8 a.m.–6 p.m.* MAJOR CREDIT CARDS; LIQUOR LICENSE.

Here is a world of food at your fingertips, including more than 200 international cheeses in the cheese case. You can find whatever ethnic ingredients you're looking for, whether fresh herbs, marinades, Crema Mexicana, or Middle Eastern specialties. The market has excellent meats, fresh fish, and crustaceans.

EL FENIX

6219 S. Central Avenue, South Phoenix (602-276-9104). *Open Monday–Friday, 8 a.m.–7 p.m.; Saturday, 7 a.m.–7 p.m.; Sunday, 7 a.m.–2 p.m.* NO CREDIT CARDS; NO LIQUOR.

El Fenix specializes in *bolillos*, sweetcakes, pumpkin candy, and tortillas, but also has some hot sauces and Mexican grocery items.

FOOD CITY

1648 S. 16th Street (602-258-3781). *Open Monday–Saturday, 7 a.m.–9 p.m.; Sunday, 7 a.m.–7 p.m.* NO CREDIT CARDS; LIQUOR LICENSE.

In addition to carrying a complete line of Mexican food ingredients (chorizo, beans, chiles, dozens of sauces and salsas, tripe, etc.), Food City, open since 1931, has an eye-popping, automated tortilla maker that turns out the thinnest, most delicious product in town.

11-2 Welcome to El Fenix Mexican Bakery in South Phoenix

PARK AND SWAP

40th Street, at East Washington and the Greyhound Race-track (602-273-1250). *Open Wednesday, 4 p.m.–10 p.m.; Saturday and Sunday, 6 a.m.–4 p.m.*

Although this flea market or swap meet does not specialize in food, vendors often sell food items "imported" from Mexico, bottled Arizona foods, and fresh produce.

Retail Shops

ARIZONA TERRITORY

The Scottsdale Fashion Square, 7014 E. Camelback Road, Scottsdale (602-949-9232). *Open Monday–Saturday, 10 a.m.–9 p.m.; Sunday, 11 a.m.–6 p.m.* VISA, MC; NO LIQUOR.

Every imaginable gift item relating to Arizona is in this store, including T-shirts, cookbooks, guidebooks, souvenirs, postcards, recipe card holders, platters, and cookie jars. Food items are Southwestern salsas, mustards, jellies, and yes, even spicy popcorn. They do mail-order sales—call for details.

Desert Botanical Gardens Gift Shop

1201 N. Galvin Parkway, Phoenix (602-941-1225). *Open daily, 9 a.m. to sunset (8 a.m. to sunset in June, July, and August).*

Just about everything concerning the desert, including plants, guidebooks, T-shirts, cookbooks, and more, is available here. The gift shop also has a good collection of Arizona foods, such as salsas.

Peppers

7128 E. Fifth Avenue, Scottsdale (602-990-8347). *Open Monday–Saturday, 9 a.m.–6:30 p.m.; Sunday, 10:30 a.m.– 5 p.m.* MAJOR CREDIT CARDS; NO LIQUOR.

In addition to a fine collection of Southwestern salsas, hot sauces, and other food products, Peppers, the self-proclaimed "hottest little gift shop in Scottsdale," offers *ristras* and wreaths, well-designed Southwestern memorabilia, cookbooks, and dinnerware.

Pinnacle Peak General Store

8711 E. Pinnacle Peak Road, Scottsdale (602-991-1822). *Open daily, 7 a.m.–8 p.m.* MAJOR CREDIT CARDS; LIQUOR LICENSE.

The setting is nice here: a courtyard and plaza modeled after Alamos, Mexico, and a lovely cactus garden. Stephen Simonson, general manager since 1974, says modestly that the general store is "even more than a legend—it's an institution." Well, this institution even has its own bakery and soda fountain and sells a wide variety of specialty foods, such as saguaro honey and mesquite honey, plus jellies, jams, salsas, and hot sauces. It's worth a trip to this interesting store.

SHALIMAR DATE GARDENS

7021 Main Street, Scottsdale (602-945-0833). *Open Monday–Friday, 10 a.m.–6 p.m.; Saturday, 10 a.m.–5 p.m.* VISA, MC; NO LIQUOR.

With the motto "date time is anytime," Shalimar obviously has plenty of dates, especially top-of-the-line *medjool* dates. It also offers a fine selection of prunes, figs, apricots, pecans, and Arizona-grown pistachios. Other specialties include macadamia nuts and pecan-stuffed dates. Call for mail-order information.

SOUTHWEST GOURMET GALLERY

320 N. Highway 89A, Sedona (602-282-2682). *Open daily, 9 a.m.–5 p.m. (winter); 9 a.m.– 8 p.m. (summer).* MAJOR CREDIT CARDS; NO LIQUOR.

In addition to Mesa Verde pottery and designer jewelry by contemporary artists, this shop has a teriffic selection of Southwestern gourmet foods, including chiles in all forms (pods, powders, canned, *ristras*), hot and spicy candy, pumpkin and blueberry butters, prickly pear products (prickly pear coffee beans?) and a great selection of honeys. They will sell by mail order—call for information.

SPHINX DATE RANCH

3039 N. Scottsdale Road, Scottsdale (602-941-2261). *Open Monday–Saturday, 9 a.m.–5 p.m.* MAJOR CREDIT CARDS; NO LIQUOR.

At Sphinx, *medjool* dates are harvested and packed during September and October, but they're available throughout the year because of proper cold storage techniques. Besides *medjools*, they have dates you've never heard of (*dayri, zahidi, barhi*, and *khadrawy*, for example), as well as a huge selection of nuts, fruits, honey, Southwestern salsas, and jams and jellies. They'll ship anywhere, so call for mail-order information.

CHIMICHANGA: TRANSLATED AT LAST?

It has long been written that the word *chimichanga* has no translation into English except as the vague thingamajig. But recently, word sleuths have been tracking down its meaning.

Since the word *changa* means female monkey in Spanish, that was the logical place to begin. Idiomatic slang was suspected, and a Tucson freelance writer, Janet Mitchell, put the question to Jim Griffith, director of the University of Arizona Southwest Folklore Center. "No doubt about it," he answered, the word *chimichanga* is a polite version of an unmentionable Mexican expletive that mentions a monkey."

So, a monkey was a part of the translation, but what did it mean? And how was it connected to a deep-fried burro? The next step was to look at the first part of the word, *chimi*. The closest Spanish word seemed to be *chimenea*, meaning chimney or hearth—and both words indicated heat.

Investigator Mitchell had heard tales about the first *chimichanga* being created when a burro was accidentally knocked into a deep-fat fryer, and the the cook exclaimed, *"Chimichanga!"* She had also heard that a baked burro cooked in a bar in Nogales in the 1940s had been called a toasted monkey.

The logical conclusion, then, was that the idiom *chimichanga* means toasted monkey and is an allusion to the golden-brown color of the deep-fried burro.

Restaurants

ADRIAN'S

2234 E. McDowell Road, Phoenix (602-273-7957). *Open Monday–Thursday, 8 a.m.–8 p.m.; Friday–Sunday, 8 a.m.– 10 p.m.* NO CREDIT CARDS; BEER AND WINE.

The weird boulder-and-blue-grout construction belies Adrian's immaculate, plain interior. The servers speak limited English, but you can get by with restaurant Spanish. The food is true Sonoran, including Pork with Nopalitos and *lengua*. Try the seafood cocktails, too.

AJO AL'S

9393 N. 90th Street, Scottsdale (602-860-2611) and 6990 E. Shea Blvd., Scottsdale (602-998-1734). *Open Monday– Friday, 11 a.m.–9 p.m.; Saturday, 11 a.m.–10 p.m.* MAJOR CREDIT CARDS; LIQUOR LICENSE.

These yuppie family restaurants serve some pretty good Sonoran-style dishes. Try the Salad Carbón with Grilled Shrimp and Avocado or the Shredded Beef Enchiladas. Also recommended are the Steak Picado with Salsa and Cheese and the best *chile con queso* ever found in a restaurant.

COYOTE CAFE

7373 Scottsdale Mall, Scottsdale (602-947-7081). *Open Tuesday–Thursday, 11 a.m.–10 p.m.; Friday and Saturday, 11 a.m.–11 p.m.; Sunday, 2 p.m.–9 p.m.; Monday, 5 p.m.– 10 p.m.* MAJOR CREDIT CARDS; LIQUOR LICENSE.

This tiny cafe, with its spacious, attractive patio, has a great view of the greenbelt surrounding Scottsdale Center for the Arts. Its interesting New Southwest menu includes Black Bean Cakes, Salmon with Tomatillo Sauce, and—for dessert—Tequila-Grapefruit Sorbet with a Cactus Cookie.

Don José

3734 E. Thomas Road, Phoenix (602-955-7870). *Open Wednesday–Sunday, 11 a.m.–9:45 p.m.* NO CREDIT CARDS; BEER ONLY.

The limited menu selections of Sonoran dishes at Don José are all done superbly. There is no ambience to speak of, but the service is speedy and friendly, and the food is ultraconsistent.

Los Dos Molinos

8646 S. Central Avenue, Phoenix (602-243-9113). *Open Tuesday–Thursday, and Sunday, 11 a.m.–9 p.m.; Friday and Saturday, 11 a.m.–10 p.m.* NO CREDIT CARDS; LIQUOR LICENSE.

This is the third location of a minichain that originated in Springerville, a small town near the New Mexico border. The other is in the Phoenix suburb of Mesa. The newest Los Dos Molinos is located in an old adobe once owned by silent film cowboy star Tom Mix. It serves a terrific hot sauce and great *adovada*; anything with green chiles is good.

La Familia

3145 W. Indian School Road, Phoenix (602-265-2912). *Open Monday–Saturday, 10:30 a.m.–8 p.m.* VISA, MC; BEER ONLY.

Tacos, tamales, enchiladas, and extraordinary hot sauce are served in this family restaurant with unpretentious, consistent, speedy service and 1970s prices.

Guedo's Taco Shop

71 E. Chandler Blvd., Chandler (602-899-7841). *Open Tuesday–Saturday, 11 a.m.–9 p.m.* NO CREDIT CARDS; BEER ONLY.

Like the name says, this shop offers tacos and a fresh salsa bar that provides all the condiments. It's a tiny place decorated in a beach shack motif, but it's worth seeking out.

11-3 Poncho's, Home of the Great Green Corn Tamale

LA HACIENDA AT THE PRINCESS RESORT

7575 E. Princess Drive, Scottsdale (602-585-4848). *Open Tuesday–Sunday, 6 p.m.–10 p.m.* MAJOR CREDIT CARDS; LIQUOR LICENSE.

Mexican goes uptown in this Rancho Elegante freestanding restaurant in the desert that is decorated in territorial style. La Hacienda serves such Mexico City–like temptations as Roasted Suckling Pig, Honey-Almond Glazed Duck, Crab-Stuffed Sea Bass, Roasted Quail Stuffed with Chorizo and Topped with Chipotle Sauce, and Beef Tenderloin Glazed with Chihuahua Cheese and Salsa.

LILY'S CAFE

6706 N. 58th Drive, Glendale (602-937-7757). *Open Wednesday–Friday, 11 a.m.–9 p.m.; Saturday, 8 a.m.– 9 p.m.; Sunday, 7 a.m.– 7 p.m.* NO CREDIT CARDS; BEER ONLY.

Since 1949, this hard-to-find suburban restaurant has been a legend among Mexican food fans. So quality-conscious is owner Zippy Hernandez that he refuses to make his famous *chiles rellenos* during peak hours because they take too long. But when things slow down, they're the specialty to try, along with the tamales.

MACAYO

4001 N. Central Avenue, Phoenix (602-264-6141); 1909 W. Thunderbird Road, Phoenix (602-866-7034); 7829 W. Thomas Road, Phoenix (602-873-0313); 7005 E. Camelback Road, Scottsdale (602-947-7641); 1920 S. Dobson Road, Mesa. *Open Sunday–Thursday, 11 a.m.–11 p.m.; Friday and Saturday, 11 a.m.–midnight.* MAJOR CREDIT CARDS; LIQUOR LICENSE.

One of the Valley's oldest Mexican food chains, Macayo was founded in 1945. The food is standard but dependable, and the restaurants always have enjoyable Cinco de Mayo celebrations and specialties. Try the tacos, tamales, enchiladas, and *chimichangas*.

MARILYN'S FIRST MEXICAN RESTAURANT

12631 N. Tatum Blvd. Phoenix (602-953-2121) and 7001 N. Scottsdale Road, Scottsdale (602-443-4399). *Open Monday– Thursday, 11 a.m.–10 p.m.; Friday and Saturday, 11 a.m.– 10:30 p.m.; Sunday, 11:30 a.m.– 9 p.m.* MAJOR CREDIT CARDS; LIQUOR LICENSE.

A very popular and "gringoized" restaurant, Marilyn's has a pretty pastel decor, a well-trained staff, and good food, on the mild side. Try the Pollo Fundido and Seafood Enchiladas.

EL NORTEÑO

1002 N. Seventh Avenue, Phoenix (602-254-4629). *Open Monday–Saturday, 9 a.m.–9 p.m.* NO CREDIT CARDS; NO LIQUOR.

This is a small take-out stand near downtown with limited seating on the patio. What it lacks in size, it more than makes up for with its excellent *machaca*, hot sauce, and tamales.

Los Olivos

7328 2nd Street, Scottsdale (602-946-2256). *Open Sunday–Thursday, 11 a.m.–10 p.m.; Friday and Saturday, 11 a.m.–11:30 p.m.* MAJOR CREDIT CARDS; LIQUOR LICENSE.

During the warm summer nights in the Valley of the Sun, owner Elvaro Corral gives the order, and the entire roof of "the olives" slides back to reveal the starry Arizona sky—a perfect environment for listening to salsa music while sipping on a Mexican beer. The menu features Sonoran specialties, plus two homemade salsas each day (one made with serranos). For dessert under the stars, try *flan* and fried ice cream.

Palo Verde Room at The Boulders Resort

34631 N. Tom Darlington Road, Scottsdale (602-488-9009). *Open daily, 11:30 a.m.–2:30 p.m. and 6 p.m.–9:30 p.m.* MAJOR CREDIT CARDS; LIQUOR LICENSE.

Lamb, veal chops, and off-beat vegetables and desserts highlight this Southwestern-influenced restaurant. It has a fresh and light-hearted decor and a charming patio. It is worth a visit just to experience this world-class resort.

La Parilla Suiza

3508 W. Peoria Avenue, Phoenix (602-978-8334). *Open Sunday–Thursday, 11 a.m.–10 p.m.; Friday and Saturday, 11 a.m.–11 p.m.* MAJOR CREDIT CARDS; LIQUOR LICENSE.

"The Swiss Grill," part of a Mexico City restaurant chain, serves mild food in a somewhat plastic environment. Try the soft tacos, *chilaquiles*, and charro beans.

La Perla

5912 W. Glendale Avenue, Glendale (602-939-7561). *Open Monday–Thursday, 7 a.m.–midnight; Friday and Saturday, 7 a.m.–2 a.m.; Sunday, 7 a.m.–10 p.m.* MAJOR CREDIT CARDS; LIQUOR LICENSE.

"The Pearl," serving Mexican food since 1946, although not fancy, is comfortable. The food is always consistent, and the expanded hours are great for folks needing a late night chile fix. Try the *albóndigas* soup, the *mole*, and *frijoles borrachos* (drunken beans).

PIÑON GRILL AT THE INN AT MCCORMICK RANCH

7401 N. Scottsdale Road, Scottsdale (602-948-5050). *Open daily, 6:30 a.m.–10 p.m.* MAJOR CREDIT CARDS; LIQUOR LICENSE.

Chef Farn Boggie has crafted a very fine Southwestern restaurant with attractive Indian motif designs and a view overlooking a small lake. Some of his specialties include Venison and Papaya in Blue Corn Tacos, Double Breast of Chicken Filled with Chorizo, and Yellow Pepper-Cilantro Rice. The salads (with homemade dressing), grilled veal chops, and desserts are all excellent.

EL POLLO SUPREMO

4221 W. University, Tempe (602-966-3713). *Open Monday–Saturday, 11 a.m.–10 p.m.; Sunday, 11 a.m.–9 p.m.* NO CREDIT CARDS; NO LIQUOR.

Here is the Valley of the Sun's answer to the Mexican fast-food "pollo" shops so common in border towns. El Pollo Supremo (the supreme chicken) offers citrus- and garlic-marinated grilled chicken served with ranch beans and chunky salsa. Very good.

PONCHO'S

7202 S. Central Avenue, Phoenix (602-276-2437). *Open Monday–Thursday, 11 a.m.–10 p.m.; Friday and Saturday, 11 a.m.–midnight; Sunday, noon–10 p.m.* MAJOR CREDIT CARDS; LIQUOR LICENSE.

This is a genuine community gathering place for all ages, races, and economic groups. One reason is cheery mariachi music on weekends, and another is their excellent Sonoran-style cuisine. Recommended are the *albóndigas* soup, green corn tamales, *machaca*, and guacamole.

11-4 The Exclusive Vincent Guerithault on Camelback

RESTAURANT MEXICO

16 E. 7th Street, Tempe (602-967-3280). *Open Monday–Thursday, 11 a.m.–9 p.m.; Friday and Saturday, 11 a.m.–10 p.m.* NO CREDIT CARDS; LIQUOR LICENSE.

This restaurant has mild, Central Mexican–style food served by folks who treat everyone like family. Recommended are the soft pork tacos, bean soup, and chunky guacamole with white cheese.

ROSITA'S PLACE

2310 E. McDowell Road, Phoenix (602-244-9779). *Open Monday–Thursday, 10 a.m.–11 p.m.; Friday, 10 a.m.–1 a.m.; Saturday, 9 a.m.–midnight.* VISA, MC; LIQUOR LICENSE.

Although Rosita's has only been in its present location since 1989, it has been around since the mid-1950s. It has some killer red and green hot sauces and some excellent Sonoran-style dishes. There is absolutely no ambience here, but it's an in-spot for hard-core local Mexican food fans.

SATISFIED FROG

6245 E. Cave Creek Road, Cave Creek (602-488-3317). *Open daily, 11 a.m.–11 p.m.* VISA, MC; LIQUOR LICENSE.

This brew pub has a pseudo-Western atmosphere that's rustic and fun. The burgers, ribs, fried chicken, and basic Mexican dishes are great, but the wonderful, made-on-the-premises beer is the keynote here. Try the chile beer with whole jalapeños afloat in the bottle.

T-BONE STEAKHOUSE

10037 S. 19th Avenue, South Phoenix (602-276-0945). *Open Sunday–Thursday, 5 p.m.–10 p.m.; Friday and Saturday, 5 p.m.–midnight.* MAJOR CREDIT CARDS; LIQUOR LICENSE.

There are plenty of cowboy steakhouses in the area. This is the least ballyhooed and the best of them all, complete with sawdust on the floor, pistol-packin' waitresses, and a great view of the city lights. The menu offers only five cuts of steak, and the best are the thirty-six-ounce porterhouse steak and the filet mignon.

TONO'S COMIDA MEXICANA

24 E. Broadway, South Phoenix (602-243-9684). *Open daily, 9 a.m.–8 p.m.* VISA, MC; LIQUOR LICENSE.

Here is the best (and only) place in town to find Jalisco-style goat. The atmosphere here is *nada*, but sweet servers make up for it. Recommended are the barbecued and stewed *cabrito*, *carnitas*, *sopas*, and *moles*.

VINCENT GUERITHAULT ON CAMELBACK

3930 E. Camelback Road, Phoenix (602-224-0225). *Open Monday–Friday, 11:30 a.m.–2:30 p.m.; Sunday–Friday, 6 p.m.–10:30 p.m.; Saturday, 5:30 p.m.–10:30 p.m.; closed Sunday May to September.* MAJOR CREDIT CARDS; LIQUOR LICENSE.

With dishes such as Duck Tamales, Rack of Lamb with Spicy Pepper Jelly, Salmon with Jalapeño Honey, and Shrimp Quesadilla with Fresh Basil, this restaurant—one of the finest in Phoenix—simply blows diners away. French-born Chef Vincent seamlessly combines classic French techniques and Southwestern ingredients. The same mix of styles is evident in the sophisticated decor. Throughout their tour of the Southwest, co-authors DeWitt and Wilan picked this restaurant as the finest they encountered.

WINDOWS ON THE GREEN AT THE PHOENICIAN RESORT

6000 E. Camelback Road, Scottsdale (602-941-8200). *Open Saturday and Sunday, 10 a.m.–3 p.m. (brunch); Monday–Friday, 11 a.m.– 3 p.m. (lunch); Tuesday–Sunday, 6 p.m.–10 p.m. (dinner).* MAJOR CREDIT CARDS; LIQUOR LICENSE.

The Windows restaurant is situated above the pro shop with a wonderful view of the golf course, so you might expect Middle American–style food instead of Chef Rubin's Southwestern inventions like Lobster-Corn Chowder and Venison Chili. His off-beat and delicious fresh baked rolls and bread with flavored butters and warm syrups are to die for.

Recipes

GREEN CORN TAMALES

The "green" in this favorite Arizona *tamal* refers both to the green chiles and the fresh, or green, corn used in the filling. Tamales are usually a seasonal dish, prepared in the summer and early fall when fresh corn is available. This recipe is from Poncho's and is delicious as a side dish.

3 cups corn masa
¾ cup lard or shortening
½ teaspoon baking powder
Pinch of salt
1½ cups green chile cut into thin strips
1½ cups grated longhorn cheese
3 cups freshly cooked white corn, pureed
20 or more corn husks, rinsed

Combine the first four ingredients and mix thoroughly until the dough is very fluffy. Add the chiles, cheese, and corn and mix again, taking care not to crush the chile strips. Let the mixture sit for at least 10 minutes.

Put a large spoonful of the mixture on a corn husk, roll up, and tie each end in a bow with a thin sliver of corn husk.

Put the tamales in a steamer and steam over medium heat for about 1 hour.

To serve, place the tamales on a plate and allow the guests to unwrap their own.

YIELD: **20 OR MORE TAMALES**
HEAT SCALE: MILD

GRILLED SHRIMP SALAD WITH FRIZZLED TORTILLAS

This recipe is courtesy of Vincent Guerithault on Camelback, a restaurant that serves perhaps the finest New Southwestern cuisine in the region. It was interesting to visit a restaurant where French ambience is combined with Southwestern tastes.

2 blue corn tortillas, cut into thin strips
2 yellow corn tortillas, cut into thin strips
½ cup olive oil
1 tablespoon each red, green, and yellow bell peppers, diced
1 tablespoon fresh ginger, julienned
2 tablespoons chopped fresh basil
2 tablespoons sherry wine vinegar

1 **tablespoon diced tomato**
Salt and pepper to taste
Assorted greens such as lamb lettuce, red oak leaf, argula, and watercress
1 **pound large fresh shrimp (or the equivalent of 4 large shrimp per person)**

Sauté the tortilla strips in olive oil to frizzle them. When they are crisp, remove from the oil and drain thoroughly. Reserve the oil.

In a large bowl, combine the peppers, ginger, basil, vinegar, tomato, and the reserved olive oil (save 2 teaspoons for the shrimp). Season the mixture to taste. Add the greens and the tortilla strips and gently mix. Divide the salad onto four salad plates.

Brush each shrimp lightly with the remaining olive oil and grill them over a very hot fire for about 30 seconds per side, taking care not to overcook them. Serve the hot shrimp over the mixed greens and tortilla strips.

SERVES: **4**

MACHACA

Common throughout the Southwest in home cooking but not so common in restaurants (who knows why?), this savory shredded meat is a versatile ingredient for tacos, enchiladas, and burritos. The word is derived from the Spanish *machacar* (to pound), an apt description of the appearance of the meat. This recipe is from our late friend, Barbara Graham.

3 - **pound arm roast**
   Water
1½ **cups coarsely chopped green chile**
1 **cup tomatoes, chopped**
½ **cup onion, diced**
½ **teaspoon garlic powder**

Place the roast in a large pan with water to cover and simmer covered until tender and the meat begins to fall apart,

11-5 Southwestern Food Items at Peppers in Scottsdale

about 3 to 4 hours. Remove the roast from the pan, remove the fat and bone, and shred the meat by hand or with a fork.

Return the meat to the pan, add the remaining ingredients, stir well, and simmer until all the liquid has been absorbed by the meat.

SERVES: **6 TO 8**
HEAT SCALE: MEDIUM

SERVING SUGGESTION: Place the meat in a large flour tortilla with lettuce, tomato, cheese, and sour cream for a super burro.

SOUTHWESTERN GREEN CHILE CORN BREAD WITH PRICKLY PEAR BUTTER

This intriguing combination of recipes is courtesy of Chef Lenard Rubin, who is responsible for the Southwestern dishes at the Windows on the Green restaurant, at the exclusive Phoenician Resort in Scottsdale.

Corn Bread

  1 **cup butter**
  ¾ **cup sugar**
  4 **eggs**
  ½ **cup chopped green chile**
1½ **cups cream-style corn**
  ½ **cup grated cheddar cheese**
  ½ **cup grated jack cheese**
  1 **cup flour**
  1 **cup yellow corn meal**
  2 **tablespoons baking powder**
  1 **teaspoon salt**

Cream the butter and sugar and add the eggs slowly, one at a time. Add the remaining ingredients and mix well. Pour the mixture into a 9-inch, buttered square pan. Bake at 325° for approximately 1 hour. Serve with Prickly Pear Butter.

SERVES: **6 TO 8**
HEAT SCALE: **MILD**

Prickly Pear Butter

  1 **pound unsalted butter**
  2 **ripe prickly pear fruits (*tunas*, or substitute ½ cup strawberries or raspberries)**
  1 **bunch cilantro, chopped fine**
  ½ **cup honey**
  Salt to taste

Let the butter soften slightly at room temperature. Peel the cactus fruits, puree in a blender, and strain the juice through a fine sieve. Combine the juice and the remaining ingredients in a blender or food processor and blend until smooth.

Put the mixture in a bowl and refrigerate until it begins to harden. Spread the butter in a wide strip on a sheet of waxed paper. Roll up the paper as you would a cigar to make a cylinder of butter. Freeze this cylinder; before serving, return it to the refrigerator to soften slightly for easy slicing.

YIELD: 1¼ POUNDS

ADOVADO RIBS

From Victoria Chavez at Los Dos Molinos comes this Phoenix version of pork baked with red chiles. Increase the spiciness by adding a few chiltepins to the sauce.

- **10 red New Mexican chile pods, stems and seeds removed**
- **4 cloves garlic**
- **2 cups water**
- **1 teaspoon Mexican oregano**
- **½ teaspoon freshly ground black pepper**
- **4 pounds country-style pork ribs**
  Garlic
  Salt
- **1 cup chopped onions**

Puree the first 5 ingredients in a blender. Rub the ribs with fresh garlic and salt and place them in a shallow baking pan. Pour the chile sauce over the ribs and top with the onions.

Cover and bake at 325° for 6 hours.

SERVES: **4 TO 6**
HEAT SCALE: MEDIUM

—VICTORIA CHAVEZ

CHAPTER

◆

12

TUCSON

Tucson reminds us in many ways of Albuquerque. The cities are similar in size, and both have a major state university, an Air Force base, scenic mountain backdrops, Spanish-Indian-Anglo heritage, wonderful food, excellent zoos, and loads of history and culture. Tucson, however, has the beautiful saguaro cacti, which are not found in New Mexico.

Although Tucson has the same sprawling urban growth as Albuquerque, its compact downtown historic districts can be visited on a walking tour.

Things to Do and See

The often misspelled name of this city is derived from a Pima Indian word, *stjuk-shon*, meaning foot of a dark mountain, an allusion to Sentinel Peak—the mountain with the large "A" painted on it. The location was originally a Pima village, and Spanish Padre Eusebio Francisco Kino selected it in 1700 as the site of the first San Xavier del Bac Mission. The existing mission, which was moved from its original site a couple of miles away, was constructed between 1783 and 1797 and today is a striking example of mission architecture. The White Dove of the Desert, as it's called, is located on I-19 at San Xavier Road (602-294-2624), and is one of the most photographed missions in the Southwest.

TUCSON'S TWO GREAT OCTOBER FOOD FIESTAS

"Tucson Eat Yourself" is what most locals call Tucson Meet Yourself, an annual fiesta held in mid-October in El Presidio Park. Organized by Big Jim Griffith, director of the Southwest Folklore Center at the University of Arizona, the fiesta is a multicultural affair that features everything from Western Apache Gaan dancing to a low-rider car show. But food is the main attraction, with more than forty booths offering international specialties such as Cuban roast pork and black beans, Carolina low-country barbecue, Greek *spanikopita*, and even some Sonoran-style treats. For information, call 602-621-3392.

Also in October is the annual Fiesta de los Chiles, held at the Tucson Botanical Gardens (602-326-9255). Booths serve ready-to-eat chile cuisines from the Southwest, the South, Mexico, and the Orient; fresh, dried, and roasted chiles; and chiles growing in pots. There are dozens of kinds of jarred salsas, plus chile-inspired artifacts ranging from earrings to wind socks. Top it all off with a dish of chiltepin ice cream and take home some heirloom chile seeds for your garden.

—COLETTE AND JOHN BANCROFT

El Presidio Historic District, bounded by Alameda, Church, and Franklin streets, consists of some of the oldest buildings in Tucson. Among the district's sights are such attractions as the Tucson Museum of Art, 140 N. Main, with its permanent collection of Western, Pre-Columbian, and Spanish Colonial art; the El Charro Restaurant, one of the oldest in town; and restored private residences, mansions, galleries, and shops. South of this area, on the other side of the Convention Center, is the Barrio Viejo, Tucson's oldest neighborhood, which includes the Cushing Street Bar and Restaurant, 343 S. Meyer Street, a former country store built over 100 years ago; and El Tiradito, Main Street, a shrine commemorating a tragic love triangle.

Like Phoenix, Tucson has numerous outdoor attractions. The Tucson Botanical Gardens, 2150 N. Alvernon Way (602-326-9255), is small compared to the Desert Botanical Garden in Phoenix, but still has nice displays of cacti, succulents, native plants, and herbs. (If you want to buy cacti, try Tanque Verde Gardens, 10810 E. Tanque Verde Road.)

Just off I-10 (Speedway exit) are three unusual and fascinating outdoor fun spots: The International Wildlife Museum, 4800 W. Gates Pass Road (602-624-4024), with wild animals from six continents in 300 exhibits; Old Tucson Studios, 201 S. Kinney Road (602-883-6457), a classic movie set that features gunfights, illusion shows, shops, restaurants, and stunt demonstrations; and the Arizona-Sonora Desert Museum, Tucson Mountain Park on W. Gates Pass Road (602-883-2702), which is an absolutely fascinating zoo-museum-botanical garden with 200 animal species and 300 plant species preserved in their native Sonoran habitat.

Surrounding the Arizona-Sonora Desert Museum is the Western part of Saguaro National Monument, Kinney Road (602-883-6366), a preserve for those huge cacti that can grow forty feet tall. The monument offers spectacular vistas and wildlife such as javelinas, coyotes, and bobcats. Wildlife can also be found at the Reid Park Zoo on E. 22nd Avenue (602-791-0422), which is one of the finest small zoos in the country with more than 450 animals.

One park not to miss is Tohono Chul Park, 7366 N. Paseo Drive (602-797-1711), with its spectacular views—and a tea room. An unnamed reporter for the *Tucson Weekly* reported ecstatically: "While the courtyard is delightful, the patio facing a meandering path into the thirty-seven acre park is paradise. The umbrellas over the tables are hardly needed as you dine beneath a canopy of palo verdes, cottonwoods, and other non-thirsty trees. While you make your selection from a menu of inviting fare, you'll be entertained by hummingbirds darting among a wide variety of desert flowering shrubs like salvia, fuschia, and penstemmon. Birds sip from a shallow-tiled fountain. Monarchs and other butterflies inspect the potted greens. And the agaves in the distance look like they've been carefully sculpted. Lately, a white dove has been hanging around, waiting for crumbs." (The *Tucson Weekly* kindly provided us with the issue containing their Best of Tucson feature, and we appreciate their observations on the food scene in the Tucson area.)

Tucson has its share of fine museums. The Arizona State Museum, Park Ave. at University Blvd. (602-621-6302), has exhibits on the natural, environmental, archaeological, and cultural history of the Southwest. Arizona's history from the Spanish period to modern times is featured at the Arizona Historical Society Tucson Museum, 949 E. 2nd Street (602-628-5774). The Old Pueblo Museum in Foothills Mall, 7401 N. La Cholla Blvd. (602-742-2355), has a large collection of Southwestern art and artifacts; and the Amerind Foundation Museum, about sixty miles east of Tucson between Benson and Wilcox off I-10 (602-622-0956), is an archaeological and ethnographical museum with fine displays of jewelry, pottery, baskets, and other crafts.

Two other museums will interest aviation buffs. The Pima Air Museum, 6000 E. Valencia Road (602-574-0462), has one of the largest collections of vintage aircraft in the West, and the Titan Missile Museum, exit 69 off I-19 (602-791-2929), is a deactivated ICBM missile site that offers a guided tour of the underground launch complex complete with a Titan missile in its silo. A more otherworldly attraction is fifty-six miles from Tucson atop the Quinlan Mountains. The Kitt Peak Observatory (602-325-9200) is the world's observatory for stellar, solar, and planetary research.

Near Tucson are several interesting towns, including Bisbee, a mining boomtown complete with open pit, architectural wonders, and galleries. Also interesting is Tombstone, once one of the West's wildest towns but now a tourist resort, health center, and National Historical Landmark. Don't miss the O.K. Corral, Boothill Cemetery, and the Bird Cage Theatre. Tumacacori, forty miles south of Tucson, has a National Historical Park with a garden and a museum; and Casa Grande National Monument, about seventy miles west of Tucson, is a prehistoric, four-story pueblo with an adjacent museum.

For more information on Tucson and a map of the downtown historic district, contact the Tucson Convention and Visitors Bureau, 130 S. Scott Street, Tucson, AZ 85701 (602-624-1817).

In Search of *Carne Seca*

Food is important in Tucson. So important that in their Best of Tucson survey, *Tucson Weekly* urged readers to find the best

12-1 Cafe Terra Cotta in Tucson

food in the city and pay particular attention to regional specialties. "It is your duty," the editors wrote to the public, "to eat green corn tamales in every restaurant and report your findings to the green corn tamale hot line." Another dish to watch out for in Tucson is that unusual—but tasty—sun-dried beef.

It's fitting that *carne seca*, one of the hallmark dishes of Sonoran fare, should be prepared in part by sun-drying. Tucson, and most of southern Arizona, is part of the Sonoran Desert, one of the hottest and most arid regions of North America.

Carne seca is one of those foods that tastes a lot better than it sounds. Its name translates as dried meat. But this is no jerky. In fact, although it's called *carne seca* south of the Gila River, it's called *machaca* north of the river, and there it's not sun-dried.

When it's done right, as in Tucson, *carne seca* is a rare treat: shreds of tender but slightly chewy beef, infused with a complex, smoky savor from its marinade of garlic and citrus juices; its hours of sun-drying; and sautéing with onions, tomatoes, green chiles, and more garlic.

The dish, like much of Sonoran food, differs from other Mexican-style cuisine in several ways: its emphasis on beef and cheese (a result of the ranching heritage of the region), its more extensive use of flour tortillas, and the more subtle heat of its seasonings. Sonoran cooks usually have a deft but light hand with chiles, so we've made an effort to find some spicier recipes.

Some of the best *carne seca* in Tucson is served at El Charro, 311 N. Court Avenue. This restaurant has been run by the same family since 1922, and owners Carlotta and Ray Flores still make *carne seca* using the same method developed by Carlotta's aunt, Monica Flin, the restaurant's founder, some seventy years ago.

Each day, about fifty pounds of thinly sliced beef is marinated in pureed garlic and lemon or lime juice. Then it's placed in a wire basket and hauled to the top of El Charro's roof and spread out to dry in the sun. The drying time varies according to the weather, and the beef is usually chewier in summer than in winter.

After several hours, the beef is brought down and shredded. When a customer orders it, the *carne seca* is sauteed with chiles, onions, garlic, and tomatoes, and served in one of a myriad of ways—anything from tucked in a taco to fried inside a *chimichanga*.

There are plenty of Sonoran specialties to try if you visit Tucson's Mexican restaurants, but don't miss your chance to savor *carne seca*—it's a truly unique product of Tucson's sun and climate as well as of the city's cultural heritage.

—COLETTE AND JOHN BANCROFT

Markets and Bakeries

FOOD CONSPIRACY

412 N. 4th Avenue (602-624-4821). *Open Monday–Saturday, 9 a.m.–7:30 p.m.; Sunday, 9 a.m.–6 p.m.* NO CREDIT CARDS; BEER AND WINE.

Tucson Weekly staffers picked this "conspiratorial cooperative" as a likely spot for produce, 200 herbs and spices, bulk foods, and the large selection of salsas and hot sauces. Sandwiches and salads are available for carry-out.

LA JOLLA BAKERY

1427 S. Fourth Avenue (602-623-0360). *Open Monday–Saturday, 6:30 a.m.–7 p.m.; Sunday, 6:30 a.m.–4 p.m.* VISA, MC; NO LIQUOR.

Simply the best in Mexican baked goods here, including fruit-filled *empanadas*, sugar encrusted *lenguas*, and a selection of breads and rolls. They also make non-traditional doughnuts and long johns.

REAY'S RANCH MARKET

3360 E. Speedway (602-795-9844) and 4751 E. Sunrise Drive (602-299-8858). *Open daily, 8 a.m.–10 p.m.* VISA, MC; LIQUOR LICENSE.

This is the city's best meat, fish, and poultry market. It stocks a wide selection of freshly harvested herbs and hard-to-find specialty items. Local products, such as salsas, are sold in quantity. Both locations have small but good cafes.

RINCON FOOD MARKET

2513 E. 6th Street (602-327-6653). *Open Monday–Saturday, 7 a.m.–10 p.m.; Sunday, 8 a.m.–9 p.m.* NO CREDIT CARDS; BEER AND WINE.

Where else do you find rattlesnake in the meat case? The Rincon has expanded greatly since 1975, and the market's evolution is evident as you move from the older room to a newer, much larger Euro-style deli/bottle shop cum cafe on the east end. It is the culinary/social nexus of the affluent Sam Hughes neighborhood—known to locals as Barrio Volvo. The market has a great selection of deli meats, dried and frozen pastas, and local products, plus there's an in-house bakery offering cakes, cookies, pastries, and muffins of considerable local reputation.

Retail Shops

CHERI'S DESERT HARVEST

1840 E. Winsett Street (602-623-4141). *Open Monday–Friday, 8 a.m.–5 p.m.* NO CREDIT CARDS; NO LIQUOR.

This combination processing plant and retail location specializes in desert fruit and bread products, including prickly pear jelly, margarita marmalade, jalapeño corn bread, pecan bread, cactus syrup, pomegranate syrup, and even a Southwestern beer bread. They will ship anywhere in the United States—call for a brochure.

CHILE PEPPER

201 Tubac Road, Tubac (602-398-2921). *Open daily,*
10 a.m.–5 p.m. VISA, MC; NO LIQUOR.

This Southwestern shop has a taste of Europe with its cap-
pucino bar. It sells a wide variety of specialty foods, including
local jams and jellies, *ristras*, salsas, hot sauces, barbecue
sauces, Southwestern mustards, and English mustards. All
their foods are available for tastings, and there's a wide selection of cookbooks here, too. The Chile Pepper accepts mail
orders—call for a catalog.

DESERT ROSE SALSA

1850 W. Grant Road, Suite 102 (602-620-6227). *Open*
Monday–Friday, 8 a.m.–4 p.m. VISA, MC; NO LIQUOR.

This retail operation carries only its own product line: Desert
Rose tortilla chips, many salsas, cactus ketchup, and Tango
sauces—papaya or tamarind with Habanero chiles. Call for a
mail-order catalog, and be sure to stop by for a free jar of
salsa.

GOURMET EMPORIUM AND CHEESE SHOP

4744 E. Sunrise (602-299-5576). *Open Monday–Thursday,*
9 a.m.–7 p.m.; Friday and Saturday, 9 a.m.–6 p.m. VISA, MC;
BEER AND WINE.

This shop is headquarters for a wide variety of specialty foods
from the Southwest, including pestos, hot sauces, mustards,
and local southern Arizona wines. Other interesting items are
Pikled Garlik, jams, jellies, chile pastas, and red lime marmalade. Carry-out sandwiches, party platters, and gift baskets top off the selection at this top-notch food shop.

12-2 Mi Nidito, One of South Tucson's Best Restaurants

THE PECAN STORE

1625 East Helmet Peak Road, 15 miles south of Tucson, Exit 75 off I-19 in Sahuarita (602-791-2062). *Open Monday–Friday, 9 a.m.–5 p.m.; Sunday, 10 a.m.–4 p.m.* VISA, MC; NO LIQUOR.

In addition to fresh pecans and pecan candies, this shop, nestled in the world's largest pecan orchard, offers a complete line of Southwestern gourmet foods, including salsas, mustards, jellies, and jams.

SANTA CRUZ CHILI & SPICE COMPANY

Highway 89, just south of Tumacacori National Monument (602-398-2591). *Open Monday–Saturday, 8 a.m.–noon and 1 p.m.–5 p.m.* NO CREDIT CARDS; NO LIQUOR.

For fifty years, this gift shop, with a small ranching museum next door, has been spicing up the lives of Arizona food lovers.

They specialize in chile, including *ristras*, pastes, pods, and powders. Their sauces include locally produced salsas, green sauces, and barbecue sauces.

TERRITORIAL GOURMET

2766 N. Country Club Road (602-323-3322). *Open Monday–Saturday, 11 a.m.–6:30 p.m.* VISA, MC; NO LIQUOR.

Territorial Gourmet has one of Arizona's most diverse collections of Southwestern food items, including fifteen salsas, unique mustards, dried soup mixes, jerky, seasonings, and chiles. Non-food items of interest are T-shirts, mugs, tiles, and pottery. If you're looking for a gift to bring back from Tucson, it's here. They'll ship anywhere UPS goes—call for information.

TOTALLY SOUTHWEST

5575 E. River Road (602-577-2295). *Open Monday–Saturday, 10 a.m.–6 p.m.; Sunday, noon–4 p.m.* VISA, MC; NO LIQUOR.

The name says it all: furniture, accessories, gifts, jewelry, and food from Arizona and nearby. Food items include barbecue sauces, Sonoran seasonings, jalapeño jellies, cactus jams, and numerous salsas.

TUBAC COUNTRY MARKET

Off I-19, south of Tucson in Tubac (602-884-1514). *Open daily, 7 a.m.–9 p.m.* VISA, MC; BEER AND WINE.

There's everything imaginable here, from Tarahumara baskets to Mexican curios, to *piñatas*, to Southwestern cookbooks. Food items include chiles (they grow their own), salsas, hot sauces, wreaths and *ristras*, powders, dried spices, jams, and jellies. The restaurant and deli serve all kinds of chile food rated "high octane hot" plus spicy and regular.

Tucson Botanical Gardens Gift Shop

2150 North Alvernon Way (602-326-9255). *Open daily, 8 a.m. to 4:30 p.m.*

This gift shop loves chile peppers and features books, T-shirts, and food products. Additionally, it carries nature books, travel guides, and calendars about Arizona and the Sonora Desert.

Restaurants

Boccata

5605 E. River Road, River Center (602-577-9309). *Open Monday–Thursday and Saturday, 5:30 p.m.–11 p.m.; Friday, 11 a.m.–2 a.m.; Sunday, 10:30 a.m.–2 p.m. and 5:30 p.m.–11 p.m.* MAJOR CREDIT CARDS; LIQUOR LICENSE.

Here's an escape from the Southwest into Tuscany. The mussels steamed in white wine and herbs sell out every evening. Boccata serves sensational pastas, seafood, and grilled meats, plus heavenly terrines. The cooking is invariably superior and inventive with impeccably fresh ingredients. The decor is lush, warm, comfortable, and witty. Boccata is one of the finest restaurants in Tucson, despite the fact it doesn't serve *carne seca.*

Cafe Poca Cosa

88 E. Broadway and 20 N. Scott Avenue (602-622-6400). *Open at Broadway Monday–Thursday, 6 a.m.–9 p.m.; Friday and Saturday, 6 a.m.–10 p.m.; Sunday, 8 a.m.–noon. Open at Scott Monday–Friday, 7:30 a.m.–3 p.m.* VISA, MC; LIQUOR AT BROADWAY, NO LIQUOR AT SCOTT.

Suzana Davila, chef and owner of this quirky restaurant, draws on her Mexican heritage to combine standard and novel ingredients in new and delightful ways. Plates come to the table brimming with terrific combinations of tropical fruits, beans, chicken, pork, fish, chocolate, chiles, tortillas, rice, or something exotic Suzana just discovered. The colorful patio

12-3 New Southwestern Cuisine Triumphs at Janos

at the Broadway location, with its splashing fountain, is a cool delight on warm summer evenings.

CAFE TERRA COTTA

4310 N. Campbell Avenue (602-577-8100). *Open daily, 11 a.m.–10 p.m.; Sunday, 11 a.m.–3 p.m. (brunch).* MAJOR CREDIT CARDS; LIQUOR LICENSE.

An aroma of wood smoke greets you at the door as you enter the casual but sophisticated setting of Terra Cotta. With a menu designed for grazing, this pioneer of New Southwestern cooking offers such eclectic dishes as pork *adobado* and warm garlic custard with hazelnuts. They also retail locally produced salsas and other food products.

EL CHARRO

311 N. Court Avenue (602-622-5465). *Open Sunday– Thursday, 11 a.m.–9 p.m.; Friday and Saturday, 11 a.m.– 10 p.m.* MAJOR CREDIT CARDS; LIQUOR LICENSE.

This restaurant, open since 1922, claims to be the birthplace of the *chimichanga*, the home of the best *carne seca*, and the site of the gigantic *USA Today chimichanga*. It could very well be all those things, but we do know it's located in a historic downtown house, has been run by the same family for decades, and serves great Sonoran-style food. Don't miss the green corn tamales in season.

CROSSROADS RESTAURANT

2602 S. Fourth Avenue (602-624-0395). *Open Sunday– Thursday, 11 a.m.–midnight; Friday and Saturday, 11 a.m.–1 a.m.* MAJOR CREDIT CARDS; LIQUOR LICENSE.

A favorite with locals, this lively weekend spot offers Guaymas shrimp in a variety of preparations (try *al mojo de ajo*) and *cabrilla* sea bass as their specialties, but also serves an assortment of Sonoran-style dishes.

ENCORE MED

5931 N. Oracle Road (602-888-1130). *Open Monday–Friday, 11 a.m.–2:30 p.m. and 5:30 p.m.–closing; Saturday, 5:30 p.m.– closing.* MAJOR CREDIT CARDS; LIQUOR LICENSE.

Probably the only restaurant in Tucson serving eels flown in from Spain, the Encore Med has authentic Old World cooking, so we can see its inspiration on the New World. Recommended are the ambrosial Paella Valenciana, tapas, Calimari alla Romana, and the outstanding sauces.

THE GRUBSTEAK

2851 W. Valencia Road (602-578-9009). *Open Monday– Thursday, 11:30 a.m.–1:30 p.m. and 5 p.m.–9 p.m.; Saturday, 5 p.m.– 10 p.m.; Sunday, 5 p.m.–9 p.m.* MAJOR CREDIT CARDS; LIQUOR LICENSE.

Jeans, boots, and stetsons are the favored attire as the bar is jammed with both genuine and wannabe cowpunchers. The favorite dish here is the Hot Steak, an inch-thick sirloin stuffed with Hatch green chiles and grilled over a mesquite fire. The green chile cheeseburger is also highly recommended.

LA INDITA

622 N. Fourth Avenue (602-792-0523) and 8578 E. Broadway (602-886-9191). *Open Monday–Thursday, 11 a.m.– 9 p.m.; Friday, 11 a.m.–6 p.m.; Saturday, 6 p.m.–9:30 p.m.; Sunday, 9 a.m.–9 p.m.* NO CREDIT CARDS; NO LIQUOR.

The roots of this restaurant are Tarascan, from the state of Michoacán, Mexico. Its homemade Indian items run the gamut from Tarascan tacos filled with *carne seca* to Tohono O'odham red chile to Navajo tacos to Sonoran *chiles rellenos.* Dine outside in warm weather.

JACK'S ORIGINAL BARBEQUE

5250 E. 22nd Street (602-750-1280). *Open Monday– Saturday, 11 a.m.–8 p.m.; Sunday, noon–8 p.m.* NO CREDIT CARDS; NO LIQUOR.

Since 1951, Jack's has been luring customers into its parking lot with the aroma of wood smoke and sizzling meats. They call this mouth-watering style of barbecued ribs, links, and sliced beef and pork 'cue "Kansas City–style," but the truth is that it has Tucson written all over it. Jack Banks sold the place a few years ago, but public outrage brought him back.

JANOS

150 N. Main Avenue (602-884-9426). *Open Monday– Saturday, 5:30 p.m.–closing (November–June); Tuesday– Saturday, 5:30 p.m.–closing (July–October).* MAJOR CREDIT CARDS; LIQUOR LICENSE.

Janos Wilder, owner and chef, has fashioned a New Southwest menu that changes half daily and half by the season. He combines impeccably fresh local ingredients with wit and imagination, and diners can expect to find everything on the menu from duck tamales to lobster in Champagne-papaya sauce, a perennial favorite. His restaurant, in the El Presidio Historic District downtown, shares a courtyard with the Tucson Museum of Art. It has thick adobe walls, high viga ceilings, fireplaces, and patio dining in nice weather.

TUCSON WEEKLY'S BEST OF TUCSON RESTAURANT TIPS

Based on the ballots of thousands of Tucson foodies who love international cuisine, here are some of the more worldly Tucson restaurants, cuisine by cuisine.

Chinese: Szechuan Omei, 2601 E. Speedway Blvd.

Indian Subcontinent: New Delhi Palace, 6751 E. Broadway Blvd.

French: Le Rendezvous, 3844 E. Fort Lowell Road

Italian: Caruso's, 434 N. Fourth Avenue

Japanese: Japanese Kitchen, 8424 Old Spanish Trail

Mexican: Mi Nidito, 1813 S. Fourth Avenue

Middle Eastern: Tork's Cafe, 1701 N. Country Club Road

Thai: Mina's Thai Restaurant, 2746 N. Campbell Avenue

LEO'S MEXICAN RESTAURANT

5114 E. Speedway (602-325-9180). *Open Monday–Thursday, 10 a.m.–10 p.m.; Friday and Saturday, 11 a.m.–11 p.m.*
VISA, MC; LIQUOR LICENSE.

This small, storefront cafe tucked behind a convenience store has astonishingly fast service, which means that everything gets to the table within seconds of being lifted from the stove. Try Viva Villa, a trio of enchiladas (*carne seca*, cheese, and chicken with green chiles) or Zapata, a gorgeous *chile relleno* teamed with two cheese enchiladas, rice, and beans. By the way, the beans are a toothsome hybrid of refried and pot beans.

LI'L ABNER'S

8500 N. Silverbell Road (602-744-2800). *Open Sunday– Thursday, 5 p.m.–10 p.m.; Friday and Saturday, 5 p.m.– 11 p.m.* VISA, MC; LIQUOR LICENSE.

Li'l Abner's began its life in the past century as a stop on the Butterfield Stage Line, and its history shows in its scarred adobe walls. Inside are two rustic dining rooms and a bar, but a picnic table on the back patio is the place to eat. The restaurant serves a monster porterhouse steak, which is grilled over mesquite on the back patio. The trimmings of this classic ranch-style meal include ranch beans, garlic toast, salsa fresca, and salad, all washed down with Dos Equis or Negra Modelo beer.

MI NIDITO

1813 S. Fourth Avenue (602-622-5081). *Open Wednesday– Thursday, 11:30 a.m.–11:30 p.m.; Friday and Saturday; 11:30 a.m.–2 a.m.; Sunday, 11:30 a.m.–midnight.* VISA, MC; BEER AND WINE.

The universal choice by the *Tucson Weekly* readers for best in most categories of Sonoran-style food, Mi Nidito (My Little Nest) is always crowded, but the wait is worthwhile. Recommended dishes include the *chiles rellenos*, cheese crisps, and *chimichangas*. The service is brisk, the portions are large, and the prices are reasonable. It's been delighting food lovers here since 1952.

EL MINUTO CAFE

354 S. Main Avenue (602-882-4145). *Open Sunday– Thursday, 11 a.m.–11 p.m.; Friday and Saturday, 11 a.m.– 2 a.m.* MAJOR CREDIT CARDS; BEER AND WINE.

Located in Barrio Viejo since 1937 and recently renovated in a pretty pastel version of Mexican decor, El Minuto is a popular late-night spot that serves up great cheese crisps, award-winning *carne seca*, plus classic Sonoran cowboy fare. The waiters are attired in *guayaberas* (Mexican shirts), Tucson's official summer business attire.

PAINTED DESERT

3055 N. Campbell Avenue (602-795-8440). *Open Monday– Friday, 11:30 a.m.–3 p.m.; seven nights a week, 5:30 p.m.– 10 p.m.* MAJOR CREDIT CARDS; LIQUOR LICENSE.

An ever-changing menu is the hallmark of this imaginative New Southwestern restaurant, which offers such tempting dishes as Salmon in Arizona Sunset Sauce, Brie Quesadilla, and Grilled Bay Scallops in Red Pepper Cream. The South-western decor is understated and attractive, the service is attentive, and shared dishes are encouraged and nicely presented.

PAT'S DRIVE-IN

1202 W. Niagra Street, at N. Grande Avenue (602-624-0891). *Open Sunday–Thursday, 10:30 a.m.–9:30 p.m.; Friday and Saturday, 10:30 a.m.–10 p.m.* NO CREDIT CARDS; NO LIQUOR.

You'd expect the ghost of Richie Valens to drive up in a con-vertible to this traditional favorite of connoisseurs of gut-bomb fare. Pat's chili dogs—the best in Tucson—are served (believe it or not) Sonoran-style, topped with a meat and beans stew flavored with fresh chiles instead of powder. The heat scale ranges from merely blazing to nuclear meltdown. The fries are great and greasy.

PRESIDIO GRILL

3352 E. Speedway (602-327-4667). *Open Monday–Thursday, 11 a.m.–10 p.m.; Friday and Saturday, 11 a.m.–midnight; Sunday, 8 a.m.–10 p.m.* VISA, MC; LIQUOR LICENSE.

This bistro with Southwestern accents has a convivial atmo-sphere and is a great place to watch people, especially when they're enjoying the seasonally changing menu. The grilled entrees are great, as are the pastas and pizzas. Try the Chicken Santa Fe with Blue Corn Cakes.

12-4 Historic El Charro Restaurant

RANCHER'S CLUB

5151 E. Grant Road, in the Hotel Park Tucson (602-797-2624).
Open Monday–Friday, 11:30 a.m.–2 p.m. and 5:30 p.m.–
10 p.m.; Saturday, 5:30 p.m.–10:30 p.m. MAJOR CREDIT
CARDS; LIQUOR LICENSE.

Diners have to make several choices when ordering steaks in
the cowboy-kitsch, clubby atmosphere here. One is the cut of
steak or chop; the second is the type of wood it is grilled over
(mesquite to sassafras); and the third is which of the twenty
sauces, butters, or chutneys you'd like served with it. The
grilled veggies are wonderful, particularly the green chiles
and jicama.

EL RAPIDO

77 W. Washington Street (602-624-4725). *Open Monday–*
Friday, 8 a.m.–5 p.m.; Saturday, 9:30 a.m.–1:30 p.m. NO
CREDIT CARDS; NO LIQUOR.

This restaurant, open since 1933, defines the concept of the
green corn tamale—in season, of course. It's a true hole-in-
the-wall about a dozen feet wide and with room for about ten
hungry customers, but it's worth the trouble because the food

is homemade and the paper-thin tortillas are outstanding. Try the green chile burros.

EL SAGUARITO

6453 N. Oracle Road (602-297-1264). *Open Monday–Saturday, 7 a.m.–9 p.m.* VISA, MC; BEER AND WINE.

This tiny restaurant serves only non-smokers and bills itself as the "healthy Mexican food alternative" because it substitutes canola oil for lard and emphasizes fresh ingredients. Try the outstanding cheese crisps, guacamole, soups, red-hot salsa, and chicken *mole*.

TOHONO CHUL TEA ROOM

7633 N. Paseo del Norte, Tohono Chul Park (602-797-1171). *Open daily, 8 a.m.–4:45 p.m.* MAJOR CREDIT CARDS; LIQUOR LICENSE.

Although lunch is good, with the standard quiches, afternoon tea, served from 2:30 to 4:30, is a delight with a choice of various teas accompanied by pastries and freshly baked scones. The food may not be classic Southwestern, but the scenery is, as the diner is surrounded by the native flora and fauna of the Sonoran desert. The enclosed courtyard, with its fountain and bougainvillea, is delightful.

Recipes

CHILE PASADO

Translated as chile of the past, this is the original recipe for preserving green chiles before the advent of canning and freezing. Be forewarned that the result looks awful—nearly black and stringy. However, when rehydrated, it regains its greenish color and makes a fine green chile sauce for casseroles or enchiladas. It can also be used in soups and stews. Since *chile pasado* costs as much as $16 a pound in Southwestern markets, it makes sense to prepare your own. The light weight of the *chile pasado* is convenient, say, when traveling to Italy to make enchiladas for friends there, as we did once.

5 pounds green chile pods (about 35–40 pods)

Follow the instructions in Chapter 7 (Las Cruces) for roasting and peeling green chiles. When finished, cut the pods into wide strips and place them on a teflon-coated cookie sheet. Cover with cheesecloth to keep insects off and place it in the full sun. Bring the chiles in at night to prevent dew from accumulating. The number of drying days depends on the humidity. A food dehydrator can also be used. When dry, the chiles should be black and brittle. The best way to preserve *chile pasado* is to put it in Ziploc bags and freeze it, though it can be stored in jars in the pantry. To use, simply place in warm water for 30 minutes to rehydrate.

YIELD: ABOUT ½ POUND
HEAT SCALE: VARIES

ORANGE AND JICAMA SALAD WITH RED CHILE POWDER

This lively salad is not only a salute to the citrus crops of Arizona, but also includes the tasty tuber jicama, which is steadily gaining favor even outside the Southwest.

2 oranges
1 small jicama, peeled and diced into ½-inch cubes
¾ cup sliced celery
1 small red onion, peeled and thinly sliced into rings
4 raw button mushrooms, sliced
1 fresh lime
4 teaspoons red chile powder

Peel the oranges and slice thinly. Divide and arrange overlapping slices among 4 salad plates. Combine the jicama, celery, onion rings, and mushrooms and divide the mixture equally on top of the orange slices.

Squeeze fresh lime juice over each salad and sprinkle with about a teaspoon of chile powder. A mixture of lime juice and olive oil can also be used for the dressing.

SERVES: 4
HEAT SCALE: MEDIUM

12-5 Chile Pepper Boxer Shorts for the True Aficionado

CARNE ADOVADA ESTILO SONORA (SONORAN-STYLE MARINATED PORK)

This unusual recipe, courtesy of Antonio Heras-Duran, is half *carne seca* and half grilled pork. Don't worry about exposing the meat to the air; it dries well and besides, the vinegar is the high-acid preservative.

10 dried red New Mexican chiles, stems removed, seeds removed and saved

10 chiltepins (or more to taste), seeds removed and saved

3 large cloves garlic

1 teaspoon Mexican oregano

1 teaspoon salt

½ cup cider vinegar

½ cup water

4 pounds pork tenderloin, sliced into strips ¼ to ½ inch thin*

Corn or flour tortillas

*For easier slicing, freeze the pork slightly, then slice.

1 small cabbage, chopped
Juice of 4 limes

Boil the New Mexican chiles until they are soft, reserving the seeds. Add the next five ingredients and puree in a blender to make the marinade.

Add the seeds to the chile marinade and marinate the pork in the mixture for an 1 hour. Hang the strips of meat over a clothesline in the sun and arrange cheesecloth around them to keep the insects away. Dry the meat in the sun for two days in dry weather; refrigerate until ready to use.

Grill the meat strips over mesquite wood for 1 to 2 minutes per side. Dice the strips and spread the meat over thin flour or corn tortillas. Spread chopped cabbage over the meat and sprinkle with lime juice. Fold the tortilla in half and serve.

SERVES: **8**
HEAT SCALE: **HOT TO EXTREMELY HOT**

—ANTONIO HERAS-DURAN

SONORAN-STYLE ENCHILADAS, MEXICAN VERSION

Our fourth and final enchilada recipe differs greatly from the Arizona version in Chapter 10. The main differences are the use of freshly made, thick corn tortillas and the inclusion of chiltepins in the sauce. We dined on these enchiladas one night in Tucson, and as Cindy Castillo was preparing them, we wrote down her recipe exactly.

Sauce

15 to 20 chiltepins, crushed
15 dried red New Mexican chiles, seeds and stems removed
1 teaspoon salt
Water

3 **cloves garlic**
1 **teaspoon vegetable oil**
1 **teaspoon flour**

In a saucepan, combine both kinds of chiles, salt, and enough water to cover. Boil for 10 or 15 minutes or until the chiles are quite soft.

Allow the chiles to cool; add the garlic and puree in a blender. Strain the mixture, mash the pulp through a strainer, and discard the skins.

Heat the oil in a saucepan, add the flour, and brown, taking care not to burn it. Add the chile puree and boil for 5 or 10 minutes until the sauce has thickened slightly. Set aside and keep warm.

Tortillas

2 **cups masa harina**
1 **egg**
1 **teaspoon baking powder**
1 **teaspoon salt**
  Water
  Vegetable oil for deep frying
2 **cups grated queso blanco or Monterey jack cheese**
  Shredded lettuce
3 **to 4 scallions, minced (white part only)**

Mix together thoroughly the first four ingredients, adding enough water to make dough. Using a tortilla press, make the tortillas. Deep fry each tortilla until it puffs up and turns slightly brown. Remove and drain on paper towels and keep warm.

To assemble and serve, place a tortilla on each plate and spoon over a generous amount of sauce. Top with the cheese, lettuce, and onions.

SERVES: **4 TO 6**
HEAT SCALE: **HOT**

—CINDY CASTILLO

Chiltepin Ice Cream

This novelty was first served in 1988 during the symposium on wild chiles at the Desert Botanical Garden in Phoenix and at the Fiesta de Los Chiles at the Tucson Botanical Gardens. It is very hot in the proportions given (despite the tendency of ice cream to cut the heat), so cooks may want to reduce the chiltepins.

½ **cup fresh green chiltepins, thoroughly pulverized (or substitute *chiltepines en escabeche* or dried red chiltepins that have been rehydrated and pulverized)**

1 **gallon vanilla ice cream**

Combine all ingredients and mix thoroughly until green (or red) flecks appear throughout the ice cream. Serve in small portions and warn people about what they're eating.

SERVES: **20 OR MORE**
HEAT SCALE: **HOT TO EXTREMELY HOT**

PART

FIVE

APPENDICES

APPENDIX

MAIL-ORDER SOURCES FOR SOUTHWESTERN FOOD ITEMS

Seeds

Native Seeds/SEARCH, 2509 N. Campbell Avenue, #325, Tucson, AZ 85719

Plants of the Southwest, Agua Fria Rt. 6, Box 11A, Santa Fe, NM 87501

Seeds of Change, 1364 Rufina Circle #5, Santa Fe, NM 87501

Seeds West, P.O. Box 1739, El Prado, NM 87529 (505-758-7268)

Shepherd's Garden Seeds, Shipping Office, 30 Irene St., Torrington, CT 06790

Cookbooks and Publications

Chile Pepper magazine, P.O. Box 4278, Albuquerque, NM 87196 (1-800-359-1483)

Jessica's Biscuit, Box 301, Newtonville, MA 02160 (1-800-878-4264)

Out West Publishing, P.O. Box 4278, Albuquerque, NM 87196
(1-800-359-1483)

Food and Gifts

Casados Farms, P.O. Box 1269, San Juan Pueblo, NM 87566
(505-852-2433)

Los Chileros, P.O. Box 6215, Santa Fe, NM 87502 (505-471-6967)

The Chili Emporium, 328 San Felipe Road NW, Albuquerque,
NM 87104 (1-800-766-4568)

Eagle Ranch Pistachio Groves, 7288 Highway 70, Alamogordo,
NM 88310 (1-800-432-0999)

Fredericksburg Herb Farm, P.O. Drawer 927, Fredericksburg,
TX 78624 (1-800-284-0525)

Great Southwest Cuisine Catalog, 630 W. San Francisco, Santa
Fe, NM 87501 (1-800-872-8787)

Hobson Gardens, Route 2, 3656 E. Hobson Road, Roswell, NM
88201 (1-800-488-7298)

Mannon's, P.O. Box 1959, Tubac, AZ 85646 (602-398-9314)

New Canaan Farms, P.O. Box 386, Dripping Springs, TX
78620

New Mexican Connection, 2833 Rhode Island NE, Albuquerque, NM 87110 (505-292-5493)

New Mexico Catalog, P.O. Box 261, Fairacres, NM 88033
(1-800-678-0585)

Old San Antonio Style Gourmet Sauces (1-800-972-3049)

Old Southwest Trading Company, P.O. Box 7545, Albuquerque, NM 87194 (505-836-0168)

Pendery's Spices, 304 E. Belknap, Fort Worth, TX 76102
(1-800-533-1870)

Santa Fe Exotix, Route 9, Box 56C, Santa Fe, NM 87501
(505-988-7063)

Simply Southwest by Mail, 7404 Menaul NE, Albuquerque, NM 87110 (1-800-447-6177)

Southwest America, 1506-C Wyoming NE, Albuquerque, NM 87112 (505-299-1856)

Southwestern Flavor Company, P.O. Box 315, Red River, NM 87558 (505-754-2221)

Stonewall Chile Pepper Company, P.O. Box 241, Stonewall, TX 78671 (1-800-232-2995)

APPENDIX

2

GLOSSARY OF SOUTHWESTERN COOKING TERMS AND INGREDIENTS

achiote: the orange-colored seeds of the annatto tree; used as a coloring agent and seasoning

adobado or **adovada**:   in Texas, a sour marinade paste made with herbs, chiles, and vinegar; in New Mexico and El Paso, a marinade for pork made with red New Mexican chiles, garlic, and oregano

adobo: thick cooking sauce consisting of tomatoes, vinegar, and spices

aguas frescas: fresh fruit drinks

ajo: garlic

albóndigas: meatballs

al carbón: charcoal grilled

al pastór: cooked on a spit over a fire

Anaheim chiles: misnomer for New Mexican chiles; now the term for a very mild New Mexican cultivar grown only in California

ancho (wide) chiles: the dried form of poblano chiles (substitute: pasilla chiles)

antojito: (little whim) an appetizer

árbol chiles: hot, dried red chiles from Mexico (substitute: dried red New Mexican chiles or pequins)

arroz: rice

asada or **asado**:   roasted or broiled

asadero: a rubbery white cheese originally made only in the Mexican states of Chihuahua and Michoacán, but now also produced in the United States (substitute: Monterey jack)

atole: a drink made from corn

azafrán: saffron

barbacoa: in Texas, pit-barbecued meat; in Mexico, the barbecued flesh of a cow's head

biscochitos: anise-flavored cookies (sometimes bizcochitos)

bolillo: Mexican hard roll; similar to French bread

borracho: (drunken); foods containing beer or liquor

buñelos: a sweetened fry bread

burros (Ariz.) and **burritos** (N.M. and Tex.):   flour tortillas stuffed with meats, cheeses, beans, and chile sauces, or a combination thereof

cabrito: kid (young goat, that is)

calabacita: squash; usually, zucchini-types

calamari: squid

caldillo: (little soup) a thick stew with beef and chiles; commonly served in El Paso and Juárez

caldo: a broth, stock, or clear soup

canela: cinnamon

capirotada: bread pudding

carne: meat

carne seca: dried beef or jerky

carnitas: (little pieces of meat) small chunks of pork fried to a crisp texture

cascabel chiles: (jingle bells) small, round, hot chiles that rattle when shaken (substitute: árbol chiles)

ceviche: raw seafood combined with lime juice; the lime juice "cooks" the seafood by combining with its protein and turning it opaque

chalupas: (little boats) fried corn tortillas in the shape of a boat containing shredded chicken or beans topped with salsa, guacamole, or cheese

chicharrón: crisp-fried pork skin

chicos: corn kernels that are roasted, then dried

chilaca chile: fresh pasilla chiles

chilaquiles: a casserole of tortilla wedges, salsa, and cheese

chile: the plants or pods of the *Capsicum* genus

chile caribe: red chile paste made from crushed or ground red chiles, garlic, and water

chile con queso: cheese and chile dip

chile pasado: (chile of the past) roasted, peeled, and sun-dried green chiles

chile pequin or **chilipiquín**: small, dried, quite hot red chiles; also called chiltepins, or chili tepins (substitute: cayenne powder or hot red chile powder)

chiles rellenos: stuffed chiles

chili: chile sauce with meat; chili con carne

chiltepins or **chilipiquíns**: small, round, wild chiles that grow in Arizona; in Texas, a wild variety called chilipiquín

chimichanga: deep-fat fried, stuffed burro topped with cheese and chile sauce

chipotle chiles: smoked and dried jalapeños (substitute: moritas, smoked serranos)

chorizo: spicy sausage made with pork, garlic, and red chile powder

cilantro: an annual herb (*Coriandrum sativum*) with seeds known as coriander; commonly used in salsas and soups (substitute: Italian parsley, or *culantro* (*Eryngium foetidum*)

comal: griddle

cumin or **comino**: an annual herb (*Cuminum cyminum*) whose seeds have a distinctive odor—the dominant flavor in Tex-Mex dishes such as chili con carne

desayuno: breakfast

empanada: pastry turnover

enchiladas: rolled or stacked corn tortillas filled with meat or cheese and covered with chile sauce

epazote: a strong and bitter perennial herb (*Chenopodium ambrosioides*) used primarily to flavor beans (known as ambrosia in English)

escabeche: vegetables, especially chiles, marinated or pickled in vinegar

fajitas: (little belts) marinated and grilled skirt steak

flan: baked caramel custard dessert

flautas: (flutes) tightly rolled, deep-fried enchiladas

frijoles: beans

gorditas: (little fat ones) stuffed corn cakes

guacamole: (mixture of vegetables) usually a blend of avocados, tomatoes, garlic, and chiles

guajillo chiles: medium-hot Mexican red chiles (substitute: New Mexican)

Habanero chiles: (from Havana) small orange or red chiles from the Caribbean and Yucatán that resemble a tam or bonnet—the hottest in the world (substitute: jalapeños or serranos)

hongos: mushroooms

hornos: outdoor ovens

huevos rancheros: ranch-style eggs

jalapeño chiles: small, fat chiles that are pickled, stuffed, or used in fresh salsas (substitute: serranos)

jamaica: a Mexican flower that flavors drinks and teas

jamón: ham

jícama: a white tuber (*Pachyrhizus erosus*) used in salads; tastes like a cross between an apple and a potato

lengua: tongue

lima: lemon

limón: lime

machaca: meat that is stewed, roasted, or broiled and then shredded

maíz: corn

manteca: lard

masa: corn dough

menudo: tripe soup, often with chiles

mescal: a liquor distilled from the agave plant

metate: stone for grinding corn

migas: in Texas, eggs scrambled with chorizo, tortilla chips, onions, tomatoes, cheese, and serrano chiles

molcajete: mortar made from volcanic stone

mole: (mixture) usually, a thick chile sauce made with many spices and chocolate

nachos: tostados topped with cheese and sliced jalapeños

natilla: custard dessert

New Mexican chiles: "long green" chiles grown in New Mexico; varieties include Big Jim, No. 6–4, Sandia, Española, Chimayo, etc. (substitute: poblanos)

nopales or **nopalitos**:   prickly pear cactus pads, spines removed

olla: a round, earthenware pot

pan: bread

pan dulce: sweet bread

papas: potatoes

parrilla: grill or broiler

parrillada: grilled items

pasilla chiles: (little raisin) an allusion to the aroma and dark brown color of this long, thin, Mexican chile (substitute: ancho chiles)

pepitas: roasted pumpkin seeds

pescado: fish

picadillo: shredded beef, spices, and other ingredients; usually used as a stuffing

picante: hot and spicy

pico de gallo: (beak of the rooster) salsa with tomatoes, onions, cilantro, and serrano chiles

piloncillo: brown, unrefined cane sugar

piñones: nuts of the piñon tree (*Pinus edulis*)

pipián: a sauce containing ground nuts or seeds and spices

piquin: see **chile pequin**

poblano chiles: (peppers of the people) dark green, fat chiles commonly used in Mexico and the Southwest; see **ancho**

pollo: chicken

posole: a thick stew made with pork, chiles, and hominy corn

puerco: pork

quelites: spinach and bean dish seasoned with chile and bacon

quesadilla: a flour tortilla turnover; usually stuffed with cheese, then toasted, fried, or baked

queso: cheese

rajas: strips; usually, strips of chiles

refrito: refried; mainly describes beans that are mashed and fried in lard

relleno: stuffed; see **chiles rellenos**

res: beef

ristra: a string of red chile pods

saguaro: tall cactus found in Arizona; its fruit is made into jams and jellies

salpicón: Mexican shredded meat salad

salsa: (sauce) usually used to describe uncooked sauces (*salsa cruda*)

serrano chiles: small, hot Mexican chiles; usually pickled or used green or red in fresh salsas (substitute: jalapeños)

sopa: soup

sopaipilla: from *sopaipa*, a fritter soaked in honey; in New Mexico, a puffed, fried bread, served with honey or filled with various stuffings

taco: stuffed corn tortilla having either a soft or crisp, fried shell

tamal: any filling enclosed in masa, wrapped in a corn shuck, and steamed (plural, tamales)

tamarindo: tamarind

taquito: rolled, deep-fried taco

tequila: a mescal (liquor) produced near Tequila in the state of Jalisco, Mexico

tomatillo: small, green husk tomato (*Physalis ixocarpa*) (substitute: small, regular tomatoes)

torta: a sandwich; often made with a bolillo

tostados: tortilla chips

tunas: prickly pear cactus fruits

yerba buena: mint

APPENDIX

3

ADDITIONAL READING

An Insider's Guide to the Texas Hills
   1991. Annual publication. Fredericksburg, Tex.: South Star Publishing.

ARNOLD, SAMUEL P.
   1990. *Eating up the Santa Fe Trail*. Niwot, Colo.: University Press of Colorado.

CALDWELL, RED
   1990. *Pit, Pot & Skillet*. San Antonio: Corona Publishing.

Chile Pepper
   1987–. The magazine of spicy world cuisine. Albuquerque: Out West Publishing.

COX, BEVERLY, AND JACOBS, MARTIN
   1991. *Spirit of the Harvest: North American Indian Cooking*. New York: Stewart, Tabori & Chang.

DEWALD, LOUISE
   1988. *Arizona Highways Heritage Cookbook*. Phoenix: Arizona Department of Transportation.

DEWITT, DAVE
   1989. *Texas Monthly Guide to New Mexico*. Houston: Gulf Publishing.

DEWITT, DAVE, AND GERLACH, NANCY
   1990. *The Whole Chile Pepper Book*. Boston: Little, Brown.

ECKHARDT, LINDA WEST
   1985. *The Only Texas Cookbook*. New York: Gramercy.

FRANK, LOIS ELLEN
   1991. *Native American Cooking: Foods of the Southwest Indian Nations*. New York: Clarkson Potter.

HESSE, ZORA GETMANSKY

1973. *Southwestern Indian Recipe Book*, Vol. 1. Palmer Lake, Colo.: Filter Press.

MILLER, MARK

1989. *Coyote Cafe*. Berkeley, Calif.: Ten Speed Press.

MILLER, RICHARD

1988. *The Official Fajita Cookbook*. Austin: Texas Monthly Press.

NABHAN, GARY

1985. *Gathering the Desert*. Tucson: University of Arizona Press.

1989. *Enduring Seeds*. San Francisco: North Point Press.

NEELY, MARTINA, AND NEELY, WILLIAM

1981. *The International Chili Society Official Chili Cookbook*. New York: St. Martin's Press.

New Mexico Almanac

1990–. Annual travel and living publication. Santa Fe: Daniels Publishing.

NIETHAMMER, CAROLYN

1974. *American Indian Food and Lore*. New York: Macmillan.

PASCAL, CELINE-MARIE

1991. *The Blue Corn Cookbook*. Albuquerque: Out West Publishing.

SUPER, JOHN C.

1988. *Food, Conquest, and Colonization in Sixteenth Century Spanish America*. Albuquerque: University of New Mexico Press.

TATE, JOYCE L.

1971. *Cactus Cookbook*. Cactus and Succulent Society of America.

THORNE, JOHN

1985. *Just Another Bowl of Texas Red*. Boston: Jackdaw Press.

TOLBERT, FRANK X.

1966. *A Bowl of Red: A Natural History of Chili con Carne*. New York: Doubleday.

VISSER, MARGARET

1986. *Much Depends on Dinner*. New York: Grove Press.

WEINER, MELISSA RUFFNER

1982. *Arizona Territorial Cookbook*. Norfolk, Va.: Donning.

WEIR, BILL

1990. *Arizona Traveler's Handbook*. Chico, Calif.: Moon Publications.

INDEX

Abert, James, 208–209
Acoma Pueblo, 207
Acoma Pumpkin, 10
Acorns, 3, 252
Adam's Extracts, 54
Adelina's Pasta Shop, 164–165
Adovado. See also Carne adovado
    ribs, 283
Adrian's, 270
Agave, 145
    hearts, 3
Agua fresca de tamarindo, 85
Ajo Al's, 270
Alamo, Texas, 88–89
Alamo Farms Winery and Vineyard, 94
Alamogordian pistachios, 148
Albuquerque (Fergusson), 180
Albuquerque, New Mexico, 179–206
    early history of, 179–181
    markets of, 183–186
    restaurants of, 192–201
    shops in, 187–190
    sightseeing in, 181–183
Albuquerque Museum, 182
Alvarado Hotel, 181
Alvarado restaurant, 145
Amador, Don Martin, 160
Amador Hotel, 160
Amandine Bakery and Cafe, 58
Amerind Foundation Museum, 287
Anasazi culture
    squash in, 10
    trade with, 140
    wild crops and, 8
Ancho chiles, 36
    sauce, 68
Anderson Valley Vineyards, 190
Andy's "La Fiesta" Restaurant, 155
Apache Indians, 3, 244
Apple Festival, 143
Apples
    in New Mexico, 147
    winter squash and apple chowder with
        chile-dusted croutons, 174–175
Appletree Restaurant, 232
Arbol
    concentrate, 70
    sauce, 69
Arcosanti, 260–261
Arizona, 241–307
    Phoenix, 259–283
    Scottsdale, 259–283
    Tucson, 284–307

Arizona Historical Society Tucson
    Museum, 287
Arizona Museum of Science and
    Technology, 260
Arizona-Sonora Desert Museum, 286
Arizona State Museum, 287
Arizona Territory, 266
Armadillo World Headquarters, 72
Arnold, Wales, 247
Auden, Bruce, 97
Auslander Biergarten and Restaurant, 79
Austin, Stephen F., 52
Austin, Texas, 49–87
    history of cuisine in, 50–54
    sports in, 50
Austin Country Flea Market, 56
Azar Nut Factor, 118

Baca, Tom, 197
Bakeries. *See* Markets and bakeries
Balcones Escarpment, 54
Bancroft, Colette and John, 289
Banks, Jack, 297
Barbacoa, 29
Barbecue
    grilling distinguished, 29–30
    history of, 30
    spellings of, 53
    in Texas, 28–32
Barbecued brisket, 41
    dry rub for, 42
    Red's basting sauce, 43
Barela, Frank, 192
Barreiro, Antonio, 144
Barrel cactus, 251
Barrio de Analco, 212
Barrio Viejo, 286
Bat Cave archaeological site, 8
Baylor, John Robert, 160
Bazar Cook Book, 249–250
Beans, 9
    Border beans, 19
    Frijoles à la Dobie, 48
    Mesquite Bean Cake, 15
    Scholey beans, 254–255
    in Tex-Mex food, 37–38
Beard, James, 64
Bears, 252
Beck, Warren, 209
Beef. *See also* Barbecued brisket; Chili
        con carne
    barbecue, 29
    for jerky, 245–246

machaca, 280–281
Short rib chile stew, 113
South Texas fajitas, 82–83
Beer. *See also* Breweries
in Red's basting sauce, 43
Shiner Bock, 59, 71
Belgian Restaurant, The, 60–61
Bell Mountain/Oberhellmann Vineyards, 76
Benavidez, Pete, 156
Benny, Jack, 181
Bent Street Deli and Cafe, 232–233
Berries, 3
Best Buy Tortilla Factory, 120
Best of Texas Specialties, 77
Bibliography, 320–321
Bieganowski Cellars, 117
Biga, 91, 97
Big Jim chiles, 163
Big John's Barbecue, 168
Bill's Barbeque, 79–80
Billy the Kid, 160
Biosphere 2, 261
Bird Cage Theatre, 287
Bisbee, Arizona, 287
Biscochitos, 152
Black-eyed peas, Texas caviar, 110–111
Blue corn, 8
tamales with spiced goat cheese, 235–237
Blue Corn Cafe, 224
Bob's Smokehouse, 90, 97
Boccata, 294
Boggie, Farn, 275
Boothill Cemetery, 287
Border beans, 19
Border Patrol Museum, 116
Bosland, Paul, 163
Bosque del Apache Wildlife Refuge, 170
Botanical Center, San Antonio, 89
Boulders Resort, Palo Verde Room at, 274
Bowl o' red. *See* Chili con carne
Bowl of Red, A (Tolbert), 90
Brahma cattle, 26
Branigan Cultural Center, 1670
Braux, Alain, 58
Bread pudding, 37
Breads
Indian fry bread, 21
Pueblo blue corn-chile bread, 18
Southwestern green chile corn bread
with prickly pear butter, 281–283
Breweries. *See also* Beer
in Austin area, 59–60
in San Antonio, 93
in Santa Fe, 219–220
Brisket. *See also* Barbecued brisket
Julio's salpicón, 132
Bromberg, David, 184–185, 195

Bueno Foods Factory Store, 187
Buffalo, 26
Buffet, Jimmy, 122
*Bull Cook and Authentic Historical
Recipes and Practices* (Herter), 95
Bull ring, 116
Burgesses, Virginia, 30
Butel, Jane, 152
Buñelos, 37

Cabrito, 29
asado, 37
Cacti, 3
barrel cactus, 251
species of, 4
Cafe Abiquiu, 233
Cafe Central, 120
Cafe Poca Cosa, 294–295
Cafe Serranos, 61
Cafe Terra Cotta, 251, 288, 295
Calabacitas, 158
spicy, 20–21
Calabaza Mexicana, 10
Caldillo Paso del Norte, 133
Caldwell, Red, 29–30, 43
Camino Real, 25
Santa Fe as terminus, 208
Camino Real de Tierra Adentro, 179–180
Campbell, Jeff, 74, 78
Cantina *sopa de lima*, 204–205
Canutillo Tortilla Factory and Little
Diner, 120–121
Capirotada, 37
Captain Quackenbush's Espresso Cafe, 61
Caramel sauce, piñon flan with, 239–240
Caravan East Grower's Market, 183
Carmen's of New Mexico USA, 187
Carne adovada, 143
estilo Sonora, 304–305
Carne asada, 30
Carne seca, 246
in Tucson, 287–288
Carnival del Rio, 28
Caruso's, 298
Carson, Kit, 225, 247
Casa Blanca, 155
Casa de Valdez, 155
Casa Grande National Monument, 287
Casa Jurado, 121
Casa Vieja, 192
Casas grandes, Chihuahua, 140
Cascabel sauce, 68
Cashman, Nellie, 248
Casseroles, El Paso green chile casserole, 131
Castañeda, 144
Castle Hill Cafe, 62
Cather, Willa, 210

Cattle. *See also* Beef
  in Albuquerque, 181
  in New Mexico, 144
  in Texas, 26
Caviar, Texas, 110–111
Celis, Pierre, 59
Celis Brewery, 59
Centro Mercado, 117, 118
Channing, Carol, 80–81
Cher, 212
Cheri's Desert Harvest, 290
Chicago World's Fair, 1893, chili at, 34
Chicken
  in almond mole, 86–87
  grilled marinated chicken breasts with
    roasted poblano-piñon salsa, 202–
    203
  winter squash and apple chowder with
    chile-dusted croutons, 174–175
Chilaquiles, 173
Childbirth, chiltepins and, 6
Chile, Etc., 220
Chile caribe, 234–235
Chile Connection, The, 155, 233
"Chile Culture", 162
Chile Gourmet, 165, 175
Chile Hill Emporium, 187
Chile pasado, 140, 302
Chile Patch USA, 188
Chile Pepper, 291
Chile Pepper magazine, 20, 35, 214
Chile peppers. *See also* specific chiles
  as acquired taste, 163
  adovado ribs, 283
  agricultural work on, 162–164
  in Arizona, 244
  calabacitas, spicy, 20–21
  Caldillo Paso del Norte, 133
  chile pasado, 302–303
  Christine's hot sauce, 258
  classic New Mexico red chile sauce, 150
  corn and poblano chile relish, 238–239
  domestication of, 10
  El Paso green chile casserole, 131
  green chile pesto on red chile pasta,
    256–257
  of New Mexico, 139–144, 180
  orange and jicama salad with red chile
    powder, 303
  Pueblo blue corn-chile bread, 18
  ristras, 129–130
  roasted poblano-piñon salsa, 202–203
  with morels, 255–256
  roasting and peeling, 176–177
  Sonoran-style marinated pork, 304–305
  Southwestern green chile corn bread
    with prickly pear butter, 281–283
  in Tex-Mex, 36
  viewing New Mexican chile fields, 164

winter squash and apple chowder with
    chile-dusted croutons, 174–175
Chile Shop, The, 221
Chiles rellenos, 249–250
Chili con carne, 32–35
  Chili Queen's chili, 108
  debate as to best chili, 188
  new age version of, 95
  Pedernales River Chili, 40
  Sam Pendergrast's Original Zen Chili,
    44–45
Chili queens, 90, 34, 35
  recipe for chili, 108
Chiltepin House sauce, 17
Chiltepin ice cream, 307
Chiltepins, 3, 5–8, 16
  beans and, 39
  in chili con carne, 32
  Christine's hot sauce, 258
  Frijoles á la Dobie, 48
  ice cream, 307
  reserve for, 7–8
  salsa casera, 17
  Sonoran'style marinated pork, 304–305
  in Tex-Mex, 36–37
Chimayó chiles, 141, 231
Chimichangas, 250–251, 263–264, 295
  definition of, 269
Chipotle sauce, 69
Chokecherry, 3
Cholla buds, 11
Chope's Bar and Cafe, 168
Chorizo, 134
Christine's hot sauce, 258
Chuy's Restaurant, 37, 62
Cibola National Forest, 182
Cinco de Mayo, 28
Cinco de Mayo (San Antonio), 89
City Market, 72
Ciudad Juárez, 114–134
  markets of, 117, 118
  restaurants of, 120–128
  shops, 118–119
  wineries of, 117
Civil War
  Albuquerque during, 181
  and Santa Fe, 209
Claiborne, Craig, 35
Classic New Mexico red chile sauce, 150
Clopper, J. C., 34
Clopton, Henry, 197, 199
Cocula, 99
Commerce of the Prairies (Gregg), 245–
    246
Cookbooks, mail-order sources for, 311–
    312
Cookies, Biscochitos, 152
Cooking Place, The, 118–119
Cooking schools in Santa Fe, 218–219

Cooper's Barbecue, 80
Copperfield's Coffee Shop and Bookstore, 119
Corn. *See also* Blue corn; Tortillas
  in Albuquerque, 180
  bread with prickly pear butter, 281–283
  Calabacitas, spicy, 20–21, 158
  domestication of, 8
  green corn tamales, 278–279
  in New Mexico, 144
  and poblano chile relish, 238–239
  with morels, 255–256
Corn, Elaine, 120–121, 124, 125, 129–130
Corn bread with prickly pear butter, 281–283
Coronado, 26
Corporate Chili Challenge, 143
Corral, Elvaro, 274
Cortex, 153
Cox, Preston, 219
Coyote Cafe, 148
Coyote Cafe (Scottsdale), 270
Coyote Cafe, The (Santa Fe), 148, 225–226
Coyote Cafe General Store, 221
Crawford, Joan, 181
Creosote bush, 252
Cronkite, Walter, 80
Crook, George, 247
Crossroads Restaurant, 296
Croutons, chile-dusted, 175
Cruet Winery, 191
Cueva Enriquez, Francisco Fernandez de la, 179
Cultural Centers, 13–15
Cushing Street Bar and Restaurant, 286
Dailey, David, 62
Das Peach House, 78
Dates in Arizona, 248
Davila, Suzana, 294
Davis, W. W. H., 138, 209
De Grolyer, E. 32
De Kluis Brewery, 59
Delmonico's Restaurant, 248
Demonstration gardens, 12–13
Desert Botanical Garden, 12, 261, 307
  Gift Shop, 267
Desert Center at Pinnacle Peak, 261
Desert Rose Salsa, 291
Desserts
  biscochitos, 152
  Hill Country peach crisp, 87
  Mesilla pecan tarts, 178
  natillas, 205–206
DeWese's Tip Top Cafe, 90, 99
DeWitt, Dave, 57
Diabetes, 11

Diamondback rattlesnakes, 252
Diez y Seis (San Antonio), 28, 89
Dirty's, 52
Dobie, J. Frank, 37, 39
Doc Martin's, 233–234
Dogs, 252
Dog's breath (*xnipec*) salsa, 70, 84
Domaine Cheurlin Winery, 165–166
Dominici, Pete, 170
Doña Ana, 159
Don José, 264, 271
Dot's Place, 62–63
Dragon Room Bar of The Pink Adobe, 212
Drinks
  agua fresca de tamarindo, 85
  Margaritas, 122–124
Dry rub, 42
"Duke City," 179
Duppa, Darrel, 260
Duran Central Pharmacy, 193
Dutchman's Market, 73
Dutch ovens, 246–247
Dye, John, 115

Eagle Ranch Pistachio groves, 148
Edwards Plateau, 54
Eggs
  El Paso green chile casserole, 131
  huevos rancheros, 151, 250
Einstein, Albert, 181
E. J.'s Coffee, Tea, and Restaurant, 193
E. K. Mas, 226
El Azteca, 60
El Chaparral, 98–99
El Charro, 264, 285, 295–296, 301
  carne seca at, 288–289
El Fenix, 265, 266
El Gringo (Davis), 209
El Matador
  Hobbs, 154
  Raton, 154
El Mercado, San Antonio, 89
El Minuto Cafe, 299–300
El Mirador, 104
El Modelo Mexican Foods, 195
El Molino, 160–161
El Monterrey, 153
El Navajo, 145
El Nido, 263
El Norteño, 196, 273
El Palenque, 197
El Paso, Texas, 114–134
  history of, 25–26
  markets of, 117
  restaurants of, 120–128
  shops, 118–119
  wineries, 117
El Paso Chile Company, 119

El Paso green chile casserole, 131
El Paso Museum of History, 116
El Patio, 52–53, 197–198
El Pollo Supremo, 275
El Presidio Historic District, 285
El Rancho de las Golondrinas, 217–218
El Rapido, 301–302
El Saguarito, 302
El Tiradito, 286
El Toro Bravo, 155
Emory, William, 141–142
Enchiladas
    Arizona version, 253
    Mexican version, 305–306
    in Santa Fe, 215–217
    Sonoran style
    stacked red chile enchiladas, 156–157
    Tex-Mex enchiladas, 47
Encore Med, 296
Entre dos fuegos, 246
Epstein, Pancho, 213–214
Erlichman, John, 212
Ernesto's, 99
Española, 141
Esquire Tavern, 90, 100
Estella's Cafe, 154
Estrella Tortilla Factory, 264–265
Euro Market, 261, 265
Exhibits of native plants, 12–13

Fabian Garcia Agricultural Science
    Center, 147
Fabulous Thunderbirds, 49
Fajita King, 63
Fajitas, 30–32
    in Austin, 54
    South Texas fajitas, 82–83
Falcon, Sonny, 30–31, 54, 63
Fall Creek Vineyards, 76
Farm to Market, 92
Farmer's Market
    San Antonio, 89, 92
    Santa Fe, 223
Farmer's Market Cookbook (Olney), 57
Fergusson, Erna, 180
Fiesta de los Chiles, 285, 307
Fiesta Navidena, 89
Fiesta of San Jacinto, 89, 91
Fiesta San Antonio, 28, 91
Fiesta Texas, 89
Flan, 37
    piñon flan with caramel sauce, 239–
    240
Flea Market
    Albuquerque, 184
    Austin, 75
Flin, Monica, 289
Flores, Carlotta and Ray, 289
Fonda San Miguel, 63–64

Font, Pedro, 244
Food City, 265
Food Conspiracy, 289
Food events
    in Arizona, 245
    in New Mexico, 143
    in Texas, 28–29
    in Tucson, 285
Foods, mail-order sources for, 312–313
Fort McDowell, 260
Fort Selden, 160
Forti's Mexican Elder, 125
Fredericksburg, Texas, 55
Fredericksburg Bakery, 73
Fredericksburg Food and Wine Festival, 29
Fredericksburg Herb Farm, 77
Fred's Bread and Bagel, 193
Fremont's, 189
French Legation, 50
Frijoles. See Beans
Frijoles á la Dobie, 48
Frontier cooking hints, 257
Frontier Restaurant, The, 193–194
Fruit Basket, The, 221
Fry bread, 21

Gadsden Purchase, 159
Garbanzos, sopa seca with, 171–172
Garcia, Billy, 69
Garcia, Fabian, 162
Garcia, Rosa and Reguio, 129–130
Garcia's, 194
Garrett, Pat, 160
Garza, Jesus, 105
Gebhardt, William, 34
Gebhardt Eagle, 34
Gerlach, Nancy, 20–21, 175
Gifts, mail-order sources for, 312–313
Gila River Arts and Crafts Center, 15
Glossary of cooking terms, 314–319
Goat cheese, blue corn tamales with,
    235–237
Going Nuts in Mesilla, 166
Golden Crown Panaderia, 190–191
Golfo de Mexico, 101
Golondrinas, El Rancho de las, 217–218
Gonzales, Adam, 61
Gourmet Emporium and Cheese Shop,
    291
Governor's Mansion, 50
Gozard, Jean-Pierre, 192
Grandma's K & I Diner, 194
Grape Creek Vineyard, 76
Grapes, wild 252
Green chile
    casserole, 131
    pesto on red chile pasta, 256–257
    stew, 172–173
Green corn tamales, 278–279

Green Pastures, 54, 63
Green sauce
  at Pinch-a-Pollo, 68
  Texas green sauce, 46
Greer, Anne Lindsay, 251
Gregg, Josiah, 7, 135, 137, 245–246
Griffith, Jim, 269, 285
Grigg's Restaurant, 125
Grilled marinated chicken breasts with
    roasted poblano-piñon salsa,
    202–203
Grilled marinated pork tenderloin with
    roasted corn and poblano relish,
    237–239
Grilled shrimp salad with frizzled
    tortillas, 279–280
Grilling, barbecue distinguished, 29–30
Grocery Emporium, The, 184–185, 195
Ground meat, 52
Grubsteak, The, 296
Guacamole, 37
Guadalajara Restaurant, 153
Guadalupe Mission, 116
Guadalupe Smoked Meat Company, 80
Guadalupe Valley Winery, 27, 94
Guajillo sauce, 68
  recipe for, 84–85
Guedo's Taco Shop, 271
Guerithault, Vincent, 278, 279
Guiltless Gourmet, 54
Gulley, Boyce, 262
Gussies Tamales and Mexican Bakery,
  119

Habanero sauce, 70
Hallford, Ruby, 78
Hamburger, 52
H & H Car Wash and Coffee Shop,
  125
Harper, Roy, 162
Harvest Festival, 143
Harvey, Fred, 145, 181
Harvey House chain, 144–145
Hatch Chile Express, 166
Hatch Chile Festival, 143, 164
Heard Museum, 262, 263
Heart of the Desert pistachios, 148
Heb Marketplace, 92–93
HemisFair Plaza, 89
Hendon, Aaron, 193
Henry's Puffy Taco, 90, 101
Hepburn, Katharine, 181
Heras-Duran, Antonio, 304
Herbs, 3
Herb Store, The, 189
Heritage Square, 260
Hernandez, Zippy, 272
Herter, George, 95

Hill Country, Texas, 54–55
  markets and bakeries, 72–75
  restaurants in, 79–81
  shops, 77–79
  wineries, 76–77
Hill Country Cellars, 59–60
Hill Country peach crisp, 87
Hilltop Cafe, 80–81
Hipp's Bubble Room, 103
Hispanic Pueblo Red corn, 8
Hohokam culture, 259–260
  squash in, 10
  trade with, 140
Homestead Act of 1862, 144
Honey-drenched smoked turkey breast
    with rainbow chile-mango salsa,
    203–204
Hoover, Herbert, 181
Hornos, 15
Hot sauces
  of Austin, 54
  at Pinch-a-Pollo, 68–70
Hudson, Homer, 52
Hudson's on the-Bend, 64
Huevos rancheros, 151, 250
Huntington Art Gallery, 49–50
Hurd, Peter, 210
Hut's Hamburgers, 52
Hutson, Stuart, 164
Hyatt-Regency, Austin, 31

Ice cream, chiltepin, 307
Indian fry bread, 21
Indian Pueblo Cultural Center, 13–14
Inn at Bushy Creek, The, 64–65
Inn of the Anasazi, 226
Institute of Texas Cultures, 89
International Chili Society, 34–35
International Food Market, 93
International Wildlife Museum, 286
Island of Big Surf, 261
Isleta Blue corn, 8
Isleta Pueblo, 114
Isleta Pueblo Bread Sales, 191

Jackalope, 222
Jack's Original Barbeque, 297
Jaeger, Hermann, 26
Jalapeños
  in Arizona, 249
  fried, 37
Jalisco Cafe, 155
Jambalaya, 65
Jams and jellies
  in Hill Country, Texas, 55
  Prickly Pear Jam, 16
J&P Grocery, 166–167
Janitzio, 102–103
Janos, 251, 295, 297

Japanese Kitchen, 298
Jaramillo, Florence, 230–231, 234
Jaramillos Mexi-Catessen, 154
Jaxon's, 126
Jeffrey's, 66
Jerky, 245–246
Jicama and orange salad with red chile
    powder, 303
J. Michaels, 185
Joe's Bakery and Coffee Shop, 66
Johnson Library and Museum, 49
Johnson, Lady Bird, 23, 2552–53
Johnson, Lyndon B., 23, 25
Johnson, Woody, 263
Jojoba, 14
Jones, David, 225
Joplin, Janis, 72
José Cuervo, 122
Juanitos Restaurant, 153
Julio's Cafe Corona, 126
Julio's salpicón, 132
Juniper berries, 3
Jupiter House, 247
Juárez. See Ciudad Juárez
Juárez, Benito, 160
Juárez Museum of History and Art, 116
Juárez Racetrack, 116

Karam's Mexican Dining Room, 103
Kasper Meat Market, 73
Kellner, Rob, 192
Kid. See Cabrito
Kilborn, Steve, 223
Killer Bees, 49
Kino, Eusebio Francisco, 243–244, 284
Kirk, Martina, 188
Kitt Peak Observatory, 287
Knife Shop, The, 119
Koock, Ken, 54
Koock, Mary Faulk, 54
Kreuz Market, 36, 51, 66–67

Laboratory of Anthropology, 211
La Buca di Saint Antonio, 91, 97
La Calesa, 98
La Casa Sena, 225
La Chiripada Winery, 219
La Fagata, 121
La Familia, 184, 264, 271
La Fiesta, 154
La Fiesta de los Chiles, 245
La Fiesta de Viños, 245
La Florida, 123
La Fogata, 100–101
La Fonda, 101, 145
La Frontera, 264
La Hacienda, 154, 126, 128
La Hacienda at the Princess Resort, 272
La Indita, 297

La Jolla Bakery, 289
Lake Travis, 50
La Margarita Mexican Restaurant and
    Oyster Bar, 103
Lamb, barbecued, 29
La Mexicana Tortilla Company, 191–192
Lamy, Jean-Baptiste, 210
Lancaster, Joe, 263
La Parilla Suiza, 274
La Perla, 274–275
La Playa, 105
La Posta, 161, 170
La Pulga, 56, 75
La Ristra, 170–171
Las Cruces, New Mexico, 159–178
    markets and bakeries of, 164–165
    restaurants of, 167–171
La Tapitia, 53
La Tertulia, 229
La Villita, 89
La Viña Winery, 117
Lawrence, D. H., 210
Leo's Mexican Restaurant, 298–299
Leon Springs Cafe, 106
Leon Springs, Texas, 106
Le Rendezvous, 298
L'Estro Armonico, 60–61
Li'l Abner's, 299
Lily's Cafe, 272
Limes, Cantina sopa de lima, 204–205
Lincoln County Barbecue War, 143
Lindbergh, Charles, 181
Little Hipp's Gimmedraw Parlour, 90, 103
Livestock from Spain, 137–138
Loca Morena sauce, 69
Lone Star Brewery, 93
Longhorn cattle, 26
Long-neck pumpkin, 10
Loretto Chapel, 210
Los Arcos, 167–168
Los Barrios Mexican Restaurant, 96–97
Los Cuates, 192
Los Dos Molinos, 271
Los Olivos Restaurant, 263, 274
Los Patios, 94–95
Los Ranchos, 155
Louie's Produce, 186
Louis Mueller's Barbecue, 51, 67
Lovejoy's Kansas City Pit Bar-B-Que,
    261
Lubliner, Karen, 233
Lyndon Baines Johnson Library and
    Museum, 49
Lytle, Jo and Jimmy, 166

Macarone Grill, 106
McCarthy, Jay, 107
Macayo chain, 263, 273

McCormick Ranch, Piñon Grill at the Inn at, 275
Machaca, 249
recipe for, 280–281
Macho nachos, 48
McQuade, Darby, 222
Mad Dog & Beans, 52
Maddog Salsa, 149
Magoffin, Samuel, 163
Magoffin, Susan, 115, 163
Mail-order sources, 311–313
Maize. *See* Corn
M & J's Sanitary Tortilla Factory, 194–195
Mangos in salsa, 203–204
Margaritas, 122–124
in Arizona, 250
recipe for, 124
Marilyn's First Mexican Restaurant, 273
Marinades
dry rub, 42
Red's basting sauce, 43
Marion, John, 241
Markets and bakeries
of Albuquerque, 183–186, 190–192
of El Paso and Ciudad Juárez, 117
of Hill Country, Texas, 72–75
of Las Cruces, 164–167
of Phoenix, 264–266
of San Antonio, 92–93
of Santa Fe, 220–224
of Tucson, 289–290
Market Square, 89, 111
outside dining at, 100
Martino's, 127
Martin's Kum-Back Burgers, 52
Mary of Agreda, 95
Masa, 236
Matt's El Rancho, 53
Maverick, Maury, 34
Maxon, Jack, 126
Mayan civilization, 140
Meem, John Gaw, 196
Mel's Bakery and Chile, 191
Mendoza, Lydia, 35
Menudo, 37
Mescalero Apaches, 3
Mesilla, New Mexico, 159–160
in Confederacy, 160
Old Mesilla, 161–162
Mesilla pecan tarts, 178
Mesilla Valley, 138
Mesquite, 14
advantages/disadvantages of trees, 38–39
charcoal, 39
pod chopper, 20
seeds, 3
tea, 11

Mesquite beans
cake, 15
nutrition in, 38
Metate, 5
Mexican Cultural Institute, 89
Mexicana sauce, 69
Michener Collection, Huntington Art Gallery, 49–50
Middleton, Robert, 168
Miller, Mark, 148, 225–226
Mina's Thai Restaurant, 298
Mi Nidito, 298, 299
Mint, 3
Mission Conceptión, 89
Mission of Our Lady of Guadalupe of Paso del Norte, 114
Mission San José, 89
Mission San Juan Capistrano, 89
Mitchell, Janet, 269
Mi Tierra Cafe and Bakery, 103–104
Mitla Black Beans, 9
Mix, Tom, 271
Mole sauce
chicken in almond mole, 86–87
at Pinch-a-Pollo, 68
Money's Kitchen, 222
Monfivaiz, Manual, 171
Monroe's Restaurant, 195–196
Monte Vista Fire Station Restaurant, 196, 202
Montezuma, 144
Morales, Francisco "Pancho", 122–124
Morales, Pat, 191
Morita sauce, 70
Moyer Champagne Company, 94
Mrs. Owen's Cook Book, 34
Much Depends on Dinner (Visser), 11
Munson, Thomas, 26
Murphy, Rosalea, 212, 214
Museum of Art, San Antonio, 89
Museum of Fine Arts, Santa Fe, 211
Museum of Indian Arts and Culture, 211
Museum of International Folk Art, 211
Mushrooms, 3
My Brother's Place, 169
Mystery Castle, 262

Nabhan, Gary, 6, 7
Nachos, 37
macho nachos, 48
Nakayama, Roy, 162–163
Napier, Arch, 188
Natillas, 205–206
National Chili Museum, 95
National Fiery Foods Show, 143
National Historical Park, 287
Native Americans, 3
Native Seeds/SEARCH, 6, 7–8
diabetes research, 10

movement to preserve ancient food
    plants, 11–12
Native Southwest, 1–21
Navajos
    Gila River Arts and Crafts Center, 15
    piñon trees, use of, 4–5
    squash and, 10
Nellie's Cafe, 169
Nelson, Willie, 49
Nentvig, Juan, 252
New Delhi Palace, 298
Newman, Paul, 212
New Mexican chiles, 141
New Mexico, 135–240
    Albuquerque, 179–206
    food events of, 143
    great restaurants of, 153–155
    Las Cruces, 159–178
    Santa Fe, 207–240
New Mexico carne adovada, 201
New Mexico Chile Cookoff, 143
New Mexico College of Agriculture and
    Mechanical Arts, 162
New Mexico Museum of Natural History,
    182
New Mexico ñ La Carte, 224
New Mexico R-Naky, 163
New Mexico State Fair, 143
New Mexico State University, 161
    chile greenhouse tours, 164
New Mexico Wine Festival, 143
New Texas Cuisine, The (Pyles), 33
New world foods, 146
Night in Old San Antonio (NIOSA), 91
Nimoy, Leonard, 212, 214
Nopales, 4
Norteño cookery, 249–250
Nuevo Restaurante Martino, 127

O. Henry House and Museum, 49
O.K. Corral, 287
O'Keeffe, Georgia, 210
Oktoberfest, 29
Old Armiljo House, 160
Old Borunda Cafe, 36
Old Custom House Museum of History,
    116
Old German Bakery and Restaurant, 74
Old Mexico Grill, The, 227
Old San Antonio Style Gourmet Sauces,
    96
Old Santa Fe, 211
Old Taos Trade Fair, 143
Old Time Barbecue, 197
Old Town, Albuquerque, 182–183
Old Town, Scottsdale, 262
Old Town Plaza, 179
Old Tucson Studios, 286
Old World foods, 146

Olney, Judith, 57
Oñate, Juan de, 138, 139, 207
Opuntia cacti. See Prickly pears
Oranges
    in Arizona, 248
    and jicama salad with red chile
        powder, 303
Original Donut Shop, 90, 104
Original Mexican Restaurant, 36
Ortiz, Ramón, 162
Otermin, Antonio de, 114
Owl Bar, 169–170

Paddock, The, 153
Painted Desert, 300
Palace of Governors, Santa Fe, 144
Palo Verde Room at the Boulders Resort,
    274
Pancho Villa, 116
Papgo Indians, 6
Park and Swap, 266
Paseo de Peralta, 211
Paseo del Rio, San Antonio, 88
Pasilla sauce, 68
Paso del Norte, 127
Pasta, green chile pesto on red chile
    pasta, 256–257
Pat's Drive-In, 300
Peach Basket Natural Foods, 78
Peach crisp, Hill Country, 87
Pecans
    Mesilla pecan tarts, 178
    in New Mexico, 147–148
Pecan Store, The, 292
Pedernales River Chili, 23, 25
    recipe for, 40
Pedernales Vineyards, 76–77
Pedro's Mexican Restaurant, 154
Peeling chile peppers, 176–177
Peñasco, New Mexico, 208
Pendergrast, Sam, 35, 44–45
Pepper Emporium, The, 189
Peppers (Mesilla), 168, 170
Peppers (Scottsdale), 267, 281
Peppers Restaurant and Cantina (Santa
    Fe), 227, 236
Pesto
    green chile pesto on red chile pasta,
        256–257
    pistachios in, 148
Pete's Cafe, 198
Petroglyph National Monument, 182
Pfeffercorn, Ignaz, 7
Pharr's Roundup Restaurant, 31
Phaseolus sp. See Beans
Phoenician Resort, Windows on the
    Green at, 278
Phoenix, Arizona, 259–283
    best of, 261

dining in, 262–264
markets and bakeries, 264–266
restaurants, 270–278
roadside stands, 264
shops, 266–268
sightseeing in, 259–262
Phoenix Art Museum, 260
Phoenix Zoo, 262
Pico de Gallo, 104–105
Pico de gallo salsa, 112
Piedras Negras de Noche, 105
Pies, Mesilla pecan tarts, 178
Pima Air Museum, 287
Pima County Cooperative Extension
    Garden Center, 12–13
Pima Indians, 284
  chile pasado, 140
  diabetes among, 11
Pinch-a-Pollo, 67–70
  hot sauces of, 68–70
Ping's, 106
Pink Adobe, The, 212, 227–228
Pink Adobe Cookbook, The (Murphy), 214
Pinnacle Peak General Store, 267
Piñon Grill at the Inn at McCormick
    Ranch, 251, 275
Piñon nuts, 3, 4–5
  discovery of, 7
  flan with caramel sauce, 239–240
  grilled venison chops with piñons, 18–
    19
  roasted poblano-piñon salsa, 202–203
Piñon trees, 4
Pinto beans, 9
  Border beans, 19
  as New Mexico state vegetable, 180
  Short rib chile stew, 113
Pioneer Arizona Living History Museum,
    260
Pistachios, 148
Pit, Pot & Skillet (Caldwell), 29–30
Plateau Cafe, 81
Plaza Cafe, The, 228
Plaza Hotel, 154
Poblanos, 36
  roasted corn and poblano chile relish,
    238–239
  roasted poblano-corn salsa with
    morels, 255–256
Pochteca, 140
Pollo en mole almendrado, 86–87
Poncho's, 275
Pork
  adovado ribs, 283
  barbeque, 29
  green chile stew with, 172–173
  grilled marinated pork tenderloin with
    roasted corn and poblano chile
    relish, 237–239

New Mexico carne adovada, 201
posole with chile caribe, 234–235
sage and serrano lime cream,
    tenderloin with, 83
Sonoran-style marinated pork, 304–
    305
Posole, 37
  with chile caribe, 234–235
Potpourri, 189
Presidio Grill, 300
Preston Brewery, 219
Price, Vincent, 212
Prickly pears, 4
  jam, 16
  juice, 11
  Southwestern green chile corn bread
    with prickly pear butter, 281–283
Prince, L. Bradford, 225
Princess Resort, La Hacienda at, 272
Processing chile peppers, 176–177
Prohibition, 27
  in Ciudad Juárez, 115
  in New Mexico, 147
Publications, mail-order sources for, 311–
    312
Pueblo blue corn-chile bread, 18
Pueblo Grande Museum, 259–260
Pueblo Indians
  squash and, 10
  wild crops and, 8
Pueblo Revolt of 1680, 114, 210
Pumpkins, types of, 10
Pyles, Stephan, 33

Quarters, The, 199
Quesadillas, 37
Quinlan Mountains, 287

Rabke's Table Ready Meats, 74–75
Rainbow chile-mango salsa, 203–204
Rainbow corn, 8
Rajkovic, Rosa, 196, 202
Ramah Navajo, 4
Ramirez, Julio, 132
Ramsdell, Charles, 34
Rancher's Club, 301
Ranch O Casados, 153
Rancho de Chimayó, 230–231, 234
Rancho Encantado, 228
Rattlesnakes, 252
Ravago, Miguel, 65
Rawhide, 262
Reading suggestions, 320–321
Read On, 190
Reay's Ranch Market, 290
Red chile powder, orange and jicama
    salad with, 303
Redford, Robert, 212
Red's basting sauce, 43

Reid Park Zoo, 286
Republic of Texas Chilympiad, 29
Restaurant André, 199
Restaurant Mexico, 276
Restaurants
    of Albuquerque, 192–201
    of Austin area, 60–72
    of Ciudad Juárez, 120–128
    of El Paso, 120–128
    of Hill Country, Texas, 79–80
    of Las Cruces, 167–171
    of New Mexico, 153–155
    of Phoenix, 270–278
    of San Antonio, 96–107
    of Santa Fe, 224–232
    of Scottsdale, 270–278
    of Taos, 232–234
    traditional Native American dishes,
        13–15
    of Tucson, 294–302
Retail shops. See Shops
Return of The Chili Queens Festival, 28,
    35, 90
Reynosa, 26
Ribs, adovado, 283
Rice with garbanzos, 171–172
Richmond, Robb, 185, 200
Rincon Food Market, 289
Rio Grande Cantina, 199–200, 204
Rio Grande Nature Center, 182
Rio Grande Pueblo people, 140
Rio Grande Zoological Park, 182
Ristras, 129–130
    in New Mexico, 143
Ristras by Rosa, 129–130
Rivera's Chile Shop, 96
Rivercenter, San Antonio, 88
River Walk, San Antonio, 88, 91
Roasted poblano-corn salsa with morels,
    255–256
Roasted poblano-piñon salsa, 202–203
Roasting chile peppers, 176–177
Robb's Ribbs, 185, 200
Roberto's, 155, 171
Rockin' R Ranch, 262
Rogers, Will, 145
Roja sauce, 68
Romero, Orlando, 228
Rooftop Cantina, 226
Roosevelt, Franklin D., 181
Roosevelt, Theodore, 181
Rosario's Authentic Mexican Cuisine,
    105
Rose's Salsa, 54
Rosita's Place, 264, 276–277
Rosson House, 260
Roundhouse, 211
Routh Street Cafe, 33
Rubin, Lenard, 278, 281–282

Ruby's, 69
Rudy's Country Store and Barbecue, 53,
    105–106

Sadie's, 201
Safford, A. P. K., 241
Saguaro, 9
    fruits, 4
Saguaro National Monument, 286
St. Anthony's Day at Tigua Indian
    Reservation, 28
St. Augustine, Florida, 207
St. Francis Cathedral, 210
Salads
    grilled shrimp salad with frizzled
        tortillas, 279–280
    orange and jicama salad with red chile
        powder, 303
Saligny, Jean Peter Isidore Alphonse de,
    50
Salisbury, J. H., 52
Salman Ranch Store, 222–223
Salopek Orchards, 166
Salpicón, 132
Salsa casera, 17
Salsa jalapeño o serrano asado, 109
Salsas. See Sauces and salsas
Salt River, 259
    irrigation project, 248
Sambet's Cajun Store, 51, 58
Sam Pendergrast's Original Zen Chili,
    44–45
Sam's, 70–71
San Antonio, Texas, 88–113
    chili queens of, 34, 35, 90
    founding of, 26
    Lone Star Brewery, 93
    markets in, 92–93
    restaurants of, 96–107
    shops in, 94–96
    wineries, 94
San Antonio Missions National Historic
    Park, 88
San Antonio Zoo, 89
Sandia Mountains, 182
Sandia Peak Tramway, 182
Sandia Wilderness Area, 182
Sandoval, David and Gloria, 197
San Felipe de Neri Church, 179
San Fernando Cathedral, 89
San Miguel Chapel, 210
Santacafe, 228–229
Santa Cruz Chili & Spice Company, 292–
    293
Santa Fe, New Mexico, 207–240
    cooking schools, 218–219
    history of, 208–210
    lawlessness in, 209–210
    markets and shops, 220–224

restaurants, 212–215, 224–232
sightseeing in, 210–212
wineries and breweries in, 219–220
Santa Fe Area Farmer's Market, 223
Santa Fe Brewing, 220
Santa Fe Chile and Wine Fiesta, 143
Santa Fe Community College, 218
Santa Fe Deli, 229
Santa Fe Olé! (Epstein), 213–214
Santa Fe Railroad, 160
Santa Fe School of Cooking, 219
Santa Fe Trail, 208
Santo Domingo blue corn, 8
Santo Domingo squash, 10
San Xavier del Bac Mission, 243, 284
Satisfied Frog, 277
Sauces and salsas
  for barbecue, 30
  chile wine sauce, 100
  Christine's hot sauce, 258
  classic New Mexico red chile sauce, 150
  guajillo sauce, 84–85
  jalapeño o serrano asado, salsa de, 109
  Maddog Salsa, 149
  pico de gallo salsa, 112
  rainbow chile-mango salsa, 203–204
  roasted poblano-corn salsa with
    morels, 255–256
  roasted poblano-piñon salsa, 202–203
  Texas green sauce, 46
  xnipec (dog's breath) salsa, 84
Sausages, chorizo, 134
Schlaraffenland Winery, 27
Schneider, Dick, 189
Scholey and Stephans Saloon, 254
Scholey beans, 254–255
Scholz Garten, 41, 50, 71
  100th Anniversary Party at, 44
Schweers, Marianne and George, 148
Scottsdale Culinary Festival, 245
Scottsdale Galleria, 262
Scottsdale, Arizona, 259–283
  restaurants, 262–264, 270–278
  roadside stands, 264
  shops, 266–268
  sightseeing in, 259–262
Sea World of Texas, 89
Seeds, mail-order sources for, 311
Seis Salsas, 71
Sena, José, 225
Sentinel Peak, 284
Serranos, pork tenderloin with sage and
    serrano lime cream, 83
Shalimar Date Gardens, 268
Shelf fungus, 252
Shiner Bock, 59, 71
Shops
  in Albuquerque, 187–190
  in Ciudad Juárez, 118–119

in El Paso, 118–119
in Hill Country, Texas, 77–79
in Phoenix and Scottsdale, 266–268
in San Antonio, 94–96
in Santa Fe, 220–224
in Tucson, 290–294
Short rib chile stew, 113
Shrimp salad with frizzled tortillas, 279–
    280
Simon David, 56–57
Sister Creek Vineyards, 77
6th Street, Austin, 49
Skunks, 252
Skyliner Gallery, 153
Slaughter-Leftwich, 60
Socorro Mission, 116
Soleri, Paolo, 260–261
Sonoran-style food, 249–251
  enchiladas, Arizona version, 253
  enchiladas, Mexican version, 305–306
  marinated pork, 304–305
Sopa seca with garbanzos, 171–172
Soups
  Cantina sopa de lima, 204–205
  winter squash and apple chowder with
    chile-dusted croutons, 174–175
Sourdough starter, 246
Southside Market, 75
South Texas fajitas, 82–83
Southwestern green chile corn bread
    with prickly pear butter, 281–283
Southwest Gourmet Gallery, 268
Southwest Residential Experiment
    Center, 161
Southwest Salsa Challenge, 245
Spanish Governor's Palace, 89
Spanish Kitchen, The, 171
Sphinx Date Ranch, 268
Spicy calabacitas, 20–21
Spoetzl Brewery, 59
Squash, 10
  calabacitas, 20–21, 158
  winter squash and apple chowder with
    chile-dusted croutons, 174–175
Squashblossom necklaces, 10
Squirrels, 252
Stacked red chile enchiladas, 156–157
Stahmann's Country Store, 164, 167
State Capitol, Santa Fe, 211
State Line Barbecue, The, 127
Stews
  Caldillo Paso del Norte, 133
  green chile stew (New Mexico), 172–
    173
  short rib chile, 113
Stonewall Chili Pepper Company, 74, 78–
    79
Sumac berries, 252
Sunday House, 75

Sunland Park, 116
Super, John C., 138
Swilling, Jack, 260
Szechuan Omei, 298

Table sauce, 68
Taboos, 3
Taft, William H., 181
Taliesin West, 261
Ta Lin Supermarket, 186·
Tamale pie, 37
Tamales
    green corn tamales, 278–279
    with spiced goat cheese, 235–237
Tamarindo, agua fresca de, 85
Tanque Verde Gardens, 286
Taos, New Mexico, 208
    restaurants of, 232–234
Taos Cookery, 223
Tarahumara Indians, 6
Taste of the Sun Country, 28
Taste of Texas, A (Dobie), 37, 39
Taste of Texas Market, 96
Tatum, Raymond, 66
T-Bone Steakhouse, 277
Tecolote, 229
Tejas Specialties, 79
Tepary beans, 9
Territorial Gourmet, 293
Texan Dining Train, 102
Texas
    ethnic influences on cooking in, 33
    food celebrations in, 28–29
    Hill Country, 54–55
    Southwestern, 23–113
Texas caviar, 110–111
Texas Confederate Museum, 49
Texas Folklife Festival, 28
Texas green sauce, 46
Texas Hill Country Food and Wine
        Festival, The, 28
Texas Spice Company, 56
Tex-Mex, 35–39
    in Austin, 52–53
    enchiladas, 47
Theodore Roosevelt Dam, 260
Thompson, Chuck, 95
Threadgill's, 72
Threadgill, Kenny, 72
Three Angels Bakery, 167
*Through the Country of the Comanche
        Indians* (Abert), 208–209
Tigua Restaurant, 14–15
Tiny's Lounge, 231–232
Tip Top Cafe, 90, 99
Titan Missile Museum, 287
Tohono Chul Park, 286
Tohono Chul Tea Room, 302
Tolbert, Frank X., 90

Toltecs, 140
Tomasita's, 224, 232
Tomatillos Cafe y Cantina, 106
Tombstone, Arizona, 287
Tommy's Place, 123
Tono's Comida Mexicana, 277
Tony Lama Boot Museum, 116
Toonerville Drive-in, 53
Tork's Cafe, 298
Tortilla chips, 54
Tortillas, 8
    chilaquiles, 173
    grilled shrimp salad with, 279–280
Totally Southwest, 293
Tower of the Americas, 89
Town Lake, Auston, 50
Trail drive chili, 32
Trains, Texan Dining Train, 102
Travis County Farmer's Market, 57–58
Tritle, Frank A., 248
Tubac Country Market, 293
Tucson, Arizona, 284–307
    bakeries of, 289–290
    bests of, 298
    markets of, 289–290
    October food fests, 285
    restaurants, 294–302
    shops of, 290–294
    sightseeing in, 284–287
Tucson Botanical Gardens, 286, 12, 13
    Gift Shop, 294
Tucson Culinary Festival, 245
Tucson Meet Yourself, 245, 285
Tucson Museum of Art, 285
Tularosa Basin, 148
Tulley's Meat Market, 186
Tumacacori, Arizona, 287
    chiltepin reserve, 7
Tunas. See Prickly pears
Turkey, honey-drenched smoked turkey
        breast with rainbow chile-mango
        salsa, 203–204

University Art Gallery, 161
Upper Crust Bakery, 58

Valentino, Rudolph, 181
Val Verde of Del Rio, 27
Vaughan, Stevie Ray, 49
Venison
    piñon-grilled venison chops, 18–19
    steaks with chile wine sauce, 110
Verde sauce, 68
Verstuyft Farms, 93
Victory Club, 37
Videz, 156
Villa, Pancho, 116
Villa Acuna, 37

Villa del Mar, 128
Villalon, Ben, 37
Vincent Guerithault on Camelback, 251,
    261, 276, 278
Visser, Margaret, 11

Walker, Jerry Jeff, 49
Walsh, Robb, 33, 57
Washington, George, 30
Waterloo Ice House, 52
Weiland, Bill, 218
West, Richard, 36
Wheat, 138, 208
Wheelwright Museum, 211
White Dove of the Desert, 284
Whittemore, Earl, 168
Whole Enchilada Fiesta, 143, 164
Wilder, Janos, 297
Wilderness Park Museum, 116
Wild Oats Community Market, 223–224
Willem, Adelina, 164–165
Wilson, Eddie, 72
Wilson, Woodrow, 181
Windows on the Green at the Phoenician
    Resort, 278
Winemaking
    history of, 25–26
    Munson, Thomas and, 26–27
    in New Mexico, 138, 145–147
Wineries
    in Albuquerque, 190–192
    in Austin area, 59–60

in El Paso and Ciudad Juárez, 117
in Hill Country, Texas, 55, 76–77
in Las Cruces, 165–166
in San Antonio, 94
in Santa Fe, 219–220
Winter squash and apple chowder with
    chile-dusted croutons, 174–175
Woods, Karin, 228
World's Highest Fountain, 262
Wright, Frank Lloyd, 261
Wurstfest, 29

Xnipec (dog's breath) salsa, 70
    recipe for, 84

Y. O. Ranch, 81
Ysleta Mission, 25, 116
Yucca, 14
    fruits, 3
Yuma Indians, 244

Zito's Sandwich Shop, 106–107
Zoos
    Phoenix Zoo, 262
    Reid Park Zoo, 286
    Rio Grande Zoological Park, 182
    San Antonio Zoo, 89
Zucchini, 10, 158
    calabacitas, spicy, 20–21
Zuni Grill, 91, 98, 107
Zuniga, Garcia de San Francisco y, 114

MORE "HOT STUFF" FROM PRIMA PUBLISHING

HOT SPOTS

Spicy Recipes from America's Most
Celebrated Fiery-Foods Restaurants

Dave DeWitt

From K-Paul's in New Orleans to the Fourth Street Grill in Berkeley, from the Coyote Cafe in Santa Fe to the East Coast Grill in Cambridge, restaurants all over America are serving up hot and spicy gourmet meals. Collected by Dave DeWitt, editor of *Chile Pepper* magazine, these are recipes contributed by some of the "hottest" chefs in the country.

$14.95

JUST NORTH OF THE BORDER

From the Editors of *Chile Pepper* Magazine,
a Collection of Favorite Southwestern Dishes

Dave DeWitt and Nancy Gerlach

Every month Dave DeWitt and Nancy Gerlach, the editors of the hot and spicy magazine, *Chile Pepper*, serve up large helpings of delicious recipes that feature the humble chile pepper in a mind-boggling variety of ways. And every month their loyal readers write and ask, "What are your favorite recipes?" The answer is here! *Just North of the Border* includes dishes like Spicy Lamb Carnitas, Roasted Corn and Crab Bisque, and Grilled Lamb Chops with Pine Nuts and Red Chile. From drinks and appetizers through soups and salads, from main dishes clear through to dessert, the recipes that Dave and Nancy have collected will please Southwestern food fans around the country.

$14.95

FILL IN AND MAIL . . . TODAY

PRIMA PUBLISHING
P.O. Box 1260DEW
Rocklin, CA 95677

USE YOUR VISA/MC AND ORDER BY PHONE
(916) 786-0449
Mon.–Fri. 9–4 PST (12–7 EST)

Dear Prima,
I'd like to order copies of the following Prima cookbook titles:

_____ copies **Food Lover's Handbook to
the Southwest** at $16.95 . . . .   _____

_____ copies **Hot Spots** at $14.95 . . . .   _____

_____ copies **Just North of the Border** at $14.95 .   _____

Subtotal   _____

Postage & Handling $3.95

CA Sales Tax 7.25%   _____

TOTAL (U.S. funds only)   _____

☐ Check enclosed for $_____, payable to **Prima Publishing**
Charge my ☐ MasterCard ☐ Visa

Account No. _____ Exp. Date _____

Signature _____

Your Name _____

Address _____

City/State/Zip _____

Daytime Telephone _____

GUARANTEE
YOU MUST BE SATISFIED!
You get a 30-day, 100% money-back guarantee on all books.

Thank you for your order.